MARKETING YOUR EDITING & PROOFREADING BUSINESS

Being interesting and discoverable

Louise Harnby

in association with The Publishing Training Centre

ISBN-13: 978-1491263679

ISBN-10: 1491263679

CONTENTS

FOREWORD

This book has been written for any editorial freelancer who feels that marketing is their Achilles' heel. With it, I hope to demonstrate that marketing needn't be difficult, overwhelming or boring. The book takes proofreaders and editors through the basics of developing and implementing an effective marketing strategy that will get them noticed and generate business leads.

Some readers may be wondering why I've dedicated a book solely to marketing when there was a chapter dedicated to the task in my companion volume, *Business Planning for Editorial Freelancers* (2013a). The marketing chapter therein was longer than any other. Nevertheless, in the interests of balance and space, many of the issues I wanted to discuss in detail had to be omitted. After all, marketing is just one aspect of developing a business plan for the new proofreader or editor. The chapter in *Business Planning* thus aimed to give a taster of some of the marketing activities that can be added to the freelancer's toolkit.

Marketing Your Editing & Proofreading Business thus takes off where its companion volume started. Not only does it cover the activities (or tools) that were addressed previously (though this time in far more detail), it also addresses the concepts behind those activities.

'Marketing' continues to be a term that strikes fear into the heart of many professional editorial freelancers, newbies and more experienced folk alike. Take the following comment that was posted by a colleague on a blog entry I wrote in June 2013:

> Of all the things you say one needs to do, there is nothing I find more challenging than marketing. To think that it has to be an ongoing effort makes me feel worse!

Statements to that effect are something I hear often. I hope that by delving deeper into both the concepts (things to think about) and the activities (things to do), the reluctant or fearful marketer will find it easier to unshackle themselves from the perception of marketing as a challenge and, instead, confidently embrace it as an opportunity.

I've done my best to avoid jargon. I won't say 'customer value proposition' when I want to talk about adding value to your business. Nor will I be discussing 'gross rating points', 'category and brand development indexes', or 'operating margins'! This book isn't designed to prepare marketing students for professional exams; rather, it's a book *for* editorial business owners, *by* an editorial business owner – and I've therefore used the language that we use when talking to each other on a day-to-day level.

Promoting our small businesses may be the most exciting thing we can do on a professional level, because from it we can see the direct benefits of our hard work. Every email we receive from a potential client, every project we secure, every contract we sign – all are proof that our marketing plans are working and that our editorial businesses are growing.

Louise Harnby, 2014

INTRODUCTION

'But I'm not a marketer ...'

If you think you're not a marketer, reconsider. Everyone is a marketer. Every time you've filled in and mailed an application form, every time you've tried to persuade someone to make one particular choice over another, every time you've gone that extra mile for a client or tried to anticipate his or her needs in order to do a good job and make a good impression, every business card you've handed out, every time you've dressed appropriately for an interview, you've been marketing.

Must I have a marketing strategy?

If you are running your own editorial business, having a marketing strategy is essential. There's little point in investing all your valuable time and money in training, reference materials, and tools for the job if you can't sell your services to those for whom you'd like to work.

Lois Frankel (2010) notes the importance of one of the favoured phrases of California-based leadership coach, Bruce Heller – 'outta sight, outta mind, outta business'. It's worth remembering because it reminds us that we very much need to be in sight and in the minds of our customers. A marketing strategy enables us to plan how we will do this.

New editors and proofreaders enter the profession every year. And the market is already full of established professionals with excellent reputations and lots of experience. These people are your colleagues but they're also the competition. If you don't invest time planning how you are going to promote your business, you are far less likely to succeed, simply because you won't get found.

What is marketing?

Trawl the internet for advice on marketing and you'll soon find yourself knee-deep (virtually speaking) in definitions. Here are a just a few:

> Marketing is the activity, set of institutions, and processes for creating, communicating, delivering, and exchanging offerings that have value for customers, clients, partners, and society at large. *(American Marketing Association 2007)*

> Marketing is the management process responsible for identifying, anticipating and satisfying customer requirements profitably. *(Chartered Institute of Marketing n.d.)*

They're two good definitions, and you'll notice how they focus on the customer, but they're a bit of a mouthful. More digestible is Robert Clay's (2007) rather fun definition:

> If you could see the world through John Smith's eyes, you can sell to John Smith what John Smith buys.

Another is my husband's. Admittedly, he probably borrowed this from someone else – he can't remember even telling me this – but his definition of marketing is:

> Persuading someone to think they want what you've got. (John Swainston)

I like it because it's easy to remember and succinctly makes the connection between your business and your customer.

A simpler way of thinking about it ...

The myriad professional definitions of marketing can, however, make the new starter feel out of their depth. There's a danger that the impenetrable business-speak gets in the way of what is, I believe, quite a simple message. Therefore, the way I choose to define marketing can be summed up in four words: *Being interesting and discoverable.*

Being interesting and discoverable

If you are interesting to your customers, it stands to reason that you've engaged with them, caught their attention, made them feel you have something to offer in response to something they need. If you are discoverable you've enabled your customers to find you, even if that means you've gone directly to *them*.

So, even if you are new to marketing your business and feel overwhelmed by what lies ahead, by returning to the idea of being interesting and discoverable every time you order a business card, write text for a promotional leaflet, website or directory listing, engage in online or offline networks with colleagues and clients, talk to potential customers on the phone, send a letter asking to be added to someone's freelance list, or respond to a client's enquiry, then you won't go far wrong.

Whichever definition you prefer, the nub of the matter involves recognizing that marketing goes well beyond leaflets, advertisements, phone calls and letters. Marketing is about how you present yourself so that, having identified your core client base, you make yourself attractive enough that those clients feel confident about commissioning your editorial services. Furthermore, it's about maintaining those relationships so that clients come back to you repeatedly and recommend you to others.

Marketing for the introverted

Marketing doesn't have to be about hard sells, screaming sales pitches and chest thumping. It can be about gentle persuasion, good communication, excellent service delivery, professionalism and courtesy. It's about putting yourself in your customers' shoes so that you (a) instil confidence in their perception of you and (b) deliver solutions to their problems.

Being introverted certainly doesn't equate with poor marketing ability. The thought of standing face to face with a large group of people in order to present a seminar sends me into a cold sweat, but I'm still supremely confident about my ability to promote my business.

3

Bringing your personality (whether you're shy or outgoing) into the equation is part of the process. Even if you are by nature an unassuming person, with a gentle approach to those you work with, this is just as attractive to the customer when it's presented as part of an overall story about the care you take with your clients, the confidence you instil in them, the quality of your work, and your attention to their requirements.

Passive vs active marketing

One way of breaking down marketing activities is to think of them in terms of passive and active.

- Passive marketing involves doing things that enable your clients to come to you. For example, advertising in directories, building a website, developing social media profiles.

- Active marketing involves doing things that take you directly to the client. For example, cold calling, emailing, letter-writing, attending networking events.

Neither one is better than the other, but doing both is recommended. Active marketing is particularly beneficial in the start-up phase of running your editorial business, because you may not yet have developed a strong enough online presence to ensure that your website features at the top of search results, and you may not yet have the amount of experience that makes you stand out when clients are searching specialist directories.

Being active will mean you're less likely to be dependent on others. If you're always dependent on referrals from colleagues or a publisher deciding whether to book you, you run a higher risk of experiencing 'dry' patches.

Don't be lulled into a false sense of security by the idea that 'dry' patches are normal even for editorial businesses that have been up and running for a few years. For the new starter, dry patches will be inevitable unless you're very lucky. Active marketing drives your business to a position where those patches are less likely to be a part of the equation.

4

Active marketing helps to turn you into the person who makes the referrals because you don't have the capacity for all the work you're being offered. It gives you the choice about which projects to take on and which to decline, whatever your reasons and preferences.

Marketing isn't difficult …

The good news is that marketing isn't difficult (technically, that is), though it is time-consuming. While the rewards of your marketing plan may take time to bear fruit, many of the promotional strategies you use can be implemented cheaply and quickly.

But it does take time …

However comprehensive and well-thought-out your marketing strategy is, the results will not happen immediately. Marketing is a process, a journey, not a checklist that one completes and then forgets about. Some activities may take months, even a couple of years to yield results; others may generate work quite quickly. Taking the time to work out where your core client groups are and how to focus your energies on them is therefore important because it will help you to invest your time wisely.

Is there a right way?

Marketing isn't about rights and wrongs – just different approaches. Marketing is a process of exploration and learning, a chance to embrace difference concepts, apply them to a range of activities, and then assess the results. In my companion volume, *Business Planning for Editorial Freelancing* (Harnby 2013a), I suggested the following:

> If someone tells you that X approach doesn't work and Y is the best way, stop and think before you follow blindly. Perhaps X didn't work for them because they didn't carry it out as well as you could. Perhaps you can write better cold letters, design a more enticing

web home page or present a better directory listing. Or perhaps Y didn't work for them because they have a different USP to you.

The truth is this – there are no rules. There are frameworks you can use to help you develop best practice, but as you research the field and look at what your colleagues are doing, you'll come across examples that break the mould and yet deliver results.

Instead, think about marketing as something that you can experiment with. It's about coming up with ideas (however banal or outlandish) that you can juggle, test, keep and discard according to how well they increase visibility and opportunity. And as I say later in the book, 'Opportunity + visibility = increased choice', which is something we all strive for. My way certainly isn't the only way. If you want to do things a different way, or test something that hasn't been mentioned in the chapters that follow, you should do so – you'll be hard-pushed to find a consensus on what's guaranteed to deliver the best results for every editorial freelancer in every area of the market. Rather, this book aims to serve up a range of ideas, tools, frameworks and approaches for you to try.

Marketing isn't the whole story

While having a marketing strategy is, in my opinion, essential, it's of course just as important to have the skills for the job. Throughout this book, I've made the assumption that we're taking the necessary steps to ensure we're fit for the very market that our promotional plans help us to target.

Think of the marketing strategy as the river we sail upon, and the training we carry out (to give us the technical skills to do a professional editorial job) as the boat. We need both to get us from A to B. If there are holes in the boat, we won't get far along the river before we sink. And if the boat is sound, but there's no river, we remain tied to the mooring.

If in doubt about the training opportunities on offer where you live, your national association will be able to advise you appropriately.

What's in this book?

This book is divided into four parts – Part I addresses concepts (things to think about) while Part II covers activities (things to do). If you are an inexperienced or cautious marketer, and you may well be if you are reading this book, I strongly recommend you read Part I in its entirety first. The conceptual elements underpin the 'doing' elements addressed in Part II and you will feel more enthusiastic about carrying out these activities if you have embraced the conceptual framework first. The chapters in Part II, which address the various activities you might like to consider, can be read in any order.

Part III offers a sample outline marketing plan. Again, I'd like to stress that it's a guideline only – you don't have to do all the activities that the fictive marketer chooses to do. Nor do you have to do them in exactly the way he does them. Instead, use it to stimulate your own creative juices.

I've used the example of a completely new entrant to the field in this section because it's often newbies who find it most difficult to develop a structured approach to promoting their businesses and to articulating a message to their customers. However, experienced editorial freelancers who are fearful of marketing should also be able to use this example in order to develop their marketing goals.

Finally, Part IV offers a list of works cited, further reading, tools and other useful resources.

PART I:
MARKETING CONCEPTS –
THINGS TO THINK ABOUT

1 WHAT ARE YOU SELLING?

What's in it for you?

- Forces you to think in detail about the market
- Assures better communication with the customer
- Essential for brand identification

Communicating what you do

The first thing you need to be clear about is what you are selling. Are you a substantive editor, a copy-editor, a proofreader, a publishing consultant, or all or some of these? Do you offer copywriting, translation, indexing, illustration, technical writing, manuscript preparation, e-formatting, ghost writing, web content validation and project management?

If you're not clear about the services you're offering, you won't be able to articulate these to your customers.

Later in this book we will discuss in more detail the concept of putting yourself in the shoes of your clients, but, for now, suffice it to say that not all clients will understand the differences between different levels of editorial intervention (the self-publishing novelist, for example). It's important that you can articulate these different services so that you can:

- structure your pricing accordingly;
- communicate that structure to your client;
- present your skill set appropriately across the marketing channels you use;
- make yourself interesting to the types of client for whom you are fit for purpose to work with.

Examples of editorial service

The following summarizes a range of editorial freelancing skills. The list is not exhaustive by any means; these are just a few examples.

It's also worth noting that, depending on where you live, different levels of intervention may be called different things (e.g. line editing is sometimes taken to mean what I would call proofreading, in that it performs the same function but on a file that has not been typeset for the final page layout, which is traditionally called a 'proof'). Using the terminology in your marketing materials that makes sense to a particular client group is therefore essential.

Structural, substantive or developmental editing

Clients looking for deeper, more hands-on intervention might wish to work with a structural, substantive or developmental editor. Here the editor will give detailed advice about, for example, overall plot, characterization, point of view, and whether the various elements of the book are working well together and supporting each other. The editor will not be working on the book line-by-line, but taking a view of the bigger picture.

Copy-editing

When the client is happy with the overall structure and plot of a book, they will be ready to work with a copy-editor.

According to the Society for Editors and Proofreaders (SfEP),

> A copy-editor makes sure that an author's raw text, or copy, is correct in terms of spelling and grammar and is easy to read so that readers can grasp his or her ideas [for example, by querying any awkward non-standard phrasing] ... A copy-editor also tries to prevent embarrassing errors of fact, alerts the publisher [or self-publishing author] to any possible legal problems and ensures that the typesetter can do a good job. (Society for Editors and Proofreaders n.d.)

Copy-editors concentrate on working with the text line-by-line rather than viewing the body of work as a whole (as in the case of the substantive editor). Further excellent advice on what a copy-editor does can be found on the Society for Editors and Proofreaders' website.

Proofreading

The final stage of the process is proofreading – the quality check. A proofreader will work line-by-line with the text to:

- eradicate any remaining grammar, punctuation and spelling errors;

- ensure consistency from a textual (e.g. hyphenation and capitalization), typographical (e.g. size and style of fonts used for different elements of text) and layout (e.g. line spacing, text alignment, and paragraph indentation) point of view;

- ensure that any cross-references in the text are correct; check that the contents list directs the reader to the correct page;

- ensure page numbers and running heads have been rendered appropriately.

Again, the SfEP offers some more detailed advice about the role of the proofreader on its website.

Copywriting

This involves producing text (copy) for marketing materials such as brochures, leaflets, websites, advertisements, sales letters, blog posts, promotional emails, personal statements, CVs and press releases. The copy is designed to entice the reader into buying a particular product or service, or supporting a particular point of view.

Indexing

Indexing is the preparation of a systematically arranged 'map' of entries from which a reader can access specific information in a document. While there are different types of indexes and a multitude of platforms in which they exist (both digital and print), many indexers specialize in the production of back-of-book indexes.

Manuscript preparation

Manuscript preparation services vary according to freelancer but can include: formatting for e-publication (e.g. Kindle-ready); organizing chapters and creating a cross-checked table of contents; creating and enforcing styles according to the client's brief to ensure consistency; preparing or checking artwork; checking figures and tables are numbered correctly and consistently; checking and/or formatting references according to preferred style; and submission to publisher or distributor.

Website validation

This service varies widely between freelancers, depending on their technical experience, but it can include checking web content to evaluate the experience for the user; proofreading, editing or rewriting text to make it fit for purpose; checking broken links; text and image layout; spam reduction; assessing how well it loads in different browsers; and debugging.

Project management

Editorial project managers coordinate the production of the publishing project from start to finish, including scheduling, budgeting, team selection and quality control.

Guiding your customer

Making your customer feel as if you offer them superb value as well as quality of service is an important part of any marketing strategy because it helps you to stand out from the crowd.

Helping those clients outside of the publishing industry understand the role we play in helping them produce a better product – whether that be a book, report, website, brochure or thesis – makes you more interesting because it:

- Emphasizes your professionalism
- Demonstrates that you understand your customer's needs
- Ensures the service you are offering matches the client's expectations

At the very least, then, you must be able to explain what it is you do. If you want to go the extra mile, consider putting this information onto your website. You don't have to clutter up space with detailed and lengthy descriptions. Instead, create a Word document or PDF that you can embed in the site and that any potential client can download. You might also email this information, or snail mail a paper copy to those who enquire after your services.

In Chapter 8 on adding value, I'll show you some examples of good practice within our industry.

Clarity with regards to multiple skills

If you have multiple skills (e.g. copy-editing and copywriting) you'd be a fool not to advertise them. But clarity is king, especially when it comes to an online presence, argues John Espirian (closed correspondence), an experienced editorial services provider:

> This is the key point in terms of your web presence. Subject-specific pages with a razor-sharp focus on content relevant to the viewer's search will help to bump you up the rankings.

Make sure that, whatever marketing platform you're using, the different services are separately summarized so as not to confuse the customer. On websites this means using different pages, with clearly named tabs, that tell your customer where to go. Shorter pitches about overall service provision need obvious links or calls to action that direct the customer to the relevant detailed information.

Be honest with your customers

I'm sure this goes without saying, but don't offer services that you don't have the requisite skills for – if you fail to deliver through lack of expertise the best outcome is that a client will blacklist you and won't use you again. Poor service is the most detrimental marketing activity I can think of. The worst outcome is that the client will complain about your services to your national editorial society, leave a poor testimonial about your business in a public environment or pass on negative word-of-mouth references to their colleagues (or all of the above), thus damaging your relationship not only with your initial client but, in addition, everyone they are connected with.

Rich Adin's article 'Implied Promises & the Professional Editor' serves as a healthy reminder that we need to take care with even the straplines we use when we are promoting our editorial services:

> Perhaps we use a slogan, such as 'Making manuscripts perfect!' or 'Nothing slips by my eagle eyes.' Maybe it isn't in a slogan but in a company name that there is an implied promise, as in 'Roseanne's Perfect Editing Service' or 'The Perfectionist.' (Adin 2013)

Adin's concern is that we imply a level of service that could be impossible. After all, editors and proofreaders are only human – can we guarantee the lowest price, the fastest turnaround in the market, or that the edited manuscript will be absolutely error-free?

> [W]e need to eliminate as many areas of disharmony as possible by being upfront about what the client can expect when we are hired. We need to explain to the client exactly what role we will play and what the client can expect us to accomplish with the client's manuscript. (Ibid.)

Adin's advice is to take every opportunity as a professional to avoid a situation where the client makes inferences about what we are selling but, instead, makes decisions based on clear and factual communication. That's not to say that we can't promote our businesses in creative and interesting ways, but honesty and clarity must underpin the words we use.

KEY POINTS

- You can't begin to promote your business unless you're clear about what services you're offering to the market.

- Put yourself in your customer's shoes – both you and they will benefit if everyone understands the skills being offered, and the value they bring to the table.

- If you have multiple skills, make sure you explain these to your customer, or provide links or calls to action that will make it as easy as possible to access the relevant information.

- Don't worry if you only offer one service – it's quality not quantity that counts.

- Don't offer services or promises to customers that you're not fit to provide or that are humanly impossible to guarantee. They might come back to bite you! Poor service is the worst form of marketing.

- Share your knowledge and add value to your business – this promotes your professionalism and makes you stand out.

TRY IT!

Make a list of the services that you are fit for purpose to offer (e.g. proofreading, copy-editing, structural editing, illustration, translation, copywriting, indexing, transcription, etc.).

2   WHERE IS YOUR MARKET?

What's in it for you?

- Forces you to think in detail about the customer

- Assures better communication with the customer

- Embeds the understanding that your skill (e.g. editing) and your ability to sell it (marketing) are two different things

To whom am I interesting?

It's harder to develop a marketing strategy if you haven't identified your market. Some of us start out by focusing on one or two specific markets in order to build experience, perhaps because we have contacts therein that we can exploit.

If you haven't worked out which customers you want to target, you will not be in a position to put yourself in your customer's shoes (Chapter 7), create hooks, pitches and calls to action (Chapter 4), identify your customer-centric USPs (Chapter 4) and add value to your business (Chapter 8). If you can't embrace these concepts, you will find it more difficult to carry out the marketing activities in the second part of the book.

There are umpteen blog posts and advertisements arguing that, for example, since 'everyone needs a good proofreader' this is a golden career opportunity for anyone wishing to set up a small business. While it's true that most written materials will benefit from the skills of a good editor and proofreader, the reality is this: being 'good' in itself is probably not enough to get you work. If you don't know who your customer is and your customer doesn't know who you are, being a good proofreader (editor, indexer, etc.) is almost useless because you can't find each other.

Potential client groups

In *Business Planning for Editorial Freelancers* (2013a) I stated:

> Freelance editors and proofreaders work for publishers, independent self-publishing authors, academic authors preparing articles for journal submission, students writing theses, prepress project management agencies, businesses, magazines and newspapers, freelance writers and bloggers, [editing agencies,] website owners and professional associations.

But I also asked whether all of those clients were suitable customers for every editorial freelancer. Even within client groups, there are sub-levels of customer that will be more interested than others in your services.

Case study: the publisher

I used to work in the publishing industry. It therefore makes perfect sense that publishers would be a target market for me because I can sell this experience as a unique selling point (USP) when I'm pitching to them. But are all publishers my potential customers?

- I have a BA in Political Science and the publisher I worked for specialized in the social sciences during my time there.

- My colleague Anna Sharman also worked in-house, but for a science publisher. She has a BA in Natural Sciences and a PhD and postdoctoral research in developmental/evolutionary biology.

- Now consider Janet MacMillan, a practising lawyer for 20 years prior to embarking on her editorial career.

- Finally, let's add in Marcus Trower to the pot. He was a journalist, writing and sub-editing for magazines and national press. He's also a published author.

If all four of us send cold letters and CVs to all of the following publishers, asking for the opportunity to be added to their freelancer list, who has the USPs that are most likely to make their direct mail campaign effective?

- 47North (fantasy, science fiction and horror)
- Cambridge University Press (social sciences; humanities; science, technology and medicine)
- Constable (fiction and commercial non-fiction)
- Edward Elgar (economics, finance, business law, environment, public and social policy)
- Elsevier Science (science, technology and medicine)
- Hart Publishing (law)
- Lippincott Williams & Wilkins (medicine, nursing and allied health)
- Polity Press (sociology, politics and philosophy)
- Sage Publications (social sciences; humanities; science, technology and medicine)

Anna would do well to target CUP, Elsevier, LWW and Sage. I would target CUP, Edward Elgar, Polity and Sage. Janet could focus on CUP, Edward Elgar, Hart and Sage. Marcus would have a better chance than the rest of us of appearing interesting to 47North and Constable.

There is nothing wrong at all with casting your marketing net wide, but it's useful to know how to target so that you can present the customer with a pitch that tells them you understand the language of their business and offer editorial solutions that match their requirements.

These days I proofread for client groups that were originally outside my target client group. However, being able to think in a client-focused way provided me with the best preparation for all my marketing activities. Specializing first and diversifying later got my business off the ground.

Your background

Your educational and career backgrounds will help you to identify core client groups. For example, if you have a career background in IT, then in addition to publishers publishing in this area, you might also target IT businesses. If you are a former nurse, you might target nursing students, health and welfare charities, medical practices, and publishers with a nursing and allied health list.

Case study

My colleague Sophie Playle is a good example of someone who has used her educational background in order to carve out a specialist niche for her business. She offers copy-editing and manuscript critiquing services.

Following her first degree in English Literature, Sophie did a Master's in creative writing. As Sophie says:

> The focus of my MA was novel writing, and each of us on the course was plunged into the task. As with my final-year undergraduate class, each week we would critique each other's work – from sentence-level, language and grammar issues to the developing bigger issues such as point-of-view and voice as our novels progressed.
>
> Much of our course was also focused on reading and analysing critical theory related to literature and the craft of novel writing, so that our constructive criticism had a sound academic foundation. I absolutely loved the experience, and my writing and editing skills developed dramatically in the challenging environment. (Playle 2013)

This, in addition to her training as an editor, and her experience of working for a large publisher, provided her with a knowledge base that she could incorporate into her editorial business. She now offers a niche specialism that she can promote to independent writers who need their work evaluated before they go to the expense of hiring a copy-editor and/or proofreader.

Specialization vs generalization

Of course you don't have to limit yourself to specific sections of the market. However, specializing is a way of helping to focus your attention on your unique selling points and how you might use these to show a particular client group that you speak their language, share an interest in their field, and can provide editorial solutions for their business or project.

Customers seeking editorial freelancers will more often than not use keywords to help hone their searches. If you market yourself as a generalist, you risk not appearing on their radar in the first place because your marketing material, online and print, won't reflect the language they're using in their searches.

Walt Kania (2012), talking about freelancing more broadly, sums up the specialization/generalization dilemma nicely, urging us not to fear 'limiting' ourselves:

> Yes. Specialists always do better. There is no debating this. I can't think of any freelancer who made it big as a handyman. The world already has plenty of all-purpose copywriters, versatile translators, general web designers and utility infielders. Don't jump into that haystack. You will be lost forever ... you stake out your private territory, even if it's the size of a beach towel, and then own it. You're not trying to cover all bases, appeal to everyone, do everything. You have your thing.

Case study

Nick Walton is good example of an editorial business owner who is using his specialism to build a targeted client base. A former biosciences researcher and journal referee, Nick's prior career in science means he is well qualified to help primarily overseas scientific writers prepare their journal articles for peer review. He targets publishing services/language polishing agencies (recommended by mainstream science publishers). These agencies require editors like Nick to have specialist academic qualifications (such as doctorates) and a thorough knowledge of the journal article submission process.

For more information about working with academic editing agencies, see Sharman 2013.

Understanding the client's needs

Understanding the needs of different clients is also an essential first step when thinking about communication style. This is as true when we're securing work from a new client as when we have established a working relationship with them. We're still marketing ourselves to clients even once we've secured the job. For example, a publisher will not need to be hand-held and will not want to hold their freelancer's hand through a project, whereas a less experienced independent author might well need validation and encouragement from their proofreader or editor. A publisher will be used to working to strict schedules whereas the business client or independent author may need gentle but firm guidance on scheduling matters.

Some independent authors, particularly those who've never published before, feel their editorial colleagues provide safe havens in which the writer can express their insecurities. They may feel nervous about putting their work 'out there'; they may be worried that their writing isn't 'good enough'; they may ask for advice and guidance on publishing issues that stand well outside the editorial pro's knowledge base; they may want to use their editor or proofreader as a sounding board for ideas. For some independent authors, in particular those who have not embraced the online writing community, the process of self-publishing can be a lonely and isolating place. These factors will affect how we present our comments, queries and feedback so that we create and maintain trust and support.

In this sense, how we market ourselves as people, as businesses, as service suppliers, as professionals, even as counsellors, never stops.

KEY POINTS

- If you don't know where your market is, you won't be able to target the appropriate groups with the relevant marketing activities.

- Knowing where your market is enables you to match your skills with your clients' business needs.

- Thinking about your background and experience is a useful way of focusing your marketing strategy in the start-up phase and the quickest way to carve out a specialist message that you can sell on to other customers.

- Consider specializing first and diversifying later. Diversity is great, but being a generalist is a difficult message to sell with conviction when you're starting out.

- Understanding your clients' differing needs and expectations will help you to ensure that the way you present yourself (e.g. the language and tone you use) is appropriate both during the process of securing work and, later, maintaining the business relationship.

- There are benefits to search engine rankings, too. If you have more specific keywords in your online marketing materials, it's easier to become ranked by the likes of Google, and this will improve how discoverable you are.

TRY IT!

Identify the broad client groups that you think match your experience and that you would like to pitch to on your website, in a directory, or through an advertisement. Even if you're a new starter and you only have one or two, that's absolutely fine.

3   THINKING IN A JOINED-UP WAY

What's in it for you?

- Helps you to think of each part of your marketing strategy as connected to, rather than isolated from, every other
- Encourages you to think about SEO opportunities
- Improves branding and professionalism
- Enables you to recognize the multiple benefits

Everything's connected ...

One of the most useful concepts worth getting your head around early on is that of thinking about marketing in a joined-up way. Whether you're considering a concept (something to think about) or an action (something to do), the outcome will be more effective if you understand that none of the elements stand in isolation from each other. Everything is connected.

The marketing wheel

Think of your marketing strategy as a wheel on a bike. The hub of the wheel is your editorial business. The rim comprises your customers and colleagues. The hub and the rim are connected by spokes upon which lie the activities that you carry out and the concepts you've embraced in order to communicate with your customers – for example, your website, the directories in which you list your business, the résumés you create, the targeted advertisements you place, the direct mail campaigns you deliver, the networking you engage in, and the social media platforms on which you have conversations and share content.

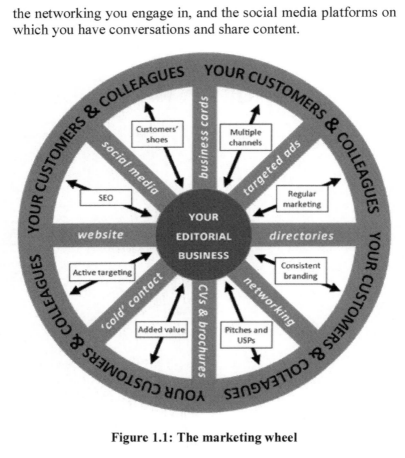

Figure 1.1: The marketing wheel

Joined-up thinking and concepts

Each of the concepts discussed in Part I is connected to many of the others. For example, you will find it much easier to work out how you can add value (Chapter 8) if you put yourself in your customer's shoes (Chapter 7). But you will find it hard to put yourself in your customer's shoes if you have not worked out who your customers are (Chapter 2).

Joined-up thinking and activities

Each of the activities discussed in Part II is also connected, both with other activities and with the concepts that underpin them. For example, your website should include your social media handles (e.g. LinkedIn and Twitter addresses; see Chapter 15), but might also include a downloadable CV (Chapter 21) and any added value you've created (Chapter 8).

As another example, a 'cold' letter that you send as part of a direct mail campaign (Chapter 20) will include a carefully targeted pitch that you've developed with your USPs and the customer's needs in mind (Chapters 4 and 7) and a link to your website (Chapter 14) in the contact information. However, you might also reference an online portfolio (Chapter 23) or include in the envelope a one-page CV or brochure (Chapter 21) that includes valuable testimonials (Chapter 24).

Joined-up thinking and people

Your potential customers are everywhere – even if you're not working for them yet, they might be working for your colleagues. It's therefore essential that you recognize this connectedness every time you communicate online.

Despite the myriad advice on taking responsibility for your privacy settings online, the safest approach is to assume that there is no such thing as privacy on the internet. Always put your professional cap on before you hit the 'post' button. The editorial world may be global in outreach, but the internet shrinks even the biggest countries to small villages. Whether you are tweeting, sharing content on Facebook or Google+, engaging in a LinkedIn discussion group thread, contributing to your national editorial society's online forum, or emailing someone privately, you are still marketing yourself, so assume the following:

• Your current clients can see what you've written.

• Your colleagues' clients can see what you've written.

- Colleagues and clients who have you on their radar, but haven't yet offered you work, can see what you've written.

- Even if you don't know a particular publisher, business owner, independent writer or fellow editorial freelancer, assume that they are using the same networks as you and that someone you do know has made a connection with them.

With all of this in mind:

- Never complain about a customer online – if they're not reading it, one of your shared connections might be.

- Never complain about a colleague online – if they're not reading it, one of your shared connections might be.

- Never moan about the fact that you've got no work. It's the equivalent of an anti-testimonial – it makes you look desperate and tells everyone that you're not pulling clients. And if no one else is using you, why would your colleagues feel confident in referring their clients to you if they're too busy to take a particular job? Instead, if you must mention the issue at all, talk in terms of having unexpected gaps in your busy schedule.

- Don't criticize colleagues on discussion groups, even if you disagree vehemently with them – healthy debate is one thing; flaming is quite another.

- Don't humiliate colleagues on social media networks or discussion forums by publically pointing out, say, a grammatical mistake they've made in their post or on their website. It's the height of rudeness (though, sadly, it happens frequently in some networks). Contact them privately if you want to help them amend the error.

If you're still not convinced, marketing veteran Ty Kiisel offers some valuable insights. I've summarized them here but his article is worth reading in full (Kiisel 2012).

- 'Don't forget your brand is every touch point': Kiisel argues that separation of the private and the public is almost impossible, so don't post anything online that would offend any company you work for or your mother.

- 'If you argue online you lose': In a nutshell, 'Arguing online is like shouting at your neighbor standing in the middle of the cul-de-sac. Everyone can hear you and you look like an idiot.'

- 'Be polite and remember the golden rule': Online postings can come across as curt so use the same rules you'd apply if you were talking to someone face-to-face.

- 'Remember that what happens online stays online': Everything you post, every comment you make and every picture you publish is stored somewhere on a server, and 'unlike your wife or your best friend, the Internet never forgets'. If Google can find it, anyone can find it.

Behaving poorly in public is simply an exercise in catastrophic public relations and counters the professionalism that you want to convey as part of your brand.

And poor PR will send your customers to your colleagues, without a doubt. Some years ago, I picked up a new publisher client after one proofreader made the mistake of criticizing the publisher's editorial staff on Facebook. The in-house editor promptly set about asking her friends in other presses for recommendations, and my name came up.

Joined-up thinking and branding

Thinking in a joined-up way also helps you to ensure that the way you brand yourself (Chapter 13) is consistent. This applies not only to your marketing activities, but also your general business practice (e.g. your letterhead, compliment slips, email signature, invoice banner, online discussion board signature, the thumbnail images you use of yourself online).

Consistent branding ensures that your customer recognizes your business name, logo, image and colourway, no matter which marketing platform they discover you on. This not only prevents confusion but also demonstrates professionalism.

Case study 1: Find a Proofreader – one platform, multiple connections

Here's an example of how one of my directory listings is connected to some other marketing activities (website; social media profiles; and networking) and how I've embraced a number of different concepts to maximize its effectiveness (SEO; putting myself in my customer's shoes; adding value; hooks, pitches and calls to action; the power of the testimonial).

I advertise on Find a Proofreader (FaP), a specialist international editorial directory that includes proofreaders, copy-editors, indexers, copywriters, ghost writers, CV writers and virtual assistants. I don't consider this to be an isolated piece of marketing – it's much more than that. Here's how it's joined up with various concepts and activities in my marketing strategy:

Website (activity)

My website (and its attached blog) includes content about FaP, and the FaP website includes not only my listing but related guest articles. There are at least 10 direct two-way links to various pages between my website and the FaP website, providing us both with valuable 'link juice' that has powerful SEO benefits.

Social media profiles (activity)

FaP, its owner and I are all on Facebook, Google+, Twitter and LinkedIn. We use these platforms to share each other's content and that of other colleagues with whom one or both of us is connected. FaP also facilitates social media networking by including a good range of follow/share buttons.

Networking (activity)

Through FaP, I connected with the directory's owner, Nick Jones, a fellow editorial freelancer. These days, we regularly bounce ideas around about different aspects of marketing and freelancing, share each other's blog content, guest blog for each other's websites, and refer clients to one another.

Putting myself in my customer's shoes (concept)

I've used my FaP listing to pitch to a range of customer groups that I don't target so deeply on my website: students, academics and business professionals looking for assistance with proofreading not only books but also reports, application forms, personal statements and CVs. I use a different directory (the SfEP's Directory of Editorial Services) to pitch to publishers. In order to decide which directories to use for which client groups, (and what information to include for each listing), I needed to put myself in my customer's shoes and ask where they might be most likely to find me and what they would want to know.

Using multiple marketing platforms (concept)

My customers use different platforms to find their proofreaders, so I use different platforms to maximize my chances of them finding me. FaP has a high Google page rank and the directory name itself incorporates the very keywords a client might use in their search.

Adding value (concept)

My FaP listing includes a link to the added value I have created for independent authors: a free booklet entitled *Guidelines for New Authors*, which is available on my website or via Smashwords.

Hooks, pitches and calls to action (concept)

I've used the 'hook, pitch, call to action' framework as a way of structuring the content of my FaP listing.

The power of the testimonial (concept)

Currently, I use my website testimonials page for publisher endorsements. However, I include a brightly coloured badge that takes readers to my FaP listing because that's where I encourage every non-publisher client to leave reviews for me (whether or not the client came via that directory listing). In my FaP listing I do the reverse by referring clients to both the internal reviews and by linking to the endorsements page on my website. FaP allows visitors to search for advertisers according to a ratings structure, so using the power of the testimonial is a way of maximizing the impact of my entry.

Case study 2: BookMachine – one platform, multiple benefits

When it comes to joined-up thinking, instead of coming from the angle of multiple connections, you might prefer to consider the various benefits on offer. Most marketing activities you carry out are worth doing for several reasons, rather than just one.

Take BookMachine for example. Founded by Laura Austin and Gavin Summers, BookMachine aims to bring together people in the publishing industry through an online hub (BookMachine.me) and a series of international face-to-face events. The website includes information about jobs, people, and events in the world of publishing. So why create a profile? There are several benefits you might like to consider:

Network expansion

Some of the people with profiles on BookMachine.me may already be in your network (members of the same professional society, Twitter followers, Facebook friends, LinkedIn connections, etc.) but some may not, particularly if they have skill sets that are outside your own. This is an opportunity to find information about people with complementary publishing skills (writers, bloggers, cover designers, publishers) and connect with them. Furthermore, if you have a 'promoted' profile, BookMachine will use their own social media contacts to share information about your business (e.g. on Twitter).

An information and learning platform

BookMachine hosts regular international events where speakers are invited to share their experiences of publishing, broadly speaking. Attendees include marketers, publishers, designers, authors, editors, app developers and publishing students. Previous events have included speakers from ALPSP, Razorbill (Penguin imprint), Macmillan Education, Little, Brown, and McGraw Hill. The settings are informal and foster a sense of collaboration and learning, providing not only face-to-face networking opportunities but also a friendly platform for continued professional development.

SEO enhancement

By creating a profile on the online hub at BookMachine.me, and including your own domain URL, you get another opportunity to build up the rich link juice, which search engines like Google love so much, between your website and others.

Portfolio showcase

BookMachine.me has a lovely portfolio platform that allows you to showcase your work. You can create links to projects on which you've worked, to key pages on your website (e.g. your home page, or testimonials), and to any added value you've created, using a one-click search tool.

KEY POINTS

- Our various marketing activities aren't isolated from each other. Our directory entries, websites, social media networks, business cards and brochures are connected in myriad ways.

- Joined-up thinking allows us to see the multiple connections and the multiple benefits.

- Try to visualize any particular marketing activity as a wheel in order to see how you might apply the concepts we've discussed with the activities you are carrying out.

- Ask yourself if there is an opportunity to add value to the given marketing activity that will enhance its effectiveness and increase the likelihood of a customer finding you indirectly or responding positively to your direct approach.

- Remember that the online world is big and small at the same time. The connections exist even if they're not obvious to you, so take care with your presentation at all times.

TRY IT!

Write down five separate marketing activities that you plan to carry out (e.g. advertisements, social media profiles and engagement, listings in directories, networking, building a website or creating business cards).

Think about the figure of the marketing wheel and how each of the activities you noted above can link you to your customers in multiple ways (e.g. in terms of concepts, connections and benefits).

4 HOOKS, USPS, PITCHES AND CALLS TO ACTION

What's in it for you?

- Enables you to structure your written content persuasively
- Forces you to put yourself in your customer's shoes
- The content you create in this chapter can be used in multiple marketing activities

Building the basics

Thinking about and developing this foundational content for your business is one of the most difficult nuts to crack, but will bring you the most benefit. This is because once you've done it you can use it (or adapt it) for many of the marketing activities discussed in Part II. In other words, you're doing a big chunk of the hard work now!

'But I don't talk like that ...'

I'm aware that if you live outside the UK, you might find my language use and style for the suggestions in this chapter rather parochial, perhaps a little too British. That's fine! By all means adapt the following framework to suit what feels comfortable for you based on the way people write and speak to each other in your own region. This chapter is not about saying exactly X or Y, but about thinking in terms of a framework that engages the customer.

The hook

The hook is the element that first captures the customer's eye or enables them to find you. It tells them enough about who you are or what you do that they are interested enough to keep reading. It might be any one of the following:

- The business name and page description that comes up in a list of search engine results

- A slogan or strapline on a website, brochure, CV or business card

- The keyword tags that you've included in a directory or in the metadata of your website

- The first line of text on the home page of your website or in the introductory paragraph of your CV

- A short, snappy testimonial that you place in a headline position

Here are some examples of best practice that I've come across in the editorial freelancing community. These are all located on the home pages of these editorial professionals' websites.

- Liz Jones Editorial Solutions: 'Making words work from concept to completion'

- Legal Proofreader: 'Professional and affordable legal proofreading and editing services'

- The Medical Editor: 'Superior medical editing and rewriting since 1991'

- Editing by Catch the Sun: 'Development and editing of educational materials, live and virtual'

- The Writer The Better!: 'Customer-friendly proofreading at comfortable prices'

There is no need to limit yourself to one hook. If you service different types of clients (e.g. publishers, independent authors, businesses, students) using different platforms (e.g. directories, printed CVs, brochures) you could develop very specialist hooks for each.

Case study

Two of my core client groups are publishers and self-publishing authors. We'll look at the concept of putting yourself in your customer's shoes in more detail in Chapter 7, and that of choosing a variety of marketing channels to talk to those various customers in Chapter 9. For now it will suffice to say that my entry in the SfEP's Directory of Editorial Services is a key tool for targeting publishers, and my website is a key tool for targeting independent authors.

The hook in my SfEP directory entry is 'Professional proofreader to the academic and trade publishing industry'. The hook on my website is the first header on the homepage: 'About Louise'. On first inspection it's not exactly the most exciting hook in the world! I thought long and hard about this. Initially, when designing my website I considered using a hook that was similar to that of my SfEP listing, but something a little more inclusive in terms of the language: 'Professional proofreader to the publishing community'.

However, the more I thought about it, the more I felt that this didn't convey the message that I wanted for my self-publishing audience. Many of my indie author clients are first-time authors. They are nervous about the editorial process, uncomfortable about being judged, don't always understand the different levels of editorial intervention, and are worried about being taken for a ride.

I was adamant that I wanted to convey a combination of professionalism and friendliness on my website. I wanted the indie author to feel how a good doctor should make their patient feel:

*   They respect the fact that the patient may feel nervous, uncomfortable or embarrassed.

*   They can offer reassurance that they've dealt with the patient's condition on many previous occasions.

- They can communicate in a comfortable manner that makes the patient feel they are welcome in the surgery.

- They are engaged with the problem that needs attending to and can offer a solution.

My intention with 'About Louise' is to give an inexperienced author the sense that they're already on first-name terms with me. I want to make them feel that they are dealing with me, and me only, that I'm a human being just like them, and that they can talk to me about what their needs are.

The lesson from this is that there are no right and wrong hooks. Rather there is the customer, and there is you. By thinking about how you want your customer to feel about you, you can start to think about the words you will use to build a bridge between the two. Hooks don't have to be complex or wordy, though they can be if you want them to be as such. All that's important is that you understand what they tell your customer.

Some wise advice ...

Bear in mind Rich Adin's (2013) advice from Chapter 1. Take care with straplines that imply impossible promises such as 'Guaranteed error-free documents', or 'Full money-back guarantee unless you are 100% satisfied'. You don't want to end up in a situation where your hooks come back to bite you because the client inferred a level of service that is not always humanly possible to achieve or because the evaluation of what is being offered is so subjective.

Unique selling points (USPs)

Making a list of your key selling points that might appeal to a range of clients is a useful early activity. You can refer to it whenever you need to identify what makes you different, what skills you have, what problems you can solve and past experience that enables you to understand your client's point of view. Some examples might include:

- Your previous career: e.g. you're a former lawyer, accountant, teacher, social worker, engineer, soldier, nurse, publishing executive, marketing manager, museum curator, or local government officer.

- Your educational background: e.g. you have a BA in politics, English literature or history; a Master's or PhD in a scientific discipline; or a specialist legal, accountancy or marketing qualification.

- You have completed a training course by a nationally recognized organization: e.g. the EAC in Canada, the IPEd in Australia, or the Publishing Training Centre (PTC) or SfEP in the UK.

- You can use professional editorial markup language: e.g. the BSI 5261 symbols in the UK. Or you can work directly in Word, using Track Changes.

- You have X years' experience.

- You can offer a fast turnaround.

- You have ancillary skills: e.g. you've written, formatted and self-published a book, you can speak a second language, you're a gifted cook.

- You're a member of a professional editorial society: e.g. the EFA in the USA, or the SfEP in the UK.

- You have a bank of clients in a relevant field.

The list is endless. The point is to think about all the things you know and all the things you can do that might make you more interesting to a particular customer.

The pitch

The pitch is the element where you provide more specific details about what you do and who you do it for. Put yourself in your customer's shoes and use the language that is relevant to them. As with the hook, you could create a number of different pitches that you can use in different situations.

The best place to start is with a short pitch that reinforces the hook and keeps the customer interested. You might hear this referred to as an 'elevator' pitch, so called because it's supposed to reflect the story you can tell your potential client during a 20-second ride between floors in an elevator (or 'lift' as we call it on my side of the pond!).

The differentiation–solution–empathy framework

Kevin Daum (2013) advises incorporating three elements into the perfect pitch: differentiation, solution and empathy. The idea is that the people on the receiving end of your pitch understand not just who you are and what you do, but why they need you.

- 'Differentiation' is about what sets you apart from the crowd or enables you to do something that your client can't do for themselves.

- 'Solution' concerns identifying what the client needs and demonstrating how you can provide it.

- 'Empathy' involves acknowledging the challenges a particular client faces and reflecting the fact that you understand what these are and can respond accordingly.

Adopting this framework when you develop your pitch enables you to work out how to communicate not only with client groups who are familiar with what you do, but also those who are not.

Case study: the 'familiar' client

Even client groups who are completely comfortable with the concept of what I do (proofreading) will still not queue up to give me a job if my pitch consists of 'I'm a freelance proofreader'. Let's imagine that I'm writing a pitch aimed at the production editor of a major academic publishing house. I'll have 20 seconds to persuade this person that my CV's worth NOT throwing in the bin.

First, I put myself in my customer's shoes. Using Daum's framework, I need to:

- Differentiate myself for them – they're targeted by hundreds of people like me every year.

- Offer solutions – they need proofreaders who are comfortable working with the kind of material they publish and in a variety of formats.

- Provide empathy – some of the biggest challenges faced by production departments in publishing companies include spiralling costs, incredibly tight schedules, and enforcing very specific house style preferences.

With these issues in mind I can now work out what I can offer.

- Differentiation: I worked in-house before I went freelance so I have experience of the publishing industry. I'm also an Advanced Member of my national editorial society – a known and highly respected organization within the industry. I'm experienced and I can prove it with testimonials from publishers who use me repeatedly.

- Solutions: I have an educational and career background in the social sciences so I'm comfortable with the language of the academic materials. I also have extensive experience of proofreading in Word and on PDF.

- Empathy: I always deliver within budget, never miss a deadline, and pride myself on being able to follow a client's brief.

Now that I've worked this out I can create my short pitch:

> I am a highly recommended professional proofreader specializing in academic and professional titles in the social sciences and humanities. I have over 20 years' publishing experience (in-house and freelance) and am an Advanced Member of the Society for Editors and Proofreaders (SfEP). To date I have proofread over 350 books, primarily from academic publishers, all of whom will supply you with outstanding references. I can proofread onscreen or on paper, and blind or against copy. I always deliver to budget and to brief, and I've never missed a deadline.

Case study: the 'unfamiliar' client

Some customers are less familiar with the kinds of service we provide. They may not have a clue about your national editorial society, and may not care that you have in-house experience or can use industry-standard hieroglyphics to mark up a text. In this study, let's develop an elevator pitch aimed at a business client. I've borrowed heavily (with permission) from my colleague Liz Jones (owner of Liz Jones Editorial Solutions) for this study because she's beautifully articulated a solution-based pitch at businesses on her website.

First, Liz puts herself in her customer's shoes. Using Daum's framework, she needs to:

- Differentiate herself for them – many commercial businesses don't understand the benefits of hiring a professional editor or proofreader. They think it can be done in-house by people who have a 'good eye'.

- Offer solutions – a commercial business whose written communications are poorly articulated and littered with spelling and grammar errors/inconsistencies looks unprofessional and less authoritative. That costs them money.

- Provide empathy – most commercial businesses' day-to-day practice is hectic and deadlines are often a huge issue; reports, marketing materials, website content and advertisements often have to be turned around quickly.

With these issues in mind, Liz has thought about what she can offer.

- Differentiation: She has more than a 'good eye' – she's a trained, experienced professional editor who is not distracted by the internal politics or business demands.

- Solutions: She can proofread, edit or rewrite their written material so that it's fit for purpose and gives the business a competitive advantage.

- Empathy: She's just as much of a professional as her business client. She understands how things can get left until the last minute because of other pressing demands.

Here's the short pitch she might write:

> I am an experienced editor who specializes in providing editorial solutions for commercial businesses. From websites to marketing materials, annual reports to training documents, I'll polish, edit or rewrite text, according to your brief, to make it error-free, fit for purpose and compelling to read. My superb attention to the details of your text's content and layout will give your product a professional edge and a competitive advantage. I understand the demands of working in a commercial environment and can offer a calm head, efficient manner, flexible attitude and, when you need it, a quick turnaround.

Real elevator pitches – having to say it out loud

If you're worried that some of these pitches might come across as too clinical or robotic in face-to-face situations, you might feel more comfortable flipping the Daum framework around. We'll look at this in more detail in Chapter 17 on face-to-face marketing.

For many, the idea of a face-to-face verbal pitch is daunting. However, we're more than comfortable with having a chat! The trick is to be well-prepared with the information but to get yourself in the mindset of talking about it in a more informal, chatty way.

- First, dive straight in with the empathy element, but this time framed rhetorically as a set of questions.
- Next, answer your own questions with a solution.
- Finally, close the pitch with your differentiation.

Let's take the example of Liz's business pitch and rework it for a verbal delivery. Just to clarify, I wouldn't feel comfortable delivering a written pitch in this style.

> Customer: Hi! Who are you and what do you do?

Liz: Hello! I'm Liz Jones. What do I do? Well, you know that feeling when you visit a website or read a brochure or report, and it's littered with errors or the text is garbled? And if you're like me, it really irritates you because all the mistakes detract from the message, and it makes you feel as if the company's sloppy and unprofessional, and that you don't want to buy from them because what they're selling might be sloppy, too? Well, I'm the person who stops that from happening. I'm an experienced professional editor and I specialize in polishing, editing or rewriting commercial businesses' written materials to make them fit for purpose and compelling to read. And that gives them a competitive edge.

- Everything up to and including '… might be sloppy, too?' is empathy.
- 'Well, I'm the person who stops that from happening' is the solution.
- 'I'm an experienced professional editor …' is differentiation. It's the thing the customer can't necessarily do for themselves.

The call to action

The call to action is where you tell your customer what you want them to do. The best calls to action compel people to do something.

Rich Brooks of Flyte New Media suggests that calls to action are 'often bland and unhelpful, such as "Click here" or "Learn more"' (Brooks n.d.). Instead, use informative statements in your promotional material (including links when online). Here are some examples of good practice from the editorial freelancing world.

- 'Call or e-mail me today so that we can discuss how I can help you with your manuscript' (KOK Edit, USA)

- 'Please contact me for a quote, for more information or to discuss your requirements, with no obligation' (The Whole Proof, UK)

- 'Help me to help you. Click on the button below and take a look at a one-page PDF that summarises what I need to know about your project. Then call or email me to discuss your proofreading requirements in more detail' (Louise Harnby | Proofreader, UK)

- 'Contact me now for more information or a non-obligatory price quote' (NEEDSer, The Netherlands)

Recycling the information

Once you've developed your hooks, USPs, pitches and calls to action, you can use and adapt them as you see fit. Whether you're developing content for the homepage of your website, creating a directory listing, designing an advertisement, writing a CV, or designing one of your social media profiles, this stock information is something you can use as a foundation and refer to again and again.

Don't think of it as static information – as your business changes, your experience grows and you acquire new client groups; think about how you can update the information so that the message you are communicating is fresh and pertinent to whom you are marketing yourself.

KEY POINTS

- Developing your hooks, pitches and calls to action can be tricky but tackling the hard work now will repay you handsomely when you come to Part II's 'doing' activities.

- Put yourself in your customer's shoes and create different content for different client groups.

- Take care to ensure you don't fall into the 'implied promises' trap.

- Use Daum's differentiation–solution–empathy framework to help you work out what information to include.

- And try flipping this round and framing it as a question if you're pitching verbally.

- Review your hooks, pitches and calls to action every few months to ensure that they are up to date and relevant to the people you're targeting.

TRY IT!

Think of two separate client groups you could target. Put yourself in the customer's shoes and jot down some keywords, concepts and USPs that will appeal to each one.

Write two one-line hooks that summarize the overall story you want to tell – one for each customer group.

Write two elevator pitches – one for each customer group.

Create corresponding calls to action for both online and print marketing materials.

Write one verbal elevator pitch that uses a set of rhetorically framed questions, or something similar.

If you haven't yet read Chapter 7 on putting yourself in your customer's shoes, you might like to repeat this exercise once you've done so to see if your hooks and pitches evolve.

5   TESTING

What's in it for you?

- Gives you the confidence to try new things
- Embeds a sense of adventure and curiosity rather than caution and fearfulness
- Enables you to gain new knowledge about your market

Stepping outside the comfort zone

Good marketers always test. This is the first thing I learned when I began my marketing career in publishing over 20 years ago. Testing involves stepping outside your comfort zone by considering new things to try and alternative ways to think.

Business advisor and broadcaster Chris Cardell (n.d.) believes that 'marketing doesn't just involve testing – marketing *is* testing'. Testing ensures that you don't get wrapped up in a mindset of believing there is only one way to do something – that only method X is correct.

> Anyone who's come from the corporate world will know the hours wasted trying to make a decision on the 'right' marketing approach.
>
> A commitment to testing ends this problem once and for all. The smart marketer knows that the only way to be certain that a specific marketing approach will work, is to test it. As long as you test small (meaning you never spend more than you're willing to lose) you have the freedom to go out to the market and test an array of marketing initiatives. (Cardell n.d.)

Don't be afraid to trial different promotion strategies, particularly those that cost you money. Set fixed time limits for how long each test will last.

If you don't get the results you hoped for, consider it as a lesson learned and move on to a different tactic. Things to test might include:

- Trying different keywords in the meta data on your website and in the tags in any searchable directories you are listed in

- Designing your pricing strategy in different ways (see Chapter 6)

- Developing different straplines targeted at various customer groups

- Trialling different advertising platforms and tracking the results

Learning from experience

My first in-house role was for a science, technology and medical (STM) publisher with a large veterinary list. I visited their offices in Philadelphia in the early 1990s as part of an ongoing knowledge-sharing strategy within the international marketing division. Our press invested heavily in direct marketing – high-gloss brochures often detailing only one book that cost hundreds of dollars. The brochures were slick and expensive to produce, but so were the books we were selling.

Our US marketing department had sent senior management into a bit of a spin – all over a small-animal surgery mailshot that had taken a rather different approach to enticing its target market. Gone were the X-ray plates, anatomical drawings, four-colour book jacket thumbnails and highly targeted scientific copy. Instead we had Spot. Spot the dog that is – a rather adorable cartoon Dalmatian puppy chasing a piece of dead tree through eight pages of simple, straight-to-the-point, widely spaced copy. Less 'slick' and more 'stick' in this case! And lots of white space.

This was a complete change of direction in terms of promotion. 'It won't work,' people cried. 'It's giving the wrong impression,' said others. 'It's too child-like.' 'It's cheesy.' 'It's the wrong market.' Actually, it turned out to be their most successful direct mail campaign ever in terms of return on investment. The veterinarians loved it and the direct sales proved the point.

Of course, the cries of alarm came in before anyone knew it was going to be the most successful direct mail campaign ever, but the marketing director, Rick, let the campaign through anyway. Not because he knew it was going to work, but precisely because he didn't know. That was the point – he didn't know and couldn't know unless he let his team test it.

Testing was one of the first things I learned, and no marketing director I worked for in the years that followed ever did anything but ram that point home. Testing is what marketers do.

Fictive case study: ParlourPods?

Here's one idea I've been toying with for the future. It came about because one of my colleagues was feeling frustrated by the gap between the amount of time she wanted to spend reading some of her favourite blogs and the amount of time she felt she had available to navigate the blogosphere. Her problem was compounded by the fact that most of the work she does is onscreen. 'I spend goodness knows how many hours each day editing my clients' files, checking emails, responding to customers' online quotation requests and responding to client queries. My eyes are done in! I'd love to grab a cup of coffee, sit back and listen to my favourite bloggers rather than having to stare at my screen AGAIN! Can't you put the Proofreader's Parlour [my blog] on the radio?!'

Well, actually I could – sort of. What if I did offer the larger blog posts as three-minute audio streams in addition to the written text on the blog? They wouldn't be to everyone's taste, certainly, but for those who want to take a break, kick back for a few minutes and use their ears to enjoy a blog, a podcast would provide an alternative channel of communication.

My feeling about this is that we all have a range of preferences when it comes to how we engage with the content we value. I love to read, but I love to listen, too. I don't see the ParlourPods as being a replacement for the written blog, but rather an expansion of how its content is delivered.

- Will audio feeds of my blog posts be welcomed by the Parlour's readers?

- Will they attract visitors who hitherto didn't feel they had the time to devote yet more eye-time to the screen, thereby increasing traffic to my website?

- Will this increased traffic improve my search rankings?

- And will those improved search rankings generate sufficient high-value job opportunities to justify the investment in time and kit?

I don't know the answers to any of these questions. However, I'd like to find out. Audio streaming is the easiest and cheapest way to experiment initially so it makes sense to add this to my testing to-do list. And it may well be something that you'd like to experiment with, too.

Summing up

There can be a tendency for owners of small businesses to worry about which is the 'right' way to promote themselves. Don't be afraid to try different methods, different platforms, different messages. If you don't get the response you hoped for, move on and try something different. Marketing isn't about rights and wrongs; it isn't about only this way or only that way. It's about getting to a position where you *do know* by exploring what you *don't*.

Test sensibly though. Use one of the frameworks for setting goals and priorities (outlined in Chapter 11) if you feel unsure about where to focus your valuable time on new strategies.

I love this quotation attributed to Thomas A. Edison (of light bulb fame), because it sums up perfectly why testing is so important:

I have not failed. I've just found 10,000 ways that won't work.

KEY POINTS

- Don't be afraid to test new strategies and concepts. See what works and what doesn't. There's no such thing as failure when it comes to marketing, only lessons learned.

- If your test involves financial outlay, put a time limit on it. Then you can decide whether to continue with the trial or shelve it.

- Track your results where possible. The more data you gather, the more informed your decisions will be.

- Testing is simply about finding answers to the questions you're asking.

TRY IT!

Think about all the different elements of your marketing strategy, from your pricing structure, to the text and design of your promotional material, the types of clients you might contact and the places you might advertise your services. Make a list of five tests that you will carry out in the next 12 months. They can be quite big ideas or really small adjustments that you'd like to try.

6　A VALUE-ON APPROACH TO PRICING

What's in it for you?

- Helps you recognize that your skills have value, and your services are worth paying for.

- Encourages you to be creative through testing different strategies with different client types

- Helps you frame the rates you charge in a customer-centric way

Show me the money!

No marketing strategy would be complete without a pricing plan. Since this is a marketing book, I've chosen to focus not on what the price should be but rather how you can sell your pricing structure to a client in a way that centres around value-on, rather than money-off, thinking.

There's nothing wrong with offering discounts or special pricing offers – these tools have been used effectively by businesses large and small for as long as people have been exchanging goods and services. However, pricing models that only focus on the discount or a low price (money-off thinking), for the purposes of competitiveness, are, in my opinion, too narrow because:

- They don't address all of our clients' concerns; most customers are interested in price, but they want other information, too.

- Concentrating only on how much the client can save isolates the fee being charged from what the editor or proofreader is bringing to the table. The two should be connected. 'Good value' isn't necessarily the same as 'lowest price'.

- If the focus is always on money-off, then editorial freelancing becomes like the high street. Our clients come to expect 'cheap', and that could lead to a race to the bottom in the long term. None of us wins in that scenario. We're business owners and I think we need to be paid as such if our businesses are to be economically viable.

- Money-off sales messages focus the client's attention in the wrong place from the word go. I want my clients to be thinking about the positive impact I can have on their writing before they consider the negative effect this will have on their bank balance. I expect a client to want to know the price, and I understand that they have a budget. I respect the fact that my fees won't always match their budget but I want us both to start from the position of what the job requires rather than the cheapest deal they can get.

- Severe under-pricing or discounting can actually damage your ability to convince a client that you're a good bet. Our customers aren't stupid and might start to wonder what they'll not be getting if the discussion revolves purely around money-off thinking.

With this in mind, it makes sense to treat money-off options with caution. I'm not advocating that we shouldn't consider them, and test them strategically, but it is critical that we see the bigger picture and understand the consequences of the message we send when we talk about money.

Different models

There are multiple ways of structuring your pricing – per word, per hour, per page, per project – and if you offer a range of services you will probably have different prices for each (e.g. copy-editing, proofreading, substantive editing will all command different rates).

Don't forget that your pricing structure is not set in stone. You can test a particular model over the course of a few jobs. If you're not earning an hourly rate that you're happy with, you can adjust it, or shelve it, and move to a new model. Here are some other ideas to consider:

- There's nothing to stop you having different models for different clients or customer groups. I offer a per-word rate for some clients and an hourly rate for others.

- You could try a hybrid model whereby you offer the customer two options and make a commitment to charge them whatever comes in cheapest (e.g £X per 1,000 words and £X per hour).

- You might decide to operate on a minimum fee basis (e.g. £20 even if the work only takes 10 minutes to complete).

- You could offer a small discount to new customers, a time-limited discount for a particular client group (e.g. students), or the promise of a discount to a returning customer (loyalty reward).

- Consider framing the 'deal' in different terms (e.g. offering a set price for a top-quality job, regardless of how long it takes you).

- An alternative would be an option package (e.g. the customer can choose from three different prices depending on the level of intervention required and their budget).

- You could offer different pricing structures for a fast turnaround. By presenting the higher fee as an option, you still give your client a choice.

Don't forget, though, that the pricing structure you use is less important than how you frame what you are offering in a way that speaks to the customer's needs and concerns.

Framing quotations around value

In a competitive market where hundreds, perhaps thousands, of editorial freelancers are competing for clients, it can be tempting, especially for the new starter, to think that 'cheap' will win the day. Certainly, there will always be customers who want the cheapest price – the question is: do you want to work with them? I don't, though I completely respect the fact that a client wants to feel they've got value for money. However, 'cheap' and 'value' are not the same thing. It's therefore useful to think about how you can instil a sense of your value in a client's mind without engaging in a race to the bottom. You're a professional business owner and you deserve to be paid like one.

I like this quotation from BizBest Media Corp.:

> [I]f you want to avoid getting beat up on price, stop trying to compete on price alone ... Strive for fabulous, standout, outrageously great service to set your startup business apart from the crowd. (2005)

This is where the added value comes in. It involves thinking about how you mould your pricing structure around your USPs so that a customer thinks you're worth the money you're charging. And it means presenting your fee structure in a way that answers the questions they have. In this way, you move your quotations beyond just a money-off mentality and into a value-on way of thinking.

What does the customer want to know?

If I put myself in the customer's shoes for a moment, it makes it easier to work out how I might frame my quotation in terms of value-on thinking. When I buy a product or service, these are the kinds of things I might want to know:

- How much will it cost?
- Why does it cost that much? What am I getting for my money?
- Might the price quoted change? How can I prevent this happening?
- Is there a discount?
- What guarantees does the price cover? How am I protected?

I had to ask myself these questions when I bought a new computer last year. Prior to visiting the store I jotted down some notes about what I wanted, in order of importance:

- 2TB memory

- Fast processing

- A 24-inch (minimum) monitor included

- A brand that I'd heard of (though it didn't have to be a PC version of a Ferrari; a Ford Focus would be fine) and that I felt would provide me with some reassurance about reliability

- Some sort of guarantee

It was obvious to me that I wasn't going to get that package by looking for the cheapest PC on the market. If I wanted cheap, I'd have to sacrifice my top three preferences. I did have a budget in mind before I started my research, but it was never going to be about just the price. This was going to be my new business computer – I needed it to do what it said on the tin, first and foremost. Price was therefore one factor among several and had to be balanced against functionality.

Case study: my value-on framework

The following is a sample of one kind of quotation I provide for my proofreading services to self-publishers. This is just one example of a pricing model, and I've found it works for me. You might prefer a different model. Again, it's not the model that is the issue, but the way you choose to frame its presentation that is key to engaging with your customer.

Dear [name],

Many thanks for getting in touch. I'd be delighted to offer you a quotation for my proofreading services.

I charge £22 per hour for proofreading, in line with the rates suggested by the Society for Editors and Proofreaders (of which I am an Advanced Member) and the NUJ.

I usually proofread at a speed of between 3,000 and 5,000 words per hour, so for your project of 100,000 words the fee would be between £440 and £733.33 (approximately 20 to 33.5 hours of work).

I always keep a track of the number of hours I spend on a client's work and I'm happy to agree to a cap on the price (based on my slowest reading rate) so that you know what the worst-case scenario will be in terms of the final bill.

While I will endeavour to complete the project in the fewest possible hours, I never place speed over quality. That's why I like to offer you a capped and ranged price structure. I want to provide you with an excellent service but I don't want you to have any surprises, even if the job takes me longer than I expected.

I'm an experienced proofreader and work with both traditional and self-publishers on fiction and non-fiction titles. If you'd like to view my online portfolio, it's available here [link]. To date, I've proofread over 350 books, including [list of three titles relevant to client's project].

In order to ensure that I'm a suitable fit for you, may I also direct you to my free author guidance booklet, particularly the chapter on selecting the appropriate editorial professional. The PDF is available from my website or you can upload it to your e-reader via Smashwords. It includes a summary of exactly what my proofreading service includes and ensures that you and I are both clear from the outset about how we'd be working together.

Just one more thing – as an Advanced Member of the SfEP, I am bound by its Code of Practice, 'Ensuring Editorial Excellence', best-practice documentation that provides clients with an assurance of editorial assistance of the very highest standards.

If you'd like to continue the conversation, please do get in touch again.

With very best wishes,

Louise

[Detailed signature]

The hourly rate I want to earn is fixed at the outset and it's rarely negotiable. Instead, I aim to justify the price I charge by framing the quotation in terms of value:

- I'm an Advanced Member of the SfEP – Message: I'm worth it and you're in safe hands.

- I'm bound by the SfEP's Code of Practice – Message: you're protected.

- The rate I charge is in line with the suggested rates of two professional organizations (the SfEP and the NUJ) – Message: it's a fair and professional rate.

- I tell them the upper- and lower-limit speeds that I tend to proofread at, and then supply a ranged fee that accords with this – Message: you know the best- and worst-case scenarios so there'll be no surprises.

- I also tell them that while I'll complete the job in the fewest hours possible, I never place speed above quality – Message: you'll get a top-notch job.

- I provide them with a few examples of related projects that I've proofread, and a link to my website portfolio – Message: I've done this before. You can be confident in my service.

- In my free advice booklet, I offer clear guidance on what 'proofreading' means (as well as lots of other useful information for self-publishers) – Message: I'm engaged with what you're doing and want to ensure that we're both clear about what you need.

Where to find your value – tangibles and intangibles

Depending on your experience and your skill base, there are lots of ways that you can add value into the quotations you offer to clients, what Adrienne Montgomerie (personal correspondence) calls tangible and intangible value – value that will focus their attention on why you are worth the price you are charging. This value might be something tangible (like a resource) or intangible (like an example of continued professional development).

Some examples of intangible value include:

- Professional accreditation, membership and any other relevant training or development.
- Specialist knowledge or experience: Examples might include specialist legal, scientific or technological experience. Or you may have ebook formatting or design experience that you can use to demonstrate your professionalism and frame your quotes within.
- Ability to work in a variety of formats (Word, paper, PDF, HTML, XML) or using particular software such as LaTeX or InDesign.

Some examples of tangible value include:

- Free booklets, newsletters, advice/guidance sheets or videos on self-publishing, self-editing, self-proofreading, using Word, formatting an ebook, working with Track Changes, etc. See Chapter 8 on adding value to your business and ask yourself if any of these tools suggested here might be of interest to a customer. If they are, you'll have a way to show that you are engaged with the client and are able to respond to their needs before you've even been asked to. It will also inspire confidence in the customer and a feeling of being nurtured.
- Add-ons: Perhaps you could offer to proofread the blurb for a self-publisher's book jacket at no extra cost. Or you could offer the same for a business's website homepage. If you have multiple editorial skills, you could decide to frame your quote in terms of offering your client a package deal for a two-stage edit, or an edit and a proofread.

- Turnaround: If you think your client would appreciate a fast turnaround, you could state that you can provide 24-hour (or weekend) project completion for up to X,000 words, and all for your standard fee.

What's the right or fair price?

I've yet to be convinced that there is a real 'right' or 'fair' price. There is only a calculation of what your costs are, what you need or want to earn, and the value you place on your service. Many professional organizations, like unions and editorial societies, suggest guidelines for pricing your services and these are incredibly useful. However, they are only suggestions and you should not be surprised if some clients (e.g. publishers) offer hourly rates that fall below these suggested minima. Nor should you be surprised if others (e.g. businesses) are willing to pay a higher rate for your services.

Buying copy-editing or proofreading services is not like buying one particular brand of washing machine from five different suppliers. It's more like visiting five different suppliers and comparing five different washing machines in each. Each supplier will be offering different deals (in terms of prices, length of guarantee or customer service support) and operating within a variety of business models. And each brand of machine will offer different levels of functionality, have different levels of brand awareness and different reputations with regards to reliability. The editorial freelancer is like the washing machine and the supplier rolled into one, and the customer makes their choice and pays their money.

The price you set (or accept) and the model you use is up to you and no one can tell you what you should charge or how you should structure your fee – it's your business and you are in control. How you decide to price your editorial services in a competitive market involves thinking creatively about the value you offer and the best way of pitching it to make yourself interesting. Don't be surprised if you can't find a unanimous answer to the question 'How much should I charge?' among your colleagues, because the likelihood is that there isn't one.

Testing

The concept of testing is just as applicable to pricing as it is to other marketing activities. One particular model might not be suitable for every client type. If you're working with clients for whom English is a second language, it will probably take you longer to work through 10,000 words than if the author is a native English speaker.

Testing different pricing structures is therefore a vital exercise in determining how you will earn an economically viable rate. Testing gives you information about what works and for whom, and allows you to build up a knowledge base that you can use to determine the way you will frame your quotations to different client groups.

Case study: learning from a bad experience

Earlier in my career I tested a price-per-1,000-words model for non-publisher clients. At the time most of my work was for publishers. Most, though not all, of my publishers tell me the hourly rate they are prepared to pay or they offer a fixed price for the job. I'd collected thousands of hours' worth of data based on this client group, and from it I determined a price per 1,000 words that I thought would work in a different market. I acknowledged that in the case of non-publisher clients I wouldn't always be dealing with text that had been copy-edited so I factored this into my rate and set it at £7 per 1,000 words in order to accommodate the extra time I'd need. I believed that this would equate to a comfortable hourly rate that was in line with the minima suggested by two UK professional organizations, the SfEP and the National Union of Journalists (NUJ).

Within the space of a month, I was contacted by two separate clients – a student and a magazine. Both provided me with samples of the work and I quoted my trial per-1,000-word rate. The magazine work, unlike the student's, consisted of monthly projects, so I viewed it as a super opportunity to add another regular income stream to my business.

Once I started work on both projects it became clear that I'd underestimated how long the work would take. By the time I'd completed the student's thesis and the magazine's monthly projects, I'd earned less than the UK's national minimum wage per hour.

The student thesis was a one-off so I put that down to a job done and a lesson learned. However, the magazine was a different matter. I had to renegotiate. Unfortunately, the client couldn't afford my adjusted rate and we parted ways amicably. I immediately set to work on rethinking a new pricing mechanism that moved away from assumptions based on the data provided by my publisher client group and started, instead, to think about how I could reframe my quotations in a way that would satisfy this other client group and protect my business.

I don't look back on this experience as a catastrophe, though at the time it was extremely frustrating. Rather, it was one of the most valuable lessons I learned and if it hadn't happened I might not have reframed my pricing model. I still believe that the per-word model can be an effective tool, and I do use it on occasion, but it's not my primary mechanism of choice (though it may be yours and it may work extremely well). Even when things go wrong, if you learn from the experience then you add your own type of value into your editorial business: wisdom!

Case study: the dangers of focusing on cheap

This case study is a super example of how good business practice won the day and how severe under-pricing was a turn off for a client.

One of my colleagues, editor Beth Hamer, was asked in 2013 (via her Find a Proofreader listing) to give a quote for proofreading some educational material for a charity. She assessed the document and, based on the fact that it was well written and for a charity, quoted £150, slightly below her standard rate of £10 per

1,000 words. Beth wanted the opportunity to broaden her skill set beyond her usual student client group and so was keen to get the job. She therefore quoted a fee that was competitive in terms of its sensitivity to the charity market, but high enough to provide her with a good return because of the initial quality of the writing.

> My quote was met with a positive response, but about half an hour later my contact came back to me to say that she had had another quote for £30. She seemed to understand that there was a price to be paid somewhere along the line for such a low fee and asked me to give her some justification for my fee.
>
> The client had to get the quote approved by her line manager, who would want to know why she was ignoring a very cheap quote in favour of a more expensive one.
>
> I told her that I was an Associate of the SfEP and adhered to their code of conduct, pointed her to the testimonials on my website and on Find a Proofreader, emphasised my training qualifications, and assured her that I always delivered on time (it was a relatively urgent job).

Beth gave some serious thought to whether she should reduce her price, but concluded that a bidding war made no sense because she'd never be able to afford to get anywhere near her competitor's pricing structure. She stood by her price.

Beth won the job. She'd justified her price in terms of the value she was bringing to the table. In doing so, her client recognized what we all recognize – that if something looks too good to be true, it probably is. Clients seeking the services of editorial freelancers don't have bottomless bank accounts, but ultimately they want a quality return on their investment. And in this example, a cheap price, framed in terms of money saved rather than quality provided, didn't communicate the message that the client wanted to hear.

Case study: am I undercutting myself?

My colleague Kate Haigh and I often lament the fact that not everyone in the editorial freelancing community is open to discussing rates. It's a shame because one can learn so much from one's colleagues. Earlier I gave the example of my ranged pricing structure. Talking to Kate made me realize that I might test an alternative fixed-rate structure that would be more beneficial to the financial side of my business.

If I offer a range between A and C, depending on how long a job takes, with A being the lowest price (fewest hours to complete the job) and C being the highest price (most hours to complete the job), and the customer commissions me on this basis, I've learned that they are prepared to pay C. If I only charge B (because the final number of hours came in somewhere in the middle of my estimated range) then I've lost out on C–B income.

There are benefits to my ranged structure in terms of the way it makes my client feel about how my fees are presented. That doesn't mean it's the only way, or the right way. I'm therefore going to test a new structure that offers one fixed rate based on my slowest reading rate and I'll monitor the response rate over a set period so that I can evaluate what the impact is on successfully turning a quotation into a commission.

Should you work for free?

My own view is that there's a time and a place for gratis work. I've never offered gratis work to a customer unless it was going to be of benefit to me. My own approach during my start-up phase included this element, but I was very targeted in my approach. I selected cottage-industry publishers who did all their proofreading in-house because they weren't in a financial position to outsource the service. I asked a few if I could do a gratis piece of work for them in return for a testimonial and their agreement to act as a referee, if they were happy with my work of course. The results varied: three never got back to me, one said no, and two said yes.

I did the work, got great feedback and secured my testimonials. I started rolling out letters to other publishers, including Publisher X, asking to be put on their freelance lists. I included my testimonials and references. Slowly, I got clients. I rolled my letters out in phases, targeting a little wider each time and using each new reference and testimonial to 'sell' myself more, though I could then start to include a small portfolio of work I'd completed, too. Some years later I found out that I secured a position on Publisher X's list based purely on my cottage-industry publisher's testimonial and reference. Many years before, they'd worked together in academic publishing. Furthermore, that same cottage-industry publisher now pays me to work for them.

To summarize, the foundation of this strategy is therefore underpinned by a clear understanding of the following:

- The target – a very small, select group of clients who will benefit from your services but who will not be re-routing paid work from your colleagues.

- The objective – a testimonial, reference or experience that you can sell on to future paying customers.

If you're discounting or working for free because you're a recent entrant to the field, don't have confidence in your value, or think that you're not worth as much as a more experienced colleague, stop, step back and reconsider. Put your insecurities to one side for a moment and think instead about what you want to achieve and how the discount or freebie can tangibly benefit the growth of your business.

The hourly rate and beyond

Focusing on the billable hourly rate is not the only indicator of the health of your business. That's because it doesn't take account of the costs of doing business, and it doesn't give you an overall picture of the amount of work you have coming in.

The effective hourly rate and tracking the data

The American Editor blog (Adin 2013a) discusses the effective hourly rate (EHR) extensively. Working out the EHR tells you not only what you earned, but what you spent, and it's a useful tool that helps you arrive at a fee that is economically viable for your business in the longer term. Briefly, if you are billing clients an average £20 for every hour that you work for them, but your costs (after training, equipment, business housekeeping, marketing, etc.) are £2.50, your EHR is actually £17.50. However, if you need £20 per hour to meet your living expenses, you'll need to adjust your business model accordingly. Either you'll need to do the same job in less time, or take on more work, or increase the billable hourly rate where it's possible to do so. That's why value-on pricing is such an important part of your marketing strategy – it helps you to think about creative ways to keep the price you charge up rather than down.

Working out the relationship between the price you charge and the health of your business is impossible if you're not tracking the data. There's a free Excel template on my website that you can try out and adapt to suit your own needs (Harnby 2012).

For more guidance on pricing a project, read Melanie Thompson's *Pricing a Project: How to prepare a professional quotation* (2013).

Value-on thinking: what the client offers

The value-on approach can be applied not only to how you communicate your price to clients, but also to how you evaluate the worth of a client to your business. Some of my most valuable clients aren't the ones that pay the highest hourly rate. I choose to have a range of clients who pay me a range of rates because they offer different types of value.

• Two of my publisher clients offer an hourly rate that is somewhat lower than the rate I charge self-publisher clients. However, the relationship is well-established, they offer me very regular work, they pay on time, they are extremely pleasant to work for, I thoroughly enjoy proofreading the books they send me, and our mutual expectations are clearly understood. Their lower rates are, to some degree, compensated for by these other factors.

- My non-publisher clients are more lucrative in terms of the hourly rate but they are never in a position to offer me the same amount of work. It takes longer to communicate a mutual understanding of what's required because often they are new to publishing and are sometimes nervous about the process. Furthermore, I have lower levels of confidence with regards to on-time payment.

- Some of my regular business clients provide a lucrative hourly rate but the jobs, while regular, are small. This means that the total amount that ends up in my bank account each month is lower than that from the two publisher clients mentioned above.

What works for me might not work for you. The important thing is to be aware of the different options available and to evaluate what your needs are, what your costs are, and the value that different clients bring to the table (e.g. confidence over payment, regularity of work, job satisfaction, mutual understanding and, of course, financial remuneration).

Thinking about pricing from a value-on perspective enables you to go beyond the data and look at the bigger picture.

KEY POINTS

- Track the basic data – this knowledge base will be an invaluable pricing tool.

- When quoting for customers, frame your bid in terms of value-on thinking. Discounts are only one of a range of hooks you can use to compel your customer to understand why the rate you are offering is a good deal.

- Put yourself in the customer's shoes to help you work out what you need to tell them in addition to the actual price.

- Test different models with different client types.

- Don't expect to find unanimity with regard to pricing within the editorial freelancing market or the publishing industry – it doesn't exist.

- Consider restricting discounts and gratis work so that they are used in a highly targeted fashion – to achieve specific objectives that will benefit your business.

- It's your editorial business and you are in control. Ultimately, you can price projects in whatever way feels comfortable for you. Just remember that high value doesn't mean the same thing as a low price. You have other options.

TRY IT!

If your current pricing mechanism focuses only on discounts (the money-off approach), try a value-on model. Think about your skills and background, and the USPs you bring to the table. Then ask yourself what you want to know when you buy a product or service – when you're the customer. Then draft a response to a client's request to quote for your services – one that incorporates not only the fee, but the value underpinning that fee. This is a particularly useful exercise if you're worried about how to compete in a crowded market, or you feel that you're consistently charging a rate that isn't viable for your business in the longer term.

If you're not keeping track of what your business is earning and spending, create a simple spreadsheet within the next week that you will update on a job-by-job basis.

7 PUTTING YOURSELF IN YOUR CUSTOMER'S SHOES

What's in it for you?

- Ensures you communicate the right message, using the appropriate language
- Encourages you to explore multiple marketing channels
- Reminds you that marketing is a dynamic process and that regular review is critical

It's not about you

Whether you're creating your CV, designing your website, tackling that directory listing, cold calling a client, or sending a response to an email offer to quote, put yourself in the shoes of your customer before you do anything else. Just two minutes spent in that head-space could make the difference between getting your pitch right or wrong, and between winning the job or losing it to a competitor.

For the proofreader or editor this means asking yourself:

- Is the marketing channel you're using appropriate to the type of client you want to attract?
- What kind of customer are you targeting or responding to (publisher, self-publisher, independent academic, student, large corporation, small business owner, etc.)?
- Do they know exactly what you do (e.g. editing, proofreading, copywriting, substantive editing)?

- What do they want/need to know?

- Are the terms that you use to articulate what you do the same as the terms your customer uses?

- Are their expectations and your expectations, based on that terminology, a good match?

- Are you including information that is broadly relevant to that client type?

- And if you're responding to an offer to quote, have you tailored that information so it's especially relevant to that particular client?

- If you're cold-contacting a specific client or business type, have you highlighted any relevant USPs (unique selling points) that match your prior work experience to their field of business?

In summary, you might use different marketing activities to target different client types, and different hooks and pitches to make yourself interesting to those client types. It's worth checking that the message matches the customer's expectations at each opportunity.

Client types

Some editors and proofreaders only work for publishers; some only work for students; some only work for businesses; some only work for independent authors. Many of us, however, take work from all of these sub-markets. Some editorial freelancers specialize in the academic field, some in fiction, and some in corporate work. However, some of us look to exploit a number of different areas both because of the variety it adds to our work streams and because it allows us to spread risk (see Chapters 9 and 10).

I'm a great believer in specializing first and diversifying later. I think that having a specialist area (e.g. science, technical and medical (STM) editing; legal proofreading; social science proofreading; business editing) for the new starter is a useful tool for building a solid pitch to potential customers. Using your prior career and educational experience, for example, can help you to demonstrate to particular client types that you understand their language.

That's not to say that you can't exploit different marketing channels and make yourself interesting to client types outside these fields. If you do decide to diversify, it's essential to put yourself in the shoes of those different customers. Consider the following client types:

- The Chinese academic who needs an editor to work on the article she's submitting to a medical journal

- The self-publishing science-fiction author who needs a structural edit

- The desk editor at the social science press who needs a copy-editor for a multi-authored political science handbook

- The Master's student who wants his geography dissertation proofread

- The corporate professional who needs her annual report formatted and edited

- The trade publishing house who needs you to copy-edit their latest mass-market paperback

These customer types have different needs and expectations. If you want to make yourself interesting to them, it's worth spending time considering how you are going to communicate with them.

Marketing channels and the customer

As a professional proofreader or editor, you know the key professional organizations, blogs, discussion groups, and directories related to your business. But does your customer?

If they're a Canadian or UK publisher, they will know about the respective searchable directories hosted by the EAC and the SfEP. But are you sure the Michigan-based student knows about the EFA? Does the South African self-publishing author know about

PEG? Does the Dutch business professional who needs her website proofreading know about SENSE? Does the Australian academic know about the IPEd?

The answers to the above questions might be 'yes', but they might be 'no'. We'll be discussing multiple marketing channels in Chapter 9, but for now it's enough to acknowledge that one marketing channel will not be sufficient if you want to attract the attention of a range of customer types.

It's worth remembering the quotation from the Introduction:

> If you could see the world through John Smith's eyes,
> you can sell to John Smith what John Smith buys.
> (Cardell n.d.)

Don't assume that John Smith knows your business like you know your business. Make it as easy as possible for him to find you by marketing yourself using a variety of channels – those that make sense to you and those you feel confident will make sense to John.

Case study

Let's take a look at my own business in order to explore how we can put ourselves in our customer's shoes. I specialize in proofreading for academic and trade publishing houses, but I also enjoy working with independent self-publishing authors when the right project comes up. Additionally, I welcome the opportunity to work with business professionals who want their websites, CVs and covering letters proofread.

- In the UK, an entry in the SfEP's Directory of Editorial Services is a must-have if one wants to maximize one's chances of picking up new publisher clients. I've been contacted by nine publishing houses in the seven years I've advertised in that directory. Now that I'm on those clients' freelance lists, they come to me with repeat offers of work; that is, I don't have to go hunting for it.

- My website has generated 80 per cent of the leads from self-publishers looking for a proofreader for their novels.

- My entry in the Find a Proofreader directory has generated 65 per cent of the leads from business professionals looking for someone to help them with their CVs and covering letters.

- The Master's and PhD students who contacted me in 2012 and 2013 came from all three of the above channels.

- One client, a children's poet, found me via Yell.com.

- Two clients came via referrals from colleagues with whom I regularly network online.

So I have a range of customer types who find me in different ways. If I limited myself to only the SfEP directory, I'd have lost out on the opportunity to work for some of those self-publishers, students, business professionals, and the poet. If I'd limited myself to Yell, I'd have lost out on the publisher clients, a customer type from whom I receive the most regular and repeat work.

Language and the customer

Having worked out which marketing channels you want to use, it's time to think about the language you use. You may understand the differences between structural editing, copy-editing, and proofreading, but does your client? A publisher will, and so might an academic author. But the self-publisher and student might not.

Take care to avoid the use of jargon. Dawn Duke (2014) uses an interesting analogy that may help you recall your own experience of jargon and the impact it had on you.

You may well have gone to the garage to have your car fixed and have a mechanic talk to you in a manner that baffles you with jargon about crankshafts and catalytic converters. How did that make you feel? Most of us feel highly suspicious of someone when they talk to us in this way. That is not how you wish to make your audience feel. Therefore, it is important to learn to translate jargon into language that is understandable to everyone.

Furthermore, the issue could be more than just understanding terminology; rather, it might be that the terminology is completely different.

Case studies

My colleague Adrienne Montgomerie runs an editing business that specializes in educational materials. Much of her work is developmental and substantive editing, though she is a certified copy-editor with the Editors' Association of Canada. She has a range of client types, from educational publishers to corporate clients. Depending on who she's talking to, she has to consider the language she uses. Says Adrienne:

> In educational publishing, what I do is called developmental editing. But in the corporate world, it is called knowledge transfer, educational design, and even technical writing. The clients I want can't find me if I'm not speaking their language. (Closed correspondence)

In my own work with traditional publishers and self-publishers, I come across similar discrepancies. My traditional publishing clients have very fixed definitions of proofreading and editing, definitions that are consistent both within and across companies, but my self-publishers often interchange these terms. And while I might discuss rectos, running heads, widows and half titles with publisher clients, this kind of language may mean nothing to a first-time indie author and could even serve to make them feel uncomfortable.

USPs/key points and the customer

You might also want to consider the key points you want to flag in order to make yourself interesting to different clients types. Consider the following:

If you're advertising in a directory from which you want to generate interest from publishers, highlight the key USPs that will mean something to publishers. For example:

- Accreditation, certification or membership of a professional editing organization

- The training you've completed that your national publishing industry recognizes
- Testimonials from other publishers
- Summary of projects you've completed for other publishers
- Ability to use industry-standard markup language (e.g. BSI 5261-2 in the UK)
- Subject areas in which you specialize
- Ability to work to deadlines, without fail (commitment statement)

If you've produced a promotional leaflet that is aimed at self-publishers, highlight the key selling points that will mean something to them. For example:

- Testimonials from other independent authors
- Summary of self-publishing projects you've worked on
- Ability to work on paper or in a Word document (it's unlikely that this client group will either know about or be interested in industry markup language)
- Spell out the services you offer and what these involve (a self-publisher might not understand the difference between proofreading, editing and manuscript critiquing)
- Ability to work in a friendly and flexible manner
- Provision of top-quality service at a customer-centric price

Case study

Compare the key points on the following two websites hosted by my colleagues Hester Higton and Jenny Drewery. Hester specializes in working with humanities publishing houses, businesses, independent academics and museums. Jenny specializes in working with self-publishing fiction writers. The two presentation styles are quite different, but each is appropriate for the market these professionals want to speak to.

Hester's key points:

- Advanced Member of the Society for Editors and Proofreaders; holds Licentiateship in Editorial Skills from the City and Guilds Institute
- Trained with Publishing Training Centre and qualified with distinction in proofreading and merit in copy-editing
- Former research and curatorial posts in national and provincial museums
- Testimonials from other publishers
- Doctorate in the history of science
- Author of two books and contributor to other books and journals
- Ability to use industry-standard markup language (e.g. BSI 5261C:2005 in the UK) on paper or edit onscreen
- Commitment statement: 'As a trained academic myself, I can edit academic writing with ease, and without introducing errors through lack of basic knowledge'
- List of humanities disciplines in which she works
- Emphasis on academic client's needs: 'I am also trained to spot the flaws in a sophisticated argument, and know how to carry out further minor research without having to raise every little question with the author'

Jenny's key points:

- Qualified professional freelance proofreader
- Numerous testimonials from independent authors and students
- Ability to work on paper or in Word
- Commitment statement: 'I won't mess with your unique style. As a writer myself, I will respect the way you express yourself'
- Quality proofreading service offered that ensures text is clear and correct

- Friendly and flexible; 'no job too small'; stepped pricing structure available to accommodate every customer; self-editing advice

- Emphasis on individual's needs: 'Customer-friendly proofreading at comfortable prices ... I believe there should be some degree of textual help available to everyone who wants to improve their written work, whatever their financial circumstances'

These two presentations are very different but both are super examples of best practice because each is targeted to the editorial freelancer's core customer requirements. It's worth visiting your colleagues' websites to see which key points they emphasize to make themselves interesting, and how they convey a sense of having put themselves in their customer's shoes.

Taking a dynamic approach

As your business develops, you might find that the bulk of your work is increasingly coming from new client types. In that case, you should consider whether there is new information you need to build in that speaks with more emphasis to this group.

Putting yourself in your customer's shoes can mean regular tweaking and targeting each and every time the opportunity arises. Or it might mean yearly (but equally important) reassessment.

CVs and brochures are two examples of things you can regularly update and then add to your website, link to in a directory listing or email/snail mail on request. On the other hand, while the overall information you elect to include on your website, or in one particular directory, might remain static, there will be opportunities to take a dynamic approach and customize the way you present this information in a way that helps the customer better evaluate whether they're a good fit for you.

Case study: a customer-centric CV

I've lost count of the CVs/résumés I've generated over the years, because each time I'm asked by a client to send one as part of my quotation, I like to tailor it specifically to that invitation to quote. My website currently includes a couple of slightly different options – one focuses on the work I've done for academic publishers, the other for trade publishers. The former includes a truncated portfolio of social science projects that I've proofread, whereas the latter includes a list of fiction and commercial non-fiction projects. Both of them emphasize the information that I believe publishers want to know.

However, I don't use either of those when a non-publisher client contacts me directly and asks me to send them a CV. Instead, I create a new one. Here are just a few examples of things I might tweak for my newly created CV, in this case for an independent writer:

- If an independent author contacts me and wants to know that I've proofread best-sellers, I'll select some of the commercial published pieces of fiction that I've worked on (perhaps *A Visit from the Goon Squad* by Jennifer Egan, or one of Ira Levin's novels), but if they want to know that I'm experienced in working with independent authors like them, I'll add in a list of self-published projects I've completed, particularly those in the same genre as the author is working.

- I'll also remove the information about my ability to use the UK publishing industry's standard markup symbols and, instead, insert something about working in Word with Tracked Changes.

- My publisher-based CVs don't include an explanation of what proofreading is – publishers already understand this. My indie author, however, might benefit from a few lines that explain exactly what my proofreading service includes.

- I like to include a couple of lines that reassure the indie writer of my commitment to do no harm and that I won't interfere with their authorial voice. A publisher-focused CV wouldn't explain this because it is taken as given for the level of intervention my service includes.

From the tone you use to the USPs (unique selling points) you highlight, the terminology you employ, the genres/subjects/experience you list, the kinds of testimonial you include, and the promises you make – ensuring they match what the customer needs and understands is the key to good communication and successful marketing. And if that means having multiple CVs, business cards, and promo brochures, so be it. If it means different pitches for different directory listings, so be it. If it means additional work to ensure you're using the right message to the right person at the right time, so be it.

Case study: website evaluation

I'm currently in the process of evaluating my website. As discussed earlier, the language of my website is, compared to others, quite publisher-focused. And yet, over the past two years the number of self-publishing authors contacting me has rocketed. I've already made some changes to the information I provide, and the value I add, based on this shift in my customer base, but I'm also taking a dynamic view to the way I structure the pages on the website. This includes thinking about:

- Creating a page dedicated to self-publishers that can be accessed by my menu ribbon

- Moving some of the added value (links to résumés and my *Guidelines for Authors*) away from the Resources section and into the dedicated self-publishing section

The point is that no website, directory listing, advertisement or résumé needs to be set in stone. When we put ourselves in our customer's shoes, change is inevitable – it's an opportunity to reassess the information we provide, the language we use and the way we present it so that we appear as interesting as possible to those who find us.

KEY POINTS

- Think about your USPs and how they relate to the client you are targeting.

- Specializing in a particular field can be an effective strategy when starting out. If you decide to focus on, say, academic work, your clients might still come from different markets (e.g. the student, the journal article author and the publisher).

- Different client types use different marketing channels. Maximize your chances of being found by putting yourself in your client's shoes and choosing the channels accordingly.

- Make sure you use the appropriate language to communicate with clients. What makes sense to a publisher might mean little to a student, business professional or independent author.

- Modify your sales pitch accordingly. Think about the key points that make you interesting to each client type. A publisher might be less interested in friendliness and pricing structure but keen to know you can use the industry-standard markup language. A self-publisher will be unlikely to give two hoots for your ability to use a proofreader's hieroglyphics but will want to feel that they can trust you and that you will respect their authorial voice.

- Research what your colleagues are doing – the language they use, the key selling points they focus on, and the channels they use to promote their businesses – to put themselves in their customer's shoes.

TRY IT!

Make a list of your customer groups and put yourself in their shoes. Are you exploiting the channels they're most likely to use to find you? If you're unsure, write down three new channels you could test.

If you haven't updated your website this year, ask yourself if the language and the structure are still the best match for your primary client groups – can they find the information they need to assess you to your best advantage?

Take a look at your CV/résumé and make sure that it's up to date and uses the language and USPs that speak to the specific customer type it's aimed at. Consider whether you need multiple versions.

8   ADDING VALUE

What's in it for you?

- Forces you to put yourself in your customer's shoes
- Increases your visibility within the editorial community and provides you with massive SEO benefits
- Communicates your professionalism through engagement with the customer's needs
- Provides you with interesting USPs that make you stand out from the crowd

Making yourself stand out

The concept of adding value is key to any successful marketing strategy and can be applied in big chunks and in tiny ones, depending on the promotional tool you're employing. When you add value you offer something to a current or future relationship that shows you are engaged with the client – you have put yourself in their shoes.

Adding value is all about offering that extra something – the wow factor that separates your letter, your website, your email response, your telephone call, your promotional leaflet, and your directory entry from those of others. Don't forget – there are lots of others, thousands of others. And now that we're operating in a global and online environment, it's easier than ever to set up a proofreading or editing business. Getting found by clients isn't a test of editorial ability; it's a test of marketing ability.

From the point of view of a current client, adding value to the relationship makes you more likely to be reselected for future work.

From the point of view of a prospective client, adding value makes you more interesting and likely to be selected for (or at least asked to quote on) a first job.

Different types of customer will appreciate different types of added value, so keep your thinking as broad-based as possible. Don't forget that your colleagues are also potential customers, so adding value for them is important. Furthermore, don't just think in terms of future customers – add value for your current clients, too. They are your most valuable resource; in addition to offering you repeat work, they might also recommend you to new clients.

Little saplings ...

How much effort you decide to expend on adding value to your editorial marketing strategy is, of course, entirely up to you. If the ideas presented here fill you with horror as you wonder how you are going to find the time to do everything, then fear not; you don't have to do it all at once. A little here, a little there – from small saplings grow large trees, as the saying goes.

The value I've attempted to build into my proofreading business certainly didn't appear overnight. I started with a few basic tenets and developed the strategy over time. I chose to add value based on what I was hearing from my particular customer types and my colleagues.

What value is worth adding?

What you add should be determined by your colleagues and customers. If it's of no interest to them, then it's no longer value – it's just stuff. And 'stuff' is wasted time and energy when it comes to a marketing strategy.

Listen to what your current and prospective customers are telling you they want. Is it a specialist skill set? Is it a particular approach or manner? Is it guidance or advice on particular issues related to what they are doing?

Who benefits?

When you add value to your editorial business, the short answer is that everyone benefits.

Benefits for you

- It shows your customer you're engaged with their needs. This demonstrates your professionalism and makes you more likely to be selected (or reselected) for work. In the case of colleagues, it's also another way of actively engaging with your business community.

- There are SEO benefits – some examples of added value are easy to share using social media. If it's good-quality, relevant added value, people will read it, share it and link to it.

- It provides you with unique selling points (USPs) that can set you apart from the crowd.

Benefits for your customer

- It doesn't (or shouldn't) cost the customer anything extra – it's their equivalent of a free lunch.

- Confidence – if a client feels that you've engaged with the challenges they face, it gives them confidence in you and confidence in their project.

- Gratitude – when someone gifts you with something that is relevant to your needs, you're thankful and you remember it. It's the same for your customer.

The stand-out perception really works. In November 2013 I was contacted by someone looking for proofreading services, and the request was urgent. The client emailed me, saying:

> So, in something of a panic, I'm searching Google. Found lots of websites offering the service of course, but yours stood out in the crowd as a place giving advice on when professional help would actually be a good idea.

I couldn't take the work, owing to the tight deadline, but I recommended a colleague whom I knew would be in a position to help. The client's response? 'Keep up the good work. Finding someone like you through Google has made me feel just as "mushy" as the Children in Need appeal [annual UK fundraising telethon].'

Using added value to stand out helps clients to feel that they want to choose you – because you're engaged on a professional level with their needs. It enhances your reputation, and that of our profession as a whole!

Added value – some substantive ideas

Many of the things you can do to add value can be considered with regard to both your current client relationships and your future customers. Don't forget that your colleagues are potential clients, too, so value added for their benefit is value added for a customer's benefit. Below, I've picked out some examples of good practice from the editorial community:

- Copyeditors' Knowledge Base (resource hub from Katharine O'Moore-Klopf/KOKEdit)
- Writers and Editors (resource hub from Pat McNees)
- *Reignite Your Writing* (Sophie Playle's free guidebook collection for writers)
- The Proofreader's Parlour (editorial business blog from Louise Harnby)
- Sharmanedit (journal publishing blog from Anna Sharman)
- Full Media (small business blog from Nick Jones)
- Beyond Paper Editing (self-publishing advice blog from Carla Douglas and Corina Koch MacLeod)
- Commas, Characters and Crime Scenes (self-editing advice blog from Marcus Trower)
- *Guidelines for New Authors* (free ebooklet from Louise Harnby)

- Free downloadable PDF proofreading stamps including installation video tutorial (from Louise Harnby on The Proofreader's Parlour)

- *Macros for Writers and Editors* (free book from Paul Beverley/Archive Publications)

- *Free Top 10 Tips Proofreading Guide* (ebooklet from John Espirian)

- Resources for Word Users (from Liz Broomfield on the Libro Editing blog)

- Video demonstrating PDF markup Adobe Acrobat Reader XI tools (Adrienne Montgomerie on the Right Angels and Polo Bears blog)

- Manuscript management tools for fiction authors and editors (available on Mary McCauley's Letters from an Irish Editor blog)

- Kateproof (Kate Haigh's blog containing advice for students and interviews with self-publishing authors)

Spotting the opportunities

Let's imagine a few examples. I've based these on both my own experience and what my colleagues have reported. They're just for illustration so, for now, don't take them as written. They're just trigger points to consider.

1. Online discussion groups are increasingly discussing the importance of copy-editors being able to use software like InDesign.

2. New proofreaders are wondering which training courses are the best in your country, whether it's worth joining a society, which are the best social media networks, how to go about setting up a Facebook business page, and so on.

3. Your colleagues report that many self-publishers don't seem to understand the difference between copy-editing, copywriting, proofreading, structural editing, and so on.

4. Your lurking on independent writer LinkedIn forums indicates that a lot of authors are worried about whether an editor will be difficult to work with, will damage their 'voice', will be inflexible or unfriendly.

5. You're constantly trying to find answers to certain recurring questions but can't find an online resource hub that houses all the answers in one place.

6. You get a rejection letter from a publisher because you can't proofread onscreen.

7. You hear fellow editors and proofreaders frequently discussing how non-publishing clients, such as businesses, don't understand what you do.

8. In your work with self-publishers, you see a range of mistakes cropping up time and again – double spaces after full points, confusion over certain points of grammar, inconsistency with regards to punctuation style, use of multiple spaces (rather than tabs) for paragraph indentation.

9. You notice that an increasing number of self-publishers are struggling to prepare their work for e-publication.

The above examples should indicate how you might begin to think about adding value based on your customer's needs. By thinking about what they want – putting yourself in their shoes – you can develop tools, resources, a pitch and a manner that gives you the wow factor.

In (1), (6) and (9) you can add value by introducing a skill into your toolkit that you can sell to a customer. You might therefore decide to carry out further training in order to expand your skill set so that it includes being able to use LaTeX or Scrivner, or you learn how to format Word documents according to Kindle or Smashwords guidelines.

Number (2) tells you that there are new entrants in the field out there who have lots of questions but few answers. We've all been newbies and there is value to be added to the business of any editorial freelancer who takes the time to share their story, their advice, their learning tips, and their top tips, tools and resources.

With (5) you may have discovered a resource gap in the market. If you can't find a central resource with the answers you're looking for, the chances are that others would like to access this information, too. This gives you the opportunity to develop a resource hub or a blog. Don't forget that regular blogging means regular fresh content on your website, which does wonders for your search engine rankings (especially if others link to this content via social media or their own websites).

In the cases of (3) and (8) you can develop valuable guidelines that aim either to help develop an understanding of the services a professional editorial freelancer supplies or to provide information about or links to valuable resources that help the client do some of the basic formatting preparation themselves. You could add these to your website in the form of a PDF, or create an ebooklet via Smashwords that clients can download to their e-reader.

Numbers (4) and (7) help you to add value to the message you communicate to one particular customer type. You can apply this to the marketing tools you use to target this particular customer (your website, a brochure, or a business network meeting), by using language that addresses those customers' concerns (or their confusion).

Helping the client understand the problems

With the boom in self-publishing, the number of independent authors looking for proofreading and editing help has increased markedly in the past few years. Self-publishing no longer has the stigma attached to it that it once had. Indeed, some writers choose this path over working with a traditional publisher because of the control it gives them. For the editorial freelancer, then, self-publishers are a potentially lucrative market.

One of the easiest ways to add value for self-publishing customers is to help the client understand the editorial process. No matter how new you are to the field, the chances are that many of the self-publishers with whom you might work have little or no experience of working with editorial professionals. It's more than simple to put together some tips and tools to help them on their journey. In doing so, you put yourself in your customer's shoes and provide accessible information that helps them make the right decisions.

It would be easy for us to take the money of every budding author who came our way. But in truth many of the indie authors who think they need a proofreader actually need at least a copy-editor, and some would benefit from more substantive structural editing prior to that stage – a professional critique by a development editor who assesses how the book works overall. In the fiction market, examples might include what the book's strengths and weaknesses are, whether the plot is structured well, the degree to which the different elements of the book support each other, and how the character point-of-view functions.

In the self-publishing market, the line between copy-editing and the final polish that a proofreader provides is often fuzzy. A lack of experience with regard to writing (let alone publishing, marketing and distribution) can leave indie writers vulnerable, with disastrous consequences: (1) they end up wasting money on a freelancing skill set that is inappropriate for their stage in the process and (2) the hard graft they've put into creating their book will be worthless because it's still not fit for market.

Creating information (either in document form or on a blog or web-based knowledge centre) that helps self-publishing clients identify what editorial skill set they require is therefore a really simple and useful way to add value and demonstrate your engagement and professionalism.

Case study

The following case study is one example of how I added value for one particular customer in a number of ways and how this led to not just one, but multiple work opportunities. For privacy reasons, I've changed the client's name.

Martin Bagott is an independent author who initially contacted me about proofreading his novel. He'd already worked with a proofreading agency who didn't allow him direct contact with the freelancer to whom they outsourced the work. This led to a number of problems with regards to formatting, and he was unhappy with the amount of errors that had been missed. Rethinking his strategy, he searched online for a proofreader with whom he could work directly. A Google search brought him to my website, whereupon he contacted me to discuss the possibility of working together. At the time I couldn't accommodate him for two and a half months, a time frame that was well outside his preference. In response to this I suggested a number of colleagues whose experience, I felt, would match his requirements. I compiled a list of names, email addresses and websites for him, and suggested a couple of searchable editorial directories that he could try.

He then emailed to ask my advice on whether he should use a literary agent, and what formats (hardback, paperback, ebook) I thought he would be wise to exploit. I also suggested, since I hadn't seen a sample of his work, that he might find my *Guidelines for New Authors* (a free advice ebooklet) useful when choosing an appropriate editorial freelancer and for accessing some links to useful resources on self-publishing in general, and marketing and formatting in particular.

Martin and I exchanged several emails over the course of a few days, and all on the understanding that he and I would not be working together, owing to him wanting to get his novel published within a month of our discussion. Or so I thought. Three days after his initial contact he told me that I'd been so helpful when there was 'nothing in it at all' for me that he'd decided he'd prefer to wait two and a half months so that I could proofread not only his first novel, but the two others he had in the pipeline. And he wrote a fabulous testimonial for me, thereby adding to my social proof (see Chapter 24).

Martin felt that I'd added value in several ways. As a first-time author he was nervous about the self-publishing process, particularly since he'd already had a bad experience with an editorial agency. By offering him advice and a referral service it gave him confidence that he could find a professional proofreader who would understand and respect his concerns. And by offering him a free advice booklet, he gained a substantive resource that he could refer to during the self-publishing process. In the end, that added value led him to feel that he didn't want to go elsewhere but was instead willing to work around my schedule.

Prioritizing

Naturally, we all have to make the decision as to how far we will go when going the extra mile. We are running businesses so while adding value is a central element of our marketing strategy, it has to be balanced with paid work. There might be days in your schedule when you are so busy with other commitments (professional or personal) that your blog has to go on the backburner or you can't fit in the time to engage with your social media platforms or online discussion groups, never mind devote your valuable time to helping someone find a colleague who'll be reaping the financial benefits of your generous referrals.

However, when you do have the time to add value, do it. There are always benefits of some sort – they're not necessarily financial, but they're always positively reputational.

KEY POINTS

- When you add value, you offer that extra something that makes you stand out from the crowd. You engage with your customers and show that you are anticipating their needs.

- Don't forget that the crowd is big, so the more effort you make, the larger the rewards you will reap.

- You don't have to do it all at once.

- Be driven by your customer – put yourself in their shoes, listen to what they want and respond accordingly. Add the value where you see the gaps.

- Added value comes in the form of small pebbles (from the smile on your face, to the reassuring tone of your voice, to the help you offer even when there's no apparent financial gain to you), big boulders (a blog, a free publication, a resource hub) and everything in between.

TRY IT!

With your different customer groups in mind, think of at least one substantive way you could add value in the next twelve months (e.g. building a blog, publishing online interviews with clients, creating a resource page, developing advice-giving documentation), and five small ways over the next six months (e.g. going the extra mile, answering a question on a discussion board, helping a customer find an editorial freelancer if you can't take on the work).

9 USING MULTIPLE PROMOTION CHANNELS

What's in it for you?

- Forces you to put yourself in your customer's shoes
- Encourages you to take a long-term view by risk-spreading
- Helps the customer to verify who you are
- SEO benefits

What are your customer's preferences?

Different client types will take different journeys to find you, so in order to maximize your opportunities and therefore the choices available to you, it makes sense to exploit the various channels available.

Let's return to the lessons from Chapter 7 on putting yourself in your customer's shoes. Let's say a self-publishing author decides they need a proofreader urgently, but they want to deal with someone who's local to them. For many people, the internet has reduced the world to the so-called global village but, for others, local still means 'you live in my town'. That person may pick up a print version of their regional business directory instead. If you're not in it, you've lost the potential opportunity to quote for what might have been a really fascinating project.

It's better to be in a position where you don't have capacity to take on all the work you are offered via several marketing channels than to be dependent on one. And you might just find that every once in a while a project comes up that is outside your specialist area but which you'd like to follow up anyway. You don't have to diversify, but you're in a far stronger position if this is by choice rather than necessity.

Spreading the risk

In *Learn How to Grow Your Business* (2007), marketing expert Robert Clay tells the story of a UK business that put all its eggs in one basket and poured its marketing budget into print advertising with the Yellow Pages. The company did extremely well using this strategy until their ad was printed with the wrong phone number. The mistake couldn't be rectified for 12 months. Considering 80 per cent of their sales came from this one marketing channel, the impact was almost catastrophic.

The lesson is simple: by spreading your marketing investment across a number of channels, you also spread the risk. Consider the following scenarios:

- Let's say many of your leads come from one particular online directory. If technical problems knock down the directory's web host server, your listing is temporarily dead. However, if you also have a website and you've invested some time on your search engine optimization (SEO), you're protected to some degree because customers searching for your skills may come across your name independently of your directory listing.

- Now let's imagine your website is your primary driver of business leads. Your web host goes out of business unexpectedly and your website is offline until you can transfer the content to a new provider. However, if you've promoted yourself on complementary online channels, your business name is still out there during this difficult transition period.

- You specialize in working for three medical publishers, both of whom you picked up by cold calling. Two of the businesses merge and there are major staff layoffs; three clients become two and you've lost 30 per cent of your business overnight. However, if you have a website and directory listings that are targeted to a range of client types, you might simply be able to accept more of the leads that you'd previously turned down in favour of your original publisher-based work.

It's not uncommon to have one primary driver, and if a particular channel is working for you then of course you should continue to exploit it. But that doesn't mean ignoring some of the myriad alternatives. One or two of these may just tide you over if disaster strikes.

Findability and verifiability

Using multiple marketing channels helps customers find you in multiple ways, but it also enables them to carry out a verification process.

Imagine for a moment that two in-house production editors working for separate presses meet on a training course. A tells B that she wants to expand her bank of top-notch copy-editors. B mentions your name to A. Production editor A trusts B's recommendation, but still wants to do a bit of research to ensure you meet the criteria.

In this situation it's important that you're findable so that A can verify that you're still in business, that you're taking on new clients, that your current skill set is a good fit for A's publishing list, that you have the training required by the publishing company she works for. The production editor may choose to do a Google search or they may look in a specialist directory. Since you don't know which option A will choose, it makes sense to cover your bases on a number of fronts. Using multiple marketing channels helps your customer find you in the first place and then verify that you're a good match.

SEO benefits

By using multiple marketing channels, you can enhance your website's SEO (search engine optimization) by utilizing an organic link-building strategy that integrates all the tools you are using to tell people about who you are and what you do, and funnelling them back to the place where you tell your big story: your website. And search engines love organic links when it comes to ranking your business.

Whether we're thinking about the letters/emails you send, the social media profiles you build, the directory listings you advertise in, the blog articles you write, the CVs you post through the mail and online, or the business cards you hand out at events, all can funnel customers and colleagues back to your website. And the more visitors you have, the more discoverable (or findable) you are.

Case study

The following pie chart illustrates a breakdown of the traffic sources to my website in a particular 24-hour period. It therefore doesn't include any contact made via direct emails or phone calls. I generated this data from the free version of StatCounter, one of the analytics tools that I use.

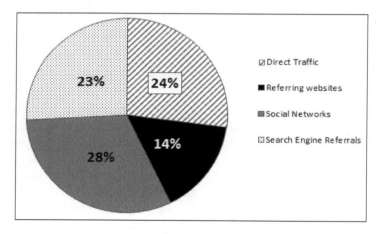

Figure 9.1: Traffic sources for louiseharnbyproofreader.com (23 July 2013)

It shows that people come to my website through different channels. Some come direct (typing in my web address), some come via mentions of my website on other websites, some come via the likes of Twitter, Facebook and LinkedIn, and some come via my business popping up in search engine results.

In this particular example, the slightly higher social networking piece of the pie can be explained by the fact that I'd recently shared an article on my blog that proved particularly popular with my colleagues.

The data remind us that even when considering just our online presence, different people use different platforms, and all those platforms have the potential to lead to us – if we utilize them effectively.

KEY POINTS

- Spread the risk so that if one of your key marketing channels fails, your business isn't stranded.

- Think about different customer types and what they know about your profession. Use the marketing channels that make sense not only to you but also to them.

- Think about what your customers want. Do all of them think globally or are they more traditional? Do they use the internet to search for service providers, or do they use printed directories or word-of-mouth recommendations?

- Giving customers multiple ways of finding you expands the opportunities that might come your way; you can always say no to a job you decide you don't fancy, but you can't say yes to a client who never found you in the first place.

- Using multiple marking channels makes you findable and verifiable.

- There are SEO benefits to being found on multiple platforms.

- By opening up your channels of communication, you start to move to a position whereby you take jobs out of choice rather than necessity.

TRY IT!

Make a list of the different promotional channels you're already exploiting. If there are fewer than five in that list, jot down three more things you can test in the next six months. Keep your target customer groups in mind and consider whether the channels you're using match the channels you think your customers are using.

10 REGULAR MARKETING

What's in it for you?

- Encourages you to take a long-term perspective
- Ensures you spread the risk and the opportunity
- Forces you to keep up to date with movements in the market outside of your control

Staying on the marketing wheel

It's important to think about marketing as an ongoing, dynamic activity, rather than a static, one-off event. At the time of writing, the global economy is struggling. Regular marketing ensures you don't make assumptions about what tomorrow will bring. If you are always thinking about how to take advantage of the many marketing opportunities appropriate to your sector, even when your client base is stable, you're proofing yourself for the future.

Using multiple marketing channels (as discussed in Chapter 9) offers you opportunity; doing this regularly offers you visibility. Combined, you are more likely to increase the number of opportunities that come your way from multiple clients, thereby spreading the risk and providing you with choices rather than ultimatums.

Spreading the risk

You can lose clients for reasons completely beyond your control, including:

- they don't need your services any more (e.g. a publisher brings the work in-house);

- they can no longer afford your services (e.g. in economic recession, a business faces general cutbacks);

- your contact moves to pastures new (and the other people in the organization have their own freelance network);

- they merge with other organizations and streamline their production processes;

- they don't have multiple jobs for you (e.g. a student with a Master's dissertation or an independent author who only self-publishes one novel).

In view of this, it's essential to protect your future interests by building a portfolio of several clients rather than focusing all your energies on one or two. If you put all your eggs in one basket and one of the above scenarios occurs, the impact on your business could be devastating.

This happened to one of my colleagues a few years ago – an experienced, highly qualified editor who'd relied on regular work from one organization for over nine years. The recession hit her client hard and the press brought all its freelancing work in-house. A decade's worth of stable workflow disappeared overnight and my colleague was left picking up the pieces.

In 2012, one of my primary publisher contacts went on maternity leave. I absolutely noticed her absence. Fortunately I had plenty of other clients in my portfolio to ensure this didn't affect my workflow. Within a month of my contact returning to work, it was business as usual and I was offered three proofreads in one hit, but I'm glad my business isn't dependent on her.

Take a 'down the road' approach to your marketing strategy

I could wax lyrical about avoiding such a disaster, but fellow freelancer Jane Ward, an experienced STM editor, said it all in an online discussion between SfEP members. The following extracts are reproduced with her permission, and the lessons she teaches are worth heeding:

When I started freelancing I was headhunted by a publisher, so I had work before I understood what a [freelance] proofreader or copy-editor was. For two years I simply did this large project and never really thought of the future.

Then a fellow SfEP member said, 'Never trust a client to be there for ever ... always have more than one egg in your basket.' This really made me think; even though that client gave me constant work, I began to look for new clients before I needed them.

Since, I have always followed the premise that a freelance business should assume they will lose one good customer a year for reasons beyond their control. I have had three clients for 20 years, but one has subsumed what had been four other clients and is now increasingly moving work to India.

Keep an eye on the market

Jane makes a crucial point, and the science publishing market is just one example of how mergers can have a huge impact on editorial freelancers if they don't keep an eye on what's happening in the market place.

My first job in publishing was for the UK arm of Williams & Wilkins, a Baltimore-based STM publisher. Prior to 1990, Wolters Kluwer, Lippincott, Raven Press, the medical division of Little, Brown, and Plenum were competitors. Over the next decade these would all be subsumed under the WK umbrella – six potential clients gradually became one.

What to do when you lose a client

Jane also offers advice on how to manage the loss of the client:

Once one is in the position of losing the client, then I recommend sending letters to lots of similar clients, detailing your work experience and making it clear that the reason you have room in your diary for additional work is because client A is no longer using freelancers or because they have merged with another company.

This is a sensible strategy because it demonstrates to the new prospect that you are reacting to changes in the market rather than suffering fall-out due to poor performance. If you are approaching similar-type clients, they'll be just as aware of the corporate changes going on around them. They'll no doubt appreciate the experience you've gained from working for a competitor, so this is a way of selling your loss in a way that demonstrates your skills and freelance employability.

Jane didn't just send out letters; she was prepared to visit, too, even if it meant travelling:

> I acquired my first new clients by writing a letter saying, 'I happen to be in X for two weeks next month and would love to pop in and see you at your convenience. I realise that you will be busy but if you could spare ten minutes to see me I would appreciate it.' To those who said yes, I then travelled to where ever it was! Out of ten letters I wrote, two did not reply; two said they did not need any one; two said they would send me a test when they next trawled for freelancers; and four invited me to visit. Of those, three offered me work after the visit and one has given me constant work, filling 50% of my diary for 20 years.

Don't stop marketing yourself

Even during the good times, it's worthwhile ensuring your profile is always high in the places where your client type finds editorial freelancers. If you're targeting the publishing market, a key society directory and cold calling may be appropriate. If you're working in the business market, regular attendance at local workshops and business networks may be crucial, as will be a website. Continue to network via social media forums, discussion groups and society chapter meetings so that you are up to date with what's going on in the marketplace and in a position to hear about any new opportunities that arise. Whatever your core marketing tools, don't let them slip.

KEY POINTS

- Whatever type of client you focus on, there's still a risk that even if you've been a trusted provider for many years, the work could dry up.

- Don't make assumptions about stability even during the good times; publishing is a dynamic sector, and mergers and acquisitions are common.

- Keep an eye on the market, even during economic booms, and react quickly by trying to replace what you've lost; clearly articulate your experience and make sure new prospects understand that your availability is for reasons beyond your control.

- Taking advantage of the myriad marketing channels appropriate to your sector increases opportunity.

- Regular use of these channels enhances visibility.

- Opportunity + visibility = increased choice (during the good times and the bad).

TRY IT!

Write down three different marketing activities that you haven't carried out in the past three months.

Create a quick schedule that encourages you to do these things regularly – can be little things each day or week, or bigger things once every few months (see Chapter 11 on time management for ideas about structuring your regular marketing using a goals-based approach).

11 TIME MANAGEMENT: GOALS AND PRIORITIES

What's in it for you?

- Reduces fearfulness by breaking tasks down in to manageable chunks

- Encourages you to promote yourself regularly – doing a little but doing it often

- Encourages you to prioritize by focusing on what works best for the most obvious client groups

- Helps you to grow in confidence, building on the small achievements first and using the information created and the lessons learned to be more creative or adventurous

'Climbing Mount Improbable'

For the nervous or inexperienced marketer, developing a substantive marketing strategy can feel like a monumental task. In 1996, evolutionary biologist Richard Dawkins published his popular-science book, *Climbing Mount Improbable*. I love the underpinning concept of this – the idea that a mammoth process, such as the development of a complex organ like the human eye, seems improbable when looked at as an end product, but becomes entirely possible when broken down into small stages.

Marketing your editorial business is far less complex than evolution, and yet the process can feel insurmountable at first sight – 'There's so much to do!'; 'How will I fit it all in?'; 'I'm never going to find the time to do all of this!'; 'I don't know where to begin.'

Setting goals allows you to break down the task into small, manageable chunks. It puts you in control of your marketing strategy, and keeps you focused on doing a little but doing it regularly. By setting yourself goals and objectives, you start the process of climbing that improbable mountain in a structured way that suits your time frame.

Goal-based marketing enables you to identify:

- What you want to achieve (goal)
- How you will achieve it (activity)
- When you will achieve it (time frame)

You are in control at all times. The point of the exercise is not to put the pressure on, but to take it off. In effect, you are creating a marketing to-do list that you can refer to as you develop your business, crossing off or rescheduling activities as necessary.

> A useful piece of advice comes from Mark Forster (2000) ... who suggests facing the task and working on it for only five minutes. Think of this as a warm-up exercise; as Forster says, we can all do something for five minutes. (Denicolo and Reeves 2014)

My colleague Mary McCauley used a goals-based strategy when she started her editorial business (McCauley 2012). Says Mary:

> Setting up a business of any kind can be a little overwhelming so, using my project management experience, I found the best way to approach it was to take things one step at a time, i.e. to set myself business objectives. I broke these objectives down into individual tasks and gave them time frames for completion.

She's now a successful editor and proofreader who regularly finds herself having to turn down work because she's so busy. And she continues to use a goals-based approach as a constructive way of managing her time.

Some objectives were met (by necessity) from the start, others were ongoing and fitted in around my client work, and some will continue to feature – in various forms – in future years' objectives. (Ibid.)

Creating a goal-based marketing schedule

A good starting point is to draw up a to-do schedule of the primary marketing goals you want to achieve. You might like to break your list into subdivisions that address daily, weekly, monthly and yearly activities. For example:

Once

- Build a website
- Create LinkedIn, Facebook, Google+ and Twitter profiles
- Generate an initial CV template
- Generate a price quotation template

Yearly

- Greetings cards to clients at Christmas and other notable holidays (if appropriate)
- Test one completely new marketing activity

Twice-yearly

- Tests re pricing structure
- Tests re new free-ads listings
- Reviewing social media profiles to ensure they are up to date and maximizing use of any newly introduced features (e.g. LinkedIn's portfolio tool)
- Review directory listings to ensure they reflect your current skill set
- Ask your indie authors how the sales of their books are doing; ask the student client how their thesis/dissertation was

received; ask the business client for feedback on the report you edited for them or whether their website traffic has increased since you helped them with their text flow and layout

Monthly

- Cold letter or email to one business
- Review your CV to ensure it reflects your skill set and current training

Twice-monthly

- Cold letter or email to one publisher
- Update your online portfolio to reflect recent projects
- Ask a client for whom you have done regular work for a testimonial

Weekly

- Write an article for your own blog or for a guest slot on one of your colleague's blogs
- Engage with regional business-based Twitter groups
- Review overall website analytics

Daily

- Check social media and online discussion groups
- Review page view data for any recent blog posts you've written

As necessary

- Advise all clients when your email/postal address or phone number changes
- Tell clients when you're going to be away, even if you haven't had work from them for a long time

Pin it!

What the schedule looks like is up to you (the above is simply an example). You can prioritize the activities as you think best and you might like to add specific dates for goal completion as an incentive. Once you've developed your schedule, you can pin it to the taskbar at the bottom of your computer screen. That way you'll have a constant and easily accessible reminder to check and tick off the various activities as you complete them.

Having a schedule of goals to hand will give you something positive to review. As Denicolo and Reeves (2014), in their discussion of Professional Development Plans, suggest:

> [It] will enable you to set little targets for where you would like to be when you next review your position and provides you with the opportunity to congratulate yourself on how far you have come.

Goal-setting in purpose-built groups

Some of us find it easier than others to garner the self-discipline needed to follow schedules. And while social media platforms such as LinkedIn are a great option for exploring marketing ideas, as are books, blogs and professional society forums, when it comes to inspiration, nothing quite beats the act of bouncing ideas around with a group of trusted friends.

Some editors and proofreaders don't feel comfortable using professional forums to chat. There are a number of reasons for this, some of the most common being:

- a lack of confidence;

- fear of exposure to strangers who may be watching the discussion without participating; and

- concern about appearing foolish or inexperienced.

If you are worried that you will find it hard to keep up your marketing momentum on your own, or you are nervous about exploring marketing in more public spaces, consider asking some colleagues if they'd like to get together with you to create a more personal online space in which you encourage each other with marketing goals – your very own online focus group.

These groups needn't be permanent. You can open them up or put them into hibernation as you all see fit. In this way, you and your colleagues can keep the interest in the group invigorated – a marketing focus group that's become a chore is no longer achieving its objective.

Case study: momentum through small-group support

In 2013 a group of editorial friends and colleagues demonstrated, over a three-week period, how the power of group support can be harnessed to encourage mutual goal-setting.

The eight freelancers concerned would have happily met for a daily lunch in a local café to discuss marketing ideas – a sandwich and a coffee to accompany the sharing of ideas. However, most live in different parts of the UK (and one member is based in Canada) so they took the challenge online. The sandwiches and drinks were virtual but the daily meet-up was very real.

The idea started when one editor mailed the following message to a small group of her trusted freelancing friends:

> I read this article last night: How to Create a Marketing Plan You'll Actually Enjoy Implementing [International Freelancers Academy n.d.]. It has inspired me to set myself a challenge to get into good marketing habits [and] I want to get better. So, I aim to do at least one marketing activity every day for the next three weeks. My definition of marketing activity is fairly loose. I'm including activities such as updating my CV because, although it's not actively marketing, it is a prerequisite to sending out emails, etc. Anyone fancy joining me and providing mutual moral support?

The response was enthusiastic and an agreement was made to 'meet', via group emails, every day for three weeks and share any activity that would fall into the initial, comfortably loose definition of business promotion.

For the next 21 days, members sent messages advising each other of the tasks they were considering for that day or that week. Examples included:

- Asking a client for a testimonial
- Sending courtesy emails to clients whom the freelancer hadn't heard from in a while
- Drafting personalized follow-up emails to recent customers, thanking them for the opportunity to work on their project
- Sending cold letters to three publishers
- Updating a CV
- Updating a LinkedIn profile to include a portfolio of works
- Reviewing an editorial directory listing

It's worth noting several rules of engagement that they decided upon:

- Size: the group was small and the contributions were quick to read and easy to digest. Any member could read the daily tip, and implement it themselves if they felt it was appropriate.
- Momentum: the goal wasn't to get into lengthy discussions of marketing strategy but rather to share quick tips and inspire each other to do one thing, once a day.
- Intimacy: the group was 'closed' so there was complete privacy. The confidence and fear factors didn't enter the equation.
- One rule: Be kind. This was not a space where people critiqued each other. The exchanges were based on professional friendship and it is unthinkable that anyone would be criticized (even politely) for sloppy spelling, poor grammar, a lack of knowledge, a failure to trim their messages, etc.

Creating purpose-built groups is an additional way for freelancers to communicate and inspire each other on a goal-by-goal basis to improve their marketing practice in a safe space. The success lies in keeping it between friends, keeping it small and keeping it kind.

Two frameworks for prioritizing

If you are still worried that there seems too much to do, consider either of the following frameworks to help you get your marketing time management on track. They both aim to help you move away from the haphazard approach to marketing, and develop instead a targeted plan that focuses your efforts on the most appropriate elements.

The Marketing Effectiveness Matrix™ (MEM)

The Marketing Effectiveness Matrix™ (MEM) is a useful framework developed by Ed Gandia, summarized in 'The 3 Pillars for Landing Progressively Better Clients' (Gandia n.d.).

The MEM encourages you to think about each marketing activity in terms of the time required to carry out the task, and the likelihood of the said task delivering its hoped-for outcome. Marketing activities are divided into four quadrants:

A: Ineffective and time-consuming: any activity that is unfocused or untargeted (e.g. cold calling to a client group whose needs don't match your skill set; concentrating on social media platforms that your colleagues and clients aren't using; over-investing time on client groups that don't understand what you do).

B: Effective and time-consuming: includes activities that are targeted at your relevant client group but take a lot of effort (e.g. business blogging, business networking).

C: Effective and efficient: relates to those activities that are quick to carry out and targeted. Gandia includes the examples of using your colleague network, targeted direct mail (e.g. cold contact with a relevant client group), and exploring opportunities with existing customers.

D: Effective (when highly targeted): requires caution because the activities are time-consuming and only work when highly targeted (e.g. advertising in a known directory that publishers use; building profiles on emerging social media platforms).

Client-focused Priority Framework (CPF)

My own preference is related to the MEM but focuses specifically on the client (rather than efficiency) for guidance about where I should be investing my marketing time and effort. In the early part of this book, we looked at what we're selling and who we're selling it to – our skill set and our core client groups.

The marketing time-management issue can be addressed by creating a list of who our primary potential clients are (in order of how core we consider them to be) and then creating a corresponding to-do list against each group. It will quickly become obvious which tasks need to be prioritized. It's a somewhat brutal approach because it forces us to focus on the present rather than the future, and what the obvious vs non-obvious client groups are.

You may think that the aeronautics company based in your town could really do with editing or proofreading assistance, but do they know? Are these obvious clients who are familiar with your services or are you better off focusing your efforts on a publishing company that specializes in publishing material in a field you have knowledge of?

Wrapping your marketing plan around the obvious client helps you to focus your activities where they are most likely to reap rewards and will help you to establish a foundational work stream, especially in the early stages of your business's life.

Here's an example based on how I perceived my situation when I started out as a freelance proofreader.

STAGE 1 CPF Skill set: Specialist proofreader with educational background in the social sciences and career experience with a social science publisher	
Primary client groups with which I have the best skill-set match	Core activities most likely to get me noticed
Social science publishers	Join SfEP and fulfil criteria for entry in its Directory of Editorial Services Cold contact to named in-house editors CV and cover letter
Student social science PhD theses and dissertations	Entry in Find a Proofreader directory Build website Join SfEP and fulfil criteria for entry in its Directory of Editorial Services Referrals from colleagues via online networking platforms (SfEP online discussion forums, LinkedIn, Facebook, Google+ and Twitter)
Individual academics writing social science books	Join SfEP and fulfil criteria for entry in its Directory of Editorial Services Build website
Individual academics writing social science journal articles	Join SfEP and fulfil criteria for entry in its Directory of Editorial Services Build website

When I was starting out, I could have devoted more time to expanding this grid to incorporate other client groups that I wanted to work for in the future (fiction publishers, for example), and other activities that might generate results, but this process is about prioritizing, so I focused purely on considering those groups with whom I had the best chance of securing work (based on my skill set) and the tools I felt were most likely to deliver the desired outcome as soon as possible.

My top marketing priorities at Stage 1 were therefore:

- Join the SfEP and work towards qualification for membership (thus fulfilling the criteria for directory entry)

- Create a CV and covering letter that I could use for cold contact to social science publishers

- Take out a listing in Find a Proofreader

- Create a website

- Create profiles on the primary online networking platforms and link with colleagues

When I'd achieved those goals (or done as much as I could do in the meantime towards their implementation) I created a Stage-2 CPF that focused on a new set of objectives that would consolidate Stage 1:

STAGE 2 CPF Skill set: Proofreader with educational background in the social sciences and career experience with a social science publisher	
Primary client groups with which I have the best skill-set match	Follow-up activities to consolidate Stage 1
Social science publishers	Ask for testimonials from existing clients Create online portfolio Update CV and cover letter

	to include testimonials Second round of cold contact to named in-house editors Add online portfolio and testimonials to website and LinkedIn profile
Student social science PhD theses and dissertations	Ask for testimonials from existing clients Create online portfolio Add online portfolio and testimonials to website, LinkedIn and Find a Proofreader directory
Individual academics writing social science books	Ask for testimonials from existing clients Create online portfolio Add online portfolio and testimonials to website, LinkedIn and Find a Proofreader directory
Individual academics writing social science journal articles	Ask for testimonials from existing clients Create online portfolio Add online portfolio and testimonials to website, LinkedIn and Find a Proofreader directory

My top marketing priorities at Stage 2 were therefore:

- Acquiring testimonials
- Creating an online portfolio
- Updating all online and print channels to include testimonials and portfolio

- Carrying out a second round of cold contact to academic publishers

There were lots of other things I wanted to explore – information-sharing with my colleagues via a blog (which would also drive my SEO), adding value that would be of interest to colleagues (PDF proofreading stamps) and new potential client groups (guidance for independent first-time authors), testing free-ads listings, expanding my client group to include fiction proofreading (for traditional presses and self-publishers) – but these were put on hold to enable me to manage my time effectively.

Having achieved the goals outlined in the first two stages, I was now ready to focus on new activities (blogging and adding value).

STAGE 3 CPF Skill set: Specialist proofreader with educational background in the social sciences and career experience with a social science publisher, but now with some fiction and commercial non-fiction (acquired via publisher word-of-mouth referrals)	
Secondary client groups	Core activities
Self-publishing authors	Update entry in UK's SfEP Directory of Editorial Services Update website and online portfolio Blog Added value
Other publishers (fiction and commercial non-fiction)	Update entry in UK's SfEP Directory of Editorial Services (to include trade proofreading experience) Cold contact to named in-house editors Revise CV and cover letter

How you would fill in your CPF at any stage will depend on your core client groups. If you're targeting businesses, and plan to attend business networking meetings, Stage 1 would require the creation of not only a CV but also business cards. If you're an STM specialist, you might want to prioritize contacting editing agencies as a way to build up a portfolio of editing experience with, for example, journal article authors. If your core client group is mainly individuals whom you want to find you on the web, blogging and other SEO activities will be more urgent, as may be selective advertising in specialist directories.

The most important thing to remember is that there is no one true way to fill in the information in these grids. How you prioritize will be specific to your skills and target markets. Be kind to yourself by using them to help you focus on what needs doing now, and by putting other activities on hold until you are ready to invest the time and effort needed for new objectives.

KEY POINTS

- If you feel overwhelmed by all the elements you want to build into your overall marketing strategy, break down the strategy into manageable chunks – individual goals that you can tackle one at a time. Consider using one of the frameworks outlined above to help you focus on what you need to do first.

- Think about who the obvious client is first and wrap your marketing plan around that, so you build a foundational work stream.

- Scheduling goals helps you stay focused and organized.

- Sharing your ideas with small groups of colleagues can help to harness motivation and keep the momentum going.

- Don't panic if you don't meet the time frame – it's your goal schedule and you are in control. Feel free to shift things around as necessary.

- Think big and think small. Your goals can be long term or short term; they can include new activities and tweaks or updates to existing ones.

Create a to-do schedule of all the marketing goals you want to achieve but haven't yet carried out. Include an approximate time frame in which you plan to achieve each one. If you don't want to do it alone, ask a group of editorial friends to join you.

Now use this list to develop your own marketing time-management matrix (based either on the MEM or my CPF).

12 SEARCH ENGINE
     OPTIMIZATION

What's in it for you?

- Turns your website from a static to a dynamic marketing tool

- Encourages you to promote yourself creatively, regularly and across multiple marketing channels

- Visibility – increases the likelihood of customers finding you and therefore the choices you have over the work you do and how much you earn

What does it mean?

If the term 'search engine optimization (SEO)' strikes fear into your soul and has you running for the hills, it's time to relax. It's just a technical way of describing how you maximize your online 'findability' (sometimes called 'discoverability') and make yourself appear 'interesting' to the likes of Google, Bing, Yahoo and Ask.

For those readers wanting a more technical definition, Wikipedia has the following to say:

> Search engine optimization (SEO) is the process of affecting the visibility of a website or a web page in a search engine's 'natural' or un-paid ('organic') search results. In general, the earlier (or higher ranked on the search results page), and more frequently a site appears in the search results list, the more visitors it will receive from the search engine's users.

Some of the marketing activities (see Part II) that you decide to pursue will automatically help your SEO. There are also steps you can take to actively increase your online visibility. Either way, SEO concerns the likelihood that when a potential client places terms like 'proofreader' or 'editor' into a search engine like Google, a link to your website pops up on the first few pages they look at.

Obviously, the higher up you come in the results listing, the better – every client will have limited reserves of patience and if your website is listed on page 137 of the results, you're unlikely to pick up leads in this way.

Optimizing your website's visibility involves embracing some of the other concepts discussed in Part I, including:

- Thinking in a joined-up way (Chapter 3)
- Adding value (Chapter 8)
- Putting yourself in your customer's shoes (Chapter 7)

and carrying out some of the activities outlined in Part II, including:

- Blogging (Chapter 16)
- Networking (Chapter 15)
- Dynamic website creation (Chapter 14)
- Directory advertising (Chapter 19)
- Using social media in a reciprocal fashion (Chapter 15)

Scanlan's 'Five simple secrets'

Gwen Moran (2008) cites 'five simple secrets' identified by SEO guru Liam Scanlan that anyone, even the uninitiated, can build into their SEO marketing plan:

Domain name

Customize your domain name so that it relates to your product but differentiates you at the same time (consider, for example, legalproofreader.co.uk and marcustrowereditor.com). Domain names that mention your big keywords have a much better chance of ranking highly in the search engines.

Rand Fishkin (2007) argues that businesses whose domain names don't tell the customer what they do need 'far more branding because of their un-intuitive names'. Since we all have enough on our plates with the myriad aspects of marketing that we need to take care of, never mind the day-to-day administrative and editorial functions that need to be carried out in order to run our businesses, it makes sense to take the load off where we can!

Page titles, descriptions and metatags

Make sure you've filled in each of your website's page titles, descriptions and tags completely and in a way that reflects the content for each particular page. So if you have a blog attached to your website, make sure that the title and keywords reflect that content. If you have a page that's dedicated to your copy-editing testimonials, the title and metatags should describe these. Says Moran, 'Plugging in page titles is an easy way to attract search engine algorithms that look for titles on multiple pages of the site' (2008).

Put yourself in your customer's shoes and think about titles and descriptions that will show up in a list of search results. Will they draw the client to your website? Do they instantly tell them what they need to know to make it worth their while to visit your site?

Inputting meta data varies from website to website, depending on which host you are using. The well-known self-build hosts (WordPress and Weebly for example) make this process quite simple. But if you're unsure, Google 'how to add meta data to a [host] website' and take a look at a YouTube video, blogger's instructions, or your host's information pages. Or ask the person who built your website to advise you.

Take a look, for example, at Yoast's WordPress SEO plugin. It is free and yet offers in-depth SEO advice for each page or post on your website (see Jones 2014 for more detailed information about this tool).

Meta data that incorporates keywords like 'science editor', 'legal proofreader' or 'fiction proofreader' are more likely to get you ranked highly than will 'holy grail' keywords such as 'proofreading' and 'editor'.

Keywords

The same applies to keywords. Try to incorporate a range of keywords into your website titles, descriptions and content that reflect your editorial business. Put yourself in your customer's shoes and think about the terms they'll use to find you. These might include general keywords (editor, proofreader, indexer) and more specific terms (fiction editor, children's book editor, academic proofreader, thesis proofreading).

By building your content (and meta data; see above) around targeted keywords such as 'structural editing', 'scientific proofreading' or 'Toronto legal editing', you're much more likely to rank highly.

Contact information

Even if you are concerned about spam, don't post your contact details in the form of a graphic. Scanlan argues that your contact information needs to be as easy as possible for search engines to find. Instead, he advises embedding emails in hotlinks in order to deter the troll programs. If you use contact forms on your website, check with your web host as to which spam filters are available.

Two-way links – being social

Chapter 14 on building a dynamic website, Chapter 16 on blogging, Chapter 8 on adding value and Chapter 15 on using social media offer more detailed guidance about building links and sharing content with your network to maximize your website's SEO. Briefly, however, the point is to build high-quality, two-way links between others' websites and your own so that you enrich your site with that organic link 'juice' that tells the search engines your site is vibrant and interesting. Sharing your added value throughout your online networks and engaging with your customers' and colleagues' content is invaluable in this respect. Guest articles relevant to your community are also a great way of generating links between your site and those of your colleagues.

To Scanlan's advice I'd add the following: don't forget to take advantage of Google Authorship opportunities. While Google+ is currently nowhere near as popular as Facebook or Twitter, the Google Authorship aspect is likely to become extremely powerful in SEO terms, so freelancers are advised to get a head start on their competitors. Even if you don't have your own blog, every time you write a guest post, ask the site owner if they'll include a mini bio about you that includes the relevant information. Be sure to update your Google+ profile to reflect the online publications for which you've written and the relevant links to the articles. See Joshua Duke (2013) for common-sense advice on this matter.

KEY POINTS

- SEO helps you to take your website from a static to a dynamic marketing tool.
- It's not as technical as it sounds.
- Scanlan's 'five simple secrets' are a useful framework for structuring your SEO activities.
- Put yourself in your customer's shoes when thinking about keywords, titles and descriptions.
- Give thought to the keywords and meta data on your website. Targeted and long-tail keywords (less common keyword phrases) are more likely to be of benefit to your search engine rankings.
- Being social is one of the most time-consuming but beneficial ways of enhancing your SEO.

TRY IT!

If the term 'search engine optimization' makes you nervous, start by looking at Scanlan's 'five simple secrets'. Even if your networking and added-value activities are some way down the line, you can attend to your meta data, keywords, contact information and domain name immediately.

13 BUILDING A PROFESSIONAL, BELIEVABLE BRAND

What's in it for you?

- Professionalism – encourages you to think of yourself as a business owner, first and foremost

- Helps you think about differentiation, clarity and consistency in how you present yourself

- Makes you recognizable and verifiable

- Allows you to bring your personality to your marketing activities

Why is branding important?

Your brand is who you are and what you stand for. It incorporates recognizable elements (e.g. logos and straplines, photographs), process elements (e.g. you're a medical editor or a humanities proofreader), and reputational elements (e.g. you're experienced, dependable, helpful, trustworthy, polite, professional, etc.).

Branding yourself is about presenting yourself in such a way that people can identify positive business-worthy characteristics about the service you offer and then recognize that service across multiple platforms.

Being believable and trustworthy

Marketing is all about making yourself interesting, and being believable and trustworthy is important if one wishes to sustain that interest.

Customers searching for editorial assistance want to believe they're in a safe pair of hands – that you and I will follow through on the claims we make about the services we provide and the benefits they'll receive as a result. They want to be able to trust us to do the job that they're paying for.

However they find you, and wherever they find you, within a matter of seconds they'll decide whether to keep your information on their computer screen, or close the window and move on to one of your colleagues.

Doing everything possible to keep that person engaged is therefore good business practice. It means ensuring that our marketing materials, online or in print, are aesthetically pleasing to the eye, engaging to read, and believable. Good branding therefore requires a consistent presentation of information and images that provides a potential customer with a gut feeling that you're a good bet. The stronger that gut feeling, the more likely they are to hit the Contact button.

Case study

In 2013 I was contacted by someone from a copywriting agency who was looking for a proofreader to check his account managers' copy prior to client handover. I make a habit of asking new contacts how they found me. Neil's response confirmed how important it is to embed a positive gut feeling in the prospecting client as soon as they hit your landing page: 'A Google search – your website looked the most professional and *trustworthy* of those on the first page of results' (my emphasis). Neil's response was a gut one – he'd not worked with me before so he couldn't know the facts. Instead, he contacted me because of how my business information made him *feel*.

Key elements to consider

So how do you brand yourself in a way that makes you believable? How do you embed a gut-based sense of trustworthiness in the way you present your business? Consider the following:

126

- Consistency – branding yourself so that you are identifiable

- Clarity – branding your skill set

- Personality and photographs – branding yourself as a real person (including using images of your face)

- Endorsements – branding yourself as someone who can deliver

- Portfolios – branding yourself as someone with experience

- Professionalism – branding yourself by your behaviour

Even if you're in the early stages of building your editorial business, most of the above elements are things you will be able to build into your brand immediately.

Consistency – branding yourself so that you are identifiable

Consistency is all about thinking in a joined-up way (see Chapter 3). Remember – your various marketing activities are not isolated. They are connected by the links you embed in them and by the fact that your colleagues and customers will reach you via different paths and on different platforms. It's therefore important to bring consistency to presentation, so that you are identifiable and visible.

- Always use the same mug shot so that customers recognize your face.

- Choose a consistent colourway that becomes synonymous with your business and apply it to your website, your Twitter profile, your Facebook banner, your website's favicon (see Chapter 14), your business cards and the featured text on your CVs, brochures, invoices, address labels, letterhead, email signature, online discussion board signature, and compliment slips.

- If you have a logo, like your colourway, this should be embedded across your social media profiles, your website, your directory advertising and your business stationery.

- Use the same email and business title, too.

Consistency in presentation and design consolidates your brand, making you and your business quickly identifiable. Being consistently recognizable will ensure that people come to trust your brand and the business attributes it represents. And if they hear about you in one way (word of mouth, for example), and then search for more information about you, you'll be more recognizable and verifiable.

Clarity – branding your skill set

A strong brand doesn't need to be over-designed. Some of the most recognizable high-street brands are based around a simple message and a simple logo. Clarity is key.

Consider your business name and corresponding domain name. Do they make it clear to your customer what you do? Take a look at the following business names and their web URLs. Whichever one a client is looking at, it should be clear what's on offer.

- KOKEdit: www.kokedit.com
- Legal Proofreader: www.legalproofreader.co.uk
- Academic Editing: www.academicedit.co.uk
- Playle Editorial Services: www.playle-editorial-services.com

Ideally, this should be extended to the business email address, too (e.g. louise@louiseharnbyproofreader.com).

Personality and photographs – branding yourself as a real person (including using images of your face)

A businesswoman contacted me at the beginning of 2013 to ask me to edit her MSc personal statement. As in the above example of the copywriter, I asked her how she found me and why she chose me. She'd spent nearly two hours searching on Google looking for the following:

- She was looking for an individual freelancer, not a company that would contract out the work to an unnamed person.

- She wanted to see a picture of the person she was going to be dealing with, rather than a stock image that looked as if it had been cut and pasted from a magazine.

- She wanted to see an appealing and professional website that told her about the freelancer's experience and that reflected their personality.

- And she wanted someone 'genuine'.

She told me she'd spent a lot of time working on the draft of her statement, and it was important to her that it communicated her story – it might have determined whether her application was successful. She wanted someone who'd made her feel that they understood what she was trying to achieve and why it was important. I got the job based on meeting the above criteria.

Bringing your personality into your marketing is important, especially when you're dealing with nervous clients. Use the first person if you're a solopreneur ('I provide editing solutions …' rather than a generic 'we'). This makes your statements personal. If you're part of an editorial partnership, by all means use 'we' but make sure it's clear who 'we' refers to – clients should be able to find bios of each partner clearly, and each person's role in the business should be explained so that the customer understands who they are dealing with.

Include a photograph of your face on your website and any other marketing channels that accept images (Facebook, LinkedIn, Twitter, advertising directories, for example). In an article published in the *Psychonomic Bulletin & Review*, the authors present experimental research that investigates how using photographs introduces a 'truth bias' – in other words, when you make a claim and attach an image to it, the people assessing that claim are more likely to judge it to be true. Images 'inflate truthiness' (Newman et al. 2012).

When your customer sees the 'real' you, in words and images, their trust increases and the likelihood of contact being made increases.

Endorsements – branding yourself as someone who can deliver

Briefly, testimonials from satisfied clients reinforce the message that your business can deliver. Saying you can do something is one thing. Other people saying you can do it is quite another. Endorsements help your customer to trust you, and being branded as trustworthy is something we all aspire to. Some online platforms allow ratings – FreeIndex, FaP, Google, Trustpilot and Facebook all allow customers to rate you out of five – this adds to trustworthiness and credibility. Chapter 24 is dedicated to the power of testimonials.

Portfolios – branding yourself as someone with experience

Again, briefly, portfolios reinforce the message that your business has experience. Like testimonials, they help the customer to trust you because they demonstrate that you've already achieved the claims that you make. More detail on the benefits of portfolios is provided in Chapter 23.

Professionalism – branding yourself by your behaviour

There are a couple of things to think about when considering professionalism. The first is your behaviour as a business owner in general, while the second concerns the way you conduct yourself while navigating the online environment in particular, though the issues at stake could easily be applied to face-to-face networking.

In the section above on consistency and clarity, we looked at the importance of ensuring that you present your business brand in a recognizable manner that enables your potential and current customers to identify who you are and what you do across a range of business activities – some marketing, others administrative.

This is important because if you want to be taken seriously as a business owner, treated like a business owner, paid promptly like a business owner, and command fees that any self-respecting business owner deems fair by industry standards, then you need to behave like one. That means having a professional business name, and corresponding domain name and email address. It means having stationery (invoices, letterhead, address labels, etc.) that is branded with your business name and logo.

US editor Rich Adin is adamant that his clients view him as a 'vendor' rather than a 'freelancer'. By ensuring that his administrative materials are professionally branded, he is reinforcing his position as a business owner, and the respect that comes with that. Talking specifically about invoices (though the point applies more broadly), Adin states:

> Your invoice should be a 'designed' form into which you enter data, and printed in PDF if sent electronically (color is not needed ... it is layout that matters). I understand that the information will be the same, but information is not what we are talking about – presentation is important in establishing credentials as a business. (Adin 2013b)

In a nutshell, if you want to be treated like a business professional, you need to behave like one. Take a look at the last invoice you received for a product you bought off the high street, the sales letter from an insurance company, the address label on the manuscript package sent by a publisher, a statement from your bank, or an appointment reminder from your dentist. These organizations brand their marketing and administrative materials consistently and professionally, and so should we.

Moving now to the second aspect of professional behaviour, it's worth recalling Kiisel's (2012) advice on taking the utmost care with your online brand (see Chapter 13). Briefly:

- Don't post anything online that would offend any company you work for or your mother
- 'If you argue online you lose'
- Be courteous
- 'What happens online stays online'

Take care with presentation on social media. Informality or laziness can lead to inattention to detail with regards to spelling or punctuation. That's fine in one sense but are your colleagues judging you? If they are project managers who might consider referring work your way, this may be the only chance they have to assess your skills. If your informal status updates frequently include a lack of attention to detail, it could work against you.

Here's a useful tip from editor Liz Broomfield in relation to protecting your business reputation.

> You are your brand ... This is particularly important if you run a small business or are a sole trader. However, even if you look at a multinational, the person at the head of the company and the reputation they personally have has an effect on the perception of the company. (Broomfield 2013a)

Building a recognizable and visible business brand is good marketing; protecting that brand through attention to your behaviour is good sense.

Examples of good editorial branding

There are some super examples of strong editorial branding in our community. Here are just three to consider:

- Averill Buchanan (of Averill Buchanan | Editor and Publishing Consultant) uses the same thumbnail image across her various online platforms, has a distinctive logo and colourway of duck-egg blue and dark grey, a professional business name that identifies her key business skills, a photograph on her website that shows her customers who she is, and website and email addresses that incorporate her business name.

- Ben Corrigan of The Whole Proof uses his distinctive logo across an array of marketing platforms (including social media), and his chosen colourway of orange and blue makes his business brand easily identifiable. His email address, web domain name and Twitter handle all incorporate this business name, too.

- Katharine O'Moore-Klopf's green colourway and recognizable KOK logo can be found on her website, her social media business profiles, and her stationery, and her digital signatures (email, web domain name, Twitter handle, etc.) – like Averill's and Ben's – incorporate her KOKEdit business name.

All three are visible, identifiable, recognizable – and impeccably behaved!

KEY POINTS

- Continual assessment of how we present ourselves in our professional lives – how we brand ourselves – is an ongoing process and something we do every day as part of our marketing strategy.

- A solid business brand with a recognizable and consistent theme increases your visibility.

- Apply your brand design across multiple marketing platforms. That way, customers can verify you.

- Branding yourself as a business owner means customers and colleagues will treat you accordingly.

- Protect your brand by always paying attention to who could be watching (and judging) you.

- Use tools like portfolios, endorsements and photographs to inject 'truthiness' to your brand. You can prove the actual truth of your claims once you've got the job.

TRY IT!

Look at your website, domain name, social media profiles, email address, email signature, invoices, business cards, letterhead, address labels, compliment slips, thumbnail photographs. Are they consistent in design and layout? Do they tell your customer who you are and what you do? Do they represent you as a professional person and as a professional business? And is the message you are communicating believable?

Consider the way you respond to requests to quote, and the way you engage with colleagues in public, online and offline. Again, does the way you communicate represent you as a professional person and as a professional business?

Tweak if and where necessary!

PART II:
MARKETING ACTIVITIES –
THINGS TO DO

14 BUILDING A DYNAMIC WEBSITE

What's in it for you?

- Provides you with a shop front
- Makes you available to a global audience (in terms of both geography and audience)
- Myriad opportunities for creativity in terms of design and content
- It's low cost, high benefit
- With good SEO, brings you customers and choice

An essential tool?

Some established editorial freelancers don't have a website and feel they don't need one. They have a solid client base, built up over many years, and their reputations alone generate referrals. For the new entrant to the field, building up a business within the context of the market as it stands today rather than 20 years ago, it's a different story. My own opinion is that not having one is a wasted opportunity (especially when one considers how inexpensive it is to build one these days, or how easy it is to build one yourself) and possibly detrimental.

Once you have a dynamic website that draws customers to you, you will have more choice. Having more choice gives you more control. If you have more opportunities than time, you are in the enviable position of turning work down. This means you can choose the projects that you *want* to work on rather than *have* to work on. It allows you to stand firm on the rates you charge and to pick the projects that you find most interesting. You can become the person who refers on work to colleagues when you don't have capacity. Like every other promotional tool you exploit, the aim is to build a dynamic presence that actively engages your customers and thereby reduces dependency.

Competition

Proofreading and editing are competitive. If your colleagues have websites but you don't, you're less likely to be found by potential customers.

No-cost promotion

Your website is a free marketing tool. If you use a self-build host such as Weebly or WordPress, to name just two, then the only cost to you is the time you spend on building and maintaining it. Once live, customers can find you rather than you always having to find them.

Create an online CV/résumé

You can use your website as an online CV/résumé. Keep your home page uncluttered, but use other pages to show off your clients, skills and portfolio of work.

Control your space

A website is more than 'having an online presence' – it's a professional space in which you control both the content and how it's presented. It's your shop front.

Content is always fresh

Websites are easy to update, meaning the content you include is always the latest content. Update your site frequently and search engines are more likely to notice you. And that means clients are more likely to find you.

It's not hard

Things have come on a long way in the past few years. Even if the idea of building your own site scares you, make the jump and at least do a bit of research. Many website hosts offer design templates that you can use and adapt to suit your own needs. You don't need any technical knowledge of computer programming or coding to get up and running.

Having said it's not hard, I should point out that some people might not find WordPress the easiest of platforms to get their heads around. If you are worried that building a website is going to give you too much of a headache, look into the possibility of paying a web designer to do it for you. You might be surprised at how inexpensive it is to have someone else do the job on your behalf.

Future-proofing

Daniel Heuman (n.d.), owner of Intelligent Editing, has some sage advice about the long-term importance of having a website: 'When you're running a small business, things can change. You may find that a big client brings in new procedures, and suddenly you could find yourself in a dry spell for work … you have the assurance of another line of marketing that's ready to go if things change.'

Become a curator

Your website can be about others as well as you – use your website as an information-sharing tool that adds value to the professional services you offer. Update your resources and useful-links sections regularly to keep your website fresh. Outbound links to relevant, well-ranked sites will also help with SEO, as this is one of the many signals to the search engines that your site is worthwhile.

Additional considerations

Favicon

Don't forget to include a favicon (the little icon that shows up on web browser tab when someone opens your site). The method of installation will depend on the host you use, so delve around in their help pages for advice on how to do this – if a reader has several tabs open at once, it enables them to locate and return to your website more easily. See 'Website Tips for Editorial Pros: Get Yourself a Favicon' (Harnby 2012a). Design your favicon so that it fits in with your overall brand design.

Analytics

Ensure you have some sort of analytics program keeping tabs on each page of your website (e.g. StatCounter or Google Analytics). That way you can see which pages are most popular. This is particularly useful if you have a blog or are using your site to curate a host of resources that you regularly promote. Nick Jones (2013c) offers some super advice on monitoring your online marketing performance:

> The average internet user leaves muddy footprints wherever they go on the web, and it is easy to track their movements, even if their data is made anonymous to some degree.

Nick recommends CuteRank, a free tool that allows you to monitor your page ranking for specific keywords across multiple online channels and in multiple countries.

Responsiveness

A responsive website 'recognises the device it is being displayed on and adapts its visual representation to match that device' (Jones 2013b). In other words, your website's layout may look different depending on whether the visitor is using a laptop, notebook, tablet or smartphone. How easy this is to do will depend on which platform you're using. For Weebly and WordPress users, for example, it's a one-click process. If in doubt, have a conversation with your web host.

EU cookie law compliance

Those of us who reside in the EU, or who target EU customers, are bound by law to ask our website visitors to explicitly consent to cookies.

> A cookie is a small file of letters and numbers downloaded on to your computer when you access certain websites. Like virtual door keys, cookies unlock a computer's memory and allow a website to recognise users when they return to a site by opening doors to different content or services. Like a key, a cookie itself does not contain information, but when it is read by a browser it can help a website improve the service delivered. (All About Cookies n.d.)

There are various options available. Which web host you use will determine what works best for you. Nick Jones (2013d) recommends CIVIC: 'their widgets are highly customisable, professional and attractive and so they don't hamper the user's experience'. If your web host doesn't easily support one of these widgets, or you're struggling with the technical aspects of installation, a possible work-around that I've opted for is provided by OpenGlobal E-commerce (2012). This is a simple HTML script that you can place on every page of your website; the script automatically places an unobtrusive pop-up in the top right-hand corner of the web page that contains customizable text and a consent button.

Sharing widgets

Allow your readers to share the content of your site easily by adding sharing widgets (Facebook, LinkedIn, StumbleUpon, Twitter, etc.). Three providers that offer a widget with a range of sharing options are AddThis, shareaholic, and ShareThis.

The short-term benefit of this is that more potential customers will be exposed to your content. The long-term benefit is that people's sharing of your content via social media is another signal to the search engines that your website is of value, thus improving your search engine rankings.

Navigation

If you want to minimize reliance on drop-down menus and instead advertise key areas of your site, buttons can be useful for helping viewers access pages easily. If you're not keen on designing them yourself, try something like CoolText Logo and Graphics Generator. After you've generated your custom buttons, simply link the graphic to the relevant page on your site.

Customize your 404 page, too – a 404 page is what your viewers see if there's a broken link. Keep it linked to your main theme, offer some suggestions of how to fix the problem (such as providing a link to your home page), and consider adding in a contact form so that people can get in touch to find what's been lost.

If you have a lot of information on your site (if you have a blog, for example) consider adding a search tool. Some providers offer this as a built-in ad-free function; others, such as Weebly (free version), don't. As a Weebly user, I therefore elected to place my search engine on a separate page and instead created a linking button. This prevented my information pages becoming cluttered. Alternatively you could decide to invest in your own custom ad-free tool and pay someone to do the design for you.

Photographs

Include a photograph of yourself so that people can see you are a real person. See Chapter 13 on branding, and Chapter 25 on using audio and video, for more information about how photographs embed a sense of your trustworthiness in the minds of your visitors.

Text placement

Think about where you place information on your website so that your readers are most likely to focus on the essential information.

Two approaches to help you lay out text are the F-shaped reading-pattern approach and the inverted-pyramid structure.

Research studies that track eye movement over web pages indicate that people predominantly scan content in an F-shaped pattern. Says Jakob Neilsen (2006):

> Users first read in a horizontal movement, usually across the upper part of the content area ... Next, users move down the page a bit and then read across in a second horizontal movement that typically covers a shorter area than the previous movement ... Finally, users scan the content's left side in a vertical movement. Sometimes this is a fairly slow and systematic scan that appears as a solid stripe on an eye-tracking heatmap. Other times users move faster, creating a spottier heatmap.

Nielsen goes on to summarize the implications for effective website placement:

- Most readers 'conducting their initial research to compile a shortlist of vendors' won't read every word on the page.

- Put the most important information in the first two paragraphs. Readers are most likely to pay more detailed attention to this, especially the first paragraph.

- Don't waste your impact-heavy space: 'Start subheads, paragraphs, and bullet points with information-carrying words that users will notice when scanning down the left side of your content in the final stem of their F-behavior. They'll read the third word on a line much less often than the first two words' (Neilsen 2006).

With regard to the inverted-pyramid approach, Jacob Gube (2011) advises placing the most important information at the top, the evidence that supports this information underneath, followed by any additional information at the bottom.

Test each approach, and ask friends or colleagues to look at your home page for 10 seconds and report back the key points they picked up. This will help you to identify whether your most important information is leaping out at them.

And don't forget to provide white space! I've discussed this on the chapters on CV creation and directory advertising, but it's equally important for online text (Gube 2011). Bullet lists, short paragraphs, clear margins and informative headings all help your reader to navigate your text easily and in a way that is easy on the eye. If your pages appear too cluttered, you're more likely to overwhelm the reader and lose their attention. It's the easiest thing in the world for a bored reader to remove your website from their screen; laying out your core information in a way that makes them want to stay is critical.

Maximizing the impact of your website

'There is no reason for any small business not to be online … in a professional, powerful way. That way, when a customer wants to find your menu of products, they will.' Those are the words of Steve Strauss (2008), USATODAY.com columnist, author and lawyer, and they're wise ones.

A website in itself is an excellent space in which to promote your business. Of all the things you can do to promote your editing and proofreading services, your website offers you the most control over how you design the space and present the content. And, yet, a website in itself is a static tool – it won't generate a steady stream of work for you if you end up on page 340 for Google searches with the keyword 'proofreader'. To turn it into the 'powerful' tool that Strauss talks about, you need to think more deeply about how you will make yourself discoverable.

Search engine optimization is founded around the idea of being interesting. Google's algorithms determine your level of 'interestingness' by crawling your website and looking at things such as:

- how much fresh content is posted regularly;
- the relevant links you embed in the content;

144

- the number of external, inbound links to your site; and

- the meta data you include.

The meta data issue is the easiest to control – you simply add in the keywords manually – but possibly the least effective in SEO terms.

In addition, you need that fresh, regular, high-quality content that will make your website rich in link juice and a popular place to come. That added-value content will be the foundation to increasing visitor numbers to your site, and therefore the sharing of your content via social media or external inbound links. This will improve your search rankings.

It takes effort to deliver regular, high-quality content that people will consider worth sharing and linking to elsewhere. And it therefore takes time to see the positive impact on your search rankings. In other words, it might take a day to build a website, but a year to generate an effective website that delivers business leads to you.

However, your hard work and patience will pay off because you're turning a static, isolated tool into a dynamic entity that will actively work on your behalf to generate opportunities for you and enable you to control the direction of your business.

Visualizing the road to a dynamic website

If you've skipped Chapter 3 on joined-up thinking or Chapter 12 on search engine optimization, go back and read them now. Figure 14.1 helps us to visualize how we can turn our websites from static to dynamic marketing tools.

You've chosen your web host, designed your page, added your content and inserted your meta data. Your content (your pitch) is focused on the message you're trying to communicate to your customers (putting yourself in your customer's shoes). Your website is still a static tool though. No customer can find it unless you actively direct them there. It's competing with the noise of thousands of other websites selling the same editorial services as you are.

Adding value is the next step. Think about information that you can add to your website that makes you more interesting. Blogs, knowledge centres, resource hubs and free (but useful) booklets that help your colleagues and customers are good examples that we discussed in Chapter 8 on adding value.

Now you need to find a way to share your added value. Chapter 15, in Part II, on networking considers in detail the importance of engaging with the wider editorial community. For our purposes in this chapter, the focus is on the opportunity networking provides to share your valuable, interesting content. Social media platforms, professional society networks and online discussion groups will provide you (when used appropriately and respectfully) with the opportunity to share the links to your content, drive visitors to your website and generate re-sharing opportunities. The more interesting your content is to your readers, the more they will share it with their own networks to which you might not be party.

In addition, by thinking in a joined-up way, you can work to build up the external links to your website. The people who value your content will do some of this work for you, for example by including links to your useful content in their knowledge centres and blog posts. But you'll have do the bulk of the work – by guest blogging, commenting on other people's high-quality e-zine/newsletter articles and blog posts, by ensuring you are included in the key, industry-recognized editorial directories, and by providing your website's URL on other marketing materials such as your business cards, advertisements, leaflets, signage, letterhead, email signature, discussion board signature, and so on.

Over time, as colleagues and customers share your content and embed links to it in their own dynamic websites, so your 'interestingness' rankings improve. The better your SEO, the more likely you are to be found by customers outside of your network who are searching generally for editorial freelancers.

If you are committed to continuously focusing on adding value to your website for the benefit of your customers and colleagues, you will see an increase in the number of leads your website generates, and gain more choice in the kind of work you take.

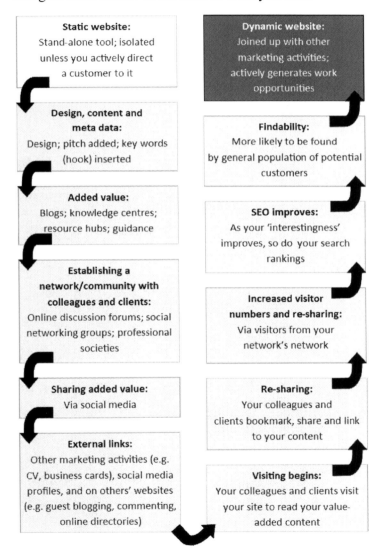

Figure 14.1: Building a dynamic website

Case study

Mine is a self-built website that I created using Weebly. The website is free to build and maintain, though I have purchased a custom domain name from Weebly. I used the framework of Figure 14.1 to optimize my findability and ensure my website is a dynamic marketing tool, not a static one.

I created the site in late November 2011, and on the day I launched it, it was a static tool whose only visitors were those I specifically directed there. If you'd typed in 'proofreader' into Google, you wouldn't have found me, so far down in the listings was I.

As of March 2014, if you'd carried out the same Google search, I was number five. Wikipedia was first, followed by three proofreading software companies. I was the first human being in the list. Typing 'proofreader training' found me at number two and a search for 'proofreading courses' listed me at number three.

StatCounter, one of the website analytics tools I use, and Google PageRank Checker provide me with the following data:

Period	Page views	PageRank
First three months November 2011–January 2012	42	0
July 2012–September 2012	18,659	1
July 2013–September 2013	44,844	3
Most recent three months January 2014–March 2014	47,989	3

Table 14.1: Analytics summary for my website

(NB. 'page views' = the number of times a page has been visited. Repeat visits of a single page by the same viewer are counted.)

Most days I receive unsolicited offers to quote for proofreading work. These come from potential clients who email me via the contact page on my website and who found me by Googling for a proofreader. I don't take up many of these offers because I'm always at capacity for at least the following six weeks and sometimes the following two months. Instead I refer these people to colleagues who have the appropriate experience, or I suggest the client searches a few core professional editorial directories (where I direct them will depend on where they live).

Most of these website leads are students and self-publishing authors. A smaller number are corporate bodies. And because an effective marketing strategy has meant that I'm never desperate for work, I never negotiate my rates downwards. Instead, I choose the projects I want to work on for the rate that I set. If a client finds my quote too expensive, I let them go elsewhere.

If the information above makes me sound as if I'm blowing my own trumpet about being a fabulous proofreader, then I haven't explained myself clearly – the important thing to remember is that this doesn't tell you anything about how good a proofreader I am. Search engines don't care about my proofreading ability; they only care about how interesting they think I am. The only thing it tells you is that I'm an effective marketer.

Now let's look at how, over 22 months, I developed my website into a powerful and dynamic marketing tool. I framed my strategy around Scanlan's 'five simple secrets', outlined in Chapter 12 on search engine optimization.

Domain name

Website domain name: www.louiseharnbyproofreader.com. My domain tells a customer who I am and what I do. I've aimed for clarity (proofreading is the service I provide) and differentiation (there are very few Harnbys in the world).

Page titles, descriptions and metatags

The search term 'proofreader' generates a list of links that include one to my site. The title appears as 'Louise Harnby | Proofreader', and the page description is listed as 'Proofreading services for publishers, businesses and authors'.

Keywords

I've embedded keywords into the content on my site (portfolio pages and subject specialism pages), and into the meta data sections. I also elected to follow Gube's (2011) advice regarding text placement and put the most important information above the fold.

Contact information

Customers are provided with a number of different ways they can contact me and one of these is a hyperlinked email address. Initially I tested a contact form, but a month after my web host (Weebly) made some backroom changes, it became apparent that many requests to quote never made it through to my email inbox. It was partly my fault for not regularly testing the form to ensure it was functioning correctly, so I decided to follow Scanlan's advice. If you do use a contact form instead of an email address, check it's working every couple of days.

Two-way links

Adding value: I added several valuable resources to my website, including:

- *Guidance for New Authors*: This is a free booklet available as a PDF on the site or as an ebooklet via Smashwords. It is aimed at independent writers who are new to the self-publishing process; it aims to direct them to useful publications and tools that will help them on their journey, and to help them make good decisions about choosing an editorial professional to work with.

- The Proofreader's Parlour: This is an information-sharing blog dedicated to providing ideas, resources and tools related to the business side of editorial freelancing. I post fresh content at least once a week.

- BSI-based PDF proofreading stamps for onscreen markup: I've uploaded these to my blog so that my colleagues (fellow freelancers and publishers) can access them for free.

- Resources: My website includes various resources including editorial tools, links to useful publications, and a list of hyperlinked national editorial societies.

Networking: I'm a member of the SfEP and regularly contribute to its member-only online discussion forum; I also attend one of the many local chapters on a bimonthly basis. I tweet daily as @LouiseHarnby. I have a detailed LinkedIn profile and I contribute to some of the publishing and editing discussion groups therein. I have a Facebook account that I use almost solely for sharing professional tips, colleagues' blog posts and useful resources for the editorial freelancer. I have a Google+ profile and a Google+ business page. All in all, I'm directly connected with hundreds of fellow editors and proofreaders (and a number of publishers and independent writers) from all over the world, and indirectly connected with thousands.

Building external links: I have a listing in two of the UK's specialist editorial directories and both entries contain a link to my website. My website URL is also included on my letterhead, address labels, email signature, discussion board signatures, business cards, social media profiles, and leaflets.

When I read excellent articles by my colleagues, I comment on their posts. I also guest write for people whose e-zines, newsletters or blogs are directly relevant to my job. I always include links to my website in these communications. And given that I hope colleagues will share my value-added content (thereby driving people to my website), I reciprocate by sharing theirs. It's a two-way process.

KEY POINTS

- A website is potentially your most powerful marketing tool. The more customers who find you, the more opportunities you will have.

- You have absolute control over your space, more so than with any other marketing tool.

- It needn't cost anything to build, so if you haven't got one, make it a priority. If you can't bear the thought of doing it yourself, investigate the costs of hiring a website designer to create one for you.

- Pay attention to the layout as well as the content of the text.

- Make sure your domain name, meta data, text, colourway, and favicon consistently represent your business brand.

- Build a dynamic site, not a static one – think of ways that you can enhance your SEO.

- Think in a joined-up way. Create links from external marketing materials in order to encourage visits so that your content will be shared and linked to.

- Make sure you're cookie-compliant!

- Use analytics tools to monitor the performance of your site.

TRY IT!

If you don't yet have a website, make it a priority to start the process within the next month.

If you already have a website, make a list of 10 things you can do to improve its findability or its effectiveness over the next six months (consider, for example, SEO activities, adding value, analytics, adding a favicon, acquiring a custom domain name or checking the structure of the text).

15 ONLINE NETWORKING: SOCIAL MEDIA PLUS

What's in it for you?

- SEO benefits via content sharing
- Promotion platform and work opportunities
- Easy access to superb, and often free, learning resources
- Reduces isolation by connecting you with fellow freelancers

What does 'social media' include?

Not all online networking is social-media networking. Social media refers to those online websites and applications that facilitate the creation and sharing of content, and that provide a shared online space in which network members can talk to each other regardless of geographical and time constraints.

Adrienne Montgomerie (2014) defines social media as follows:

> Social media must have a 'broadcast' quality to it. It must have one-to-anyone-'listening' functionality, with the ability for real-time interaction between audience and creator, and the ability to rebroadcast (re-share) the content. And, it must be accessible over the Internet.

New social media sites are springing up all the time, but established examples with a broad user base include LinkedIn, Twitter, Facebook, Google+, Pinterest, StumbleUpon, Reddit, Tumblr, Goodreads and Delicious. If you're a member of a professional editorial society, you may have access to its online networking discussion boards.

Many consider blogging to be part of the social media experience, although Montgomerie's definition places it at the margins. It's certainly a powerful online networking and communication tool so I've chosen to give this a chapter all of its own, not because I don't think it fits within the umbrella of online networking, but because it's a special case that brings more demands with it (see Chapter 16).

What are the benefits?

Information gathering

The amount and quality of information you can access via online networking is extraordinary – unprecedented, in fact. If you want advice on any aspect of editorial freelancing, you can guarantee it's been discussed somewhere on Google+, LinkedIn, Facebook, Twitter or a professional editorial discussion group at some time in the past 12 months. Someone will probably have blogged about it, asked a question about it, or shared a link to a book or article about it. And if they haven't, you can.

Online networking platforms give you instant access to what your customers and colleagues are thinking and doing. Which social media networks work best for you will depend on the kind of information you want to access, and whom you want to communicate with.

Marketing yourself to colleagues

By joining relevant social networks, you'll be engaging with potentially hundreds, even thousands, of colleagues. If they know who you are and what you do, you've made yourself discoverable for them. Many of these colleagues will not only be experienced, but also have benefited from an active marketing programme that they've sustained over a number of years. Established marketers not only get offered more work than they can take on; they also get offered work that they're not suitable for. I get offered copy-editing jobs all the time. I've also been offered opportunities to proofread scientific journal articles and architecture books, neither of which are in my skill set. That's meant I've had to refer the client to colleagues in my network – copy-editors and scientific specialists whose skills sets make them a much better fit. So engaging with a network will put you in touch with people who want to offload, or want to find a more suitable home for, a particular project.

Every year, established editorial freelancers send thousands of pounds' worth of work elsewhere – often to someone they're connected with via a professional online forum, or to someone who attends the same society meet-up, or to a number of colleagues via a jobs board. If you're not in those networks, you won't benefit from the opportunities that arise.

Be picky about which networks you focus on

Don't feel under pressure to use every social media opportunity – you'll lose the will to live! If you're new to online networking, talk to colleagues to find out what they recommend, test a few, and see what works for you. These are free resource streams, and so

> [w]hile not all will be primary drivers of your work stream, the excellent networking opportunities these platforms afford, in combination with the possibility that you might get found by a client, mean it makes sense to take advantage of them. There's no financial outlay, either, so the only costs will be on your time. Your colleagues are there – you should make it your business to be there, too. (Harnby 2013a)

Nick Jones's article 'Which social media channels are right for your business?' (2013) provides a useful overview of how the editorial business owner can make the most of a range of social media.

Professional societies and their opportunities

Professional societies and other editorially focused online discussion forums can be excellent sources of advice and job opportunities. Busy colleagues looking for a home for a job might post directly to these networks. For example, the UK's SfEP, the regional branches of Australia's IPEd, Canada's EAC, and the US's EFA all have jobs boards on their membership forums, and South Africa's PEG allows jobs to be posted on its discussion board.

Twitter and its opportunities

Twitter is an online social networking service that allows you to post messages (tweets) of no more than 140 characters to any follower, and to receive the same from anyone you follow. Many people use it as a leisure tool to text with friends and family, but for others it's a professional mode of information communication and sharing.

It's also a fabulous one-stop shop for news, events and resources from within your colleague network. I follow hundreds of fellow editorial freelancers, publishers, training organizations and marketing specialists, and many of them follow me.

Twitter ('Using Twitter Lists' n.d.) enables the user to create lists with which to categorize those they follow. So if you're short of time, and you follow a lot of people, you can access specific lists to streamline the information you're interested in at any particular point in the day. List creation reduces the 'noise' and enables you to funnel the information efficiently.

Having an active Twitter account that's connected to your editorial colleagues is invaluable when it comes to sharing your added value (see Chapter 8), and the added value created by others. Every time you write new content on your blog, update your resource hub, and add a new resource for your colleagues or clients on your website, you need to be able to let people know what you've done. Twitter's not the only way of getting the message out, but it's one exceptionally easy and productive way.

Twitter as a business networking tool

It's also a way of engaging with other small business owners, both locally and nationally.

One way in which large groups of people can communicate in a structured way involves the use of hashtags alongside keywords (#copyediting, for example). This enables users to categorize posts and follow particular threads across the message stream.

A super example of how this enables small business owners to communicate efficiently is #irishbizparty (which also now has its own Twitter account: @irishbizparty). Here Irish businesses tweet and retweet each other about their services, particularly on a Wednesday evening from 9–11 pm. It's a process of mutual promotion that encourages participation and increases awareness. In one sense it's a very broad form of marketing because of the diversity of the businesses involved, but in another it's highly targeted because all tweeters have the uniform aim of selling their brand to interested parties. Given that editorial freelancing can appeal to a wide range of business clients, taking the time to investigate Twitter-based business groups like @irishbizparty, perhaps ones that are in your region, makes perfect sense. If one doesn't yet exist, set it up.

Samantha Kelly of Funky Goddess, the person responsible for setting up @irishbizparty, has some useful advice about using Twitter effectively:

> My top tip for [the] small business on Twitter is stand out, tweet often but not too much. Make it interesting.
> Target groups that will be interested. (Whelan 2012)

Case study: the editor, the entrepreneur and the hashtag

Theo Paphitis, UK business magnate (of *Dragons' Den* fame) runs a Twitter competition every Sunday between 5 pm and 7.30 pm – you can read details on the Theo Paphitis Small Business Sunday website at www.theopaphitissbs.com, including the entry rules. In a nutshell, you tweet Theo with details about your business, followed by #sbs. He then selects his six favourites from the session and retweets those business owners' messages to his 393,000 followers.

Are you guaranteed to get new business leads by joining in? Of course not! Do you have anything to lose? Same answer! And that's exactly what my colleague Gill Pavey of Wordhouse Writing Services thought. Not only did she join in; she was selected as one of Theo's six weekly favourites, and that meant her business details were forwarded to well over a quarter of a million fellow business owners.

Hits on her website went through the roof. More importantly for SEO purposes, the spike in social media activity may well have helped her rankings and indicated to the likes of Google that her site is worthwhile and 'interesting'. This is a great example of good business practice from the editorial community – Gill used a social media tool creatively and strategically to generate awareness about her editorial services within the business community. It cost her nothing more than the time to write 140 characters' worth of catchy phrasing and a weblink.

Liz Broomfield (2013b) runs regular advanced Twitter searches to locate people actively looking for the services she provides and her efforts have resulted in the acquisition of a few long-term clients working in industries she'd not previously had access to.

Facebook and its opportunities

Facebook was the organization that put the 'social' into social media. When I first experimented with this some years back, it was purely a forum for communicating with friends and family whom I didn't have easy access to and with whom I wanted to socialize online. These days, for me, it's almost purely a professional resource. How you use it is up to you, but Facebook is a superb marketing tool if you want to take advantage of it.

Facebook as a learning and sharing tool

Facebook has a large and friendly editorial network. Most of the professional editorial groups have profiles, some more active than others. Some of the groups are open to the public; others are closed, thereby allowing members to let off steam or share a problem. One of my favourite is the Editors' Association of Earth, an active group of over 2,200 editors and proofreaders from all over the world who come together to share their experiences on a daily basis.

Once you've developed your added value (e.g. a blog or a knowledge centre) or discovered useful resources created by other editorial freelancers, you can use Facebook to share the content quickly and widely to a targeted network of readers.

One of the best features is the instant messaging option that allows private communication between you and others in just about the most efficient way possible. If I want to make a quick referral and need to find out whether my colleague has availability, Facebook is my preferred method of getting their instant attention.

Facebook as a business networking tool

Job opportunities on Facebook via non-colleagues are rarer than via LinkedIn. Given Facebook's original social focus, this isn't surprising. Nevertheless, I have been contacted by students (via my public Facebook business page) and been asked to quote for dissertation and thesis proofreading on a handful of occasions. More likely is that a colleague looking to find a professional with a particular skill set will post an enquiry on one of the editorial group pages.

Case study: two proofreaders and a message box

While Facebook will allow you to connect with hundreds, perhaps thousands, of colleagues, there may well only be a few that you really click with, just like in the offline world! I met Nick Jones via Facebook. We weren't connected via a professional society (or via Twitter or LinkedIn initially), but we had a handful of mutual connections and through their timelines noticed we were both blogging about things that the other found interesting. We made an initial connect via the 'Like' button and then began to bounce a few marketing ideas around using Facebook's messaging tool.

Over time we got to know more about each other's business models, target audiences and skill sets. Nick specializes in proofreading for businesses and students; my target group is publishers (including self-publishers). Nick operates an agency model; I'm a solopreneur. He's a technically savvy gadget-lover; I'm more of a late adopter. But we're both interested in growing our businesses and using a variety of tools to achieve this.

Nick provides me with technical help that enables me to maximize my online discoverability; and he feeds me opportunities to quote for fiction self-publishers. He, on the other hand, is one (of only a handful) of my go-to proofreading colleagues for fast-turnaround work and students (with whom I no longer work). We scratch each other's backs because we understand that while on the surface we might appear to be two competing proofreaders, at a more micro level we have distinct skills sets that provide a home for work the other doesn't want. This means we can give great customer service, even to a client we're not going to work with, and we can feed each other's work streams.

Facebook can facilitate the development of this kind of professional friendship in an unprecedented way. A decade ago, Nick and I might not have crossed paths but a tool like Facebook provides a platform for gentle, speculative engagement that can foster supportive and financially measurable rewards for all of us.

LinkedIn and its opportunities

LinkedIn is an online business networking website. Users build detailed profiles about themselves and their businesses and link with other professionals from around the globe. Added 'furniture' comes in the form of comprehensive testimonials and one-click endorsements from clients and colleagues.

LinkedIn has rolled out a number of features that enable the user to enrich their profiles. One of my favourites is the ability to add highly visible graphic-based links to external content (e.g. a website, blog, CV or portfolio).

LinkedIn as a learning and sharing tool

Once the user has created their profile and linked with a group of fellow professionals, clicking on the Home button delivers a timeline of activity from everyone in that user's network. Activity will include new discussions started on LinkedIn's discussion boards (which you have to join), and information shared from external websites such as blogs and e-zines, and some Twitter and Facebook feeds. Like Twitter, this enables the user to access relevant information in a single stream.

As with Twitter and Facebook, if you're looking for a place to promote any added value you've created, or to share useful content created by others, LinkedIn is an invaluable tool for the job.

For those looking for solutions to problems or to learn the experiences of colleagues, LinkedIn has a wide variety of editorial-focused discussion groups, including Copywriting & Copyediting, STET: Professional Copy Editors, Freelance Editing Network, Grammar Geeks, and Between the Covers Editing and Proofreading Services, to name just a few.

LinkedIn as a business networking tool

The degree to which LinkedIn provides work leads varies depending on which editorial freelancer you talk to. However, there's little doubt that LinkedIn is 'an increasingly important search tool for recruitment agents, business professionals, and writers looking for editorial service providers' (Harnby 2013a). I'd now add publishers and academic authors to that list.

I know of several publishers/project management agencies who are using the LinkedIn network to find editors and proofreaders, and this alone makes it a must-do.

I concur with my colleague, editor Liz Jones, who in my business-planning book (Harnby 2013a) stated:

> It does seem like LinkedIn has finally reached some kind of critical mass ... Just in the past couple of weeks I've had more leads and firm offers of work from that platform than in the previous five years. It feels like an essential now rather than just an extra.

Case study: the project manager's view

My colleague Hazel Harris offers some excellent advice on how to make a good impression to colleagues and customers via your LinkedIn profile. The article, published on her blog Editing Mechanics, is worth reading in full. For our purposes, the following is a brief summary:

- Make the profile comprehensive. Taking the time to do this shows the reader that you give the same attention to detail when indexing, editing and proofreading.

- Don't write an essay – be clear, readable and accessible. The most important information should come first, and generate enough interest to make the reader want to scroll down.

- Provide evidence – testimonials, client lists, professional memberships and portfolios all help to show that you practise what you preach.

- Identify your specialisms clearly – 'producing long and indiscriminate lists just says to me that you're a jack of all trades and a master of none'.

- Include other relevant expertise such as accomplishments, prior career and educational background.

- Use the right kind of images – you need to look professional, convincing, but friendly and approachable. Scary, angry, uninterested expressions won't cut the mustard. Nor will holiday snaps! Worst of all is the absent photo, which leaves the reader wondering what's being hidden.

- 'Use LinkedIn's other features intelligently, according to the client base you're marketing to' (Harris 2013).

Building an effective profile

It's worth spending time to ensure your profiles are set up in a way that will be appealing to potential customers.

Images: In addition to the thumbnail image of your face, take advantage of the free advertising space provided on the top image bars of Twitter, Facebook and Google+. You might compile an image based on some of the material you've worked on (journal covers and book jackets – though do take great care to ensure you secure permission from the copyright holders), or you could base the image around your company logo. I constructed some book-jacket images using Boxshot, an affordable software package than enables you to manipulate images in order to provide different lighting aspects, angles and staged shots. However, there's no right or wrong way. The most important thing is to ensure that the images tell the customer about what you do, reinforce the message that you want to communicate to them, and are attractive to look at.

Description and contact information: Your description should clearly state your name, business name, an outline of the professional services you provide and relevant contact information, particularly your website URL. LinkedIn allows the inclusion of more detailed information than Twitter and Facebook, so look carefully at what the options are and utilize what's available.

Reinforcing your brand: Where possible, use a colourway that matches your business brand (my Twitter profile makes use of the green and dark red I use on my website). Use the same thumbnail image across all your social media profiles. Attention to this kind of detail will help to ensure that you are identifiable and recognizable across multiple marketing platforms.

Adding value: If your chosen social media platform allows you to add value, do take advantage of this. Ideas include:

- using the image bars to visually promote any free guides or information you've created;

- creating portfolios of work completed (or linking to an already-existing online portfolio). LinkedIn, BookMachine and Google+ are good examples;

- adding links to specific pages on your website that feature the added value you've created (Google+ and LinkedIn offer multiple linking opportunities);

- adding links to any articles you've written for editorial colleagues' blogs or your own blog (see especially the information about Google Authorship in Chapter 16).

Signatures: If the social media platforms you're engaged with include editorial discussion forums, pay attention to your signature. In addition to your name, business name and website address, you might create links to your other social media profiles or any online pages that feature your added value and your online portfolio.

How to approach social media

Effective social media engagement is about:

- **Learning:** Through social media channels, you have access to masses of free online tips and resources that can make you better at your job. That's great for you and great for your clients.

- **Researching:** Effective social media use requires investigation of the opportunities. That means finding out where the groups of people are that you want to connect with. These groups might comprise your colleagues (e.g. fellow editors, proofreaders, indexers and translators) or your customers (e.g. students, independent authors and businesses).

- **Being part of a network:** Social media is, well, social. If you're not connected with fellow business professionals and potential clients, it doesn't matter how good your content is – you'll have no one to share it with.

- **Quality of content:** If the content is poor quality, it doesn't matter how strong your network is – no one will want to share it.

- **Professionalism:** It's worth repeating Kiisel's warnings from Chapter 3.

Separation of the private and the public is almost impossible, so don't post anything online that would offend any company you work for or your mother.

> Arguing online is like shouting at your neighbor standing in the middle of the cul-de-sac. Everyone can hear you and you look like an idiot. (Kiisel, 2012)

Online postings can come across as curt so use the same rules you'd apply if you were talking to someone face-to-face. Be friendly and polite.

What goes online stays online. If Google can find it, anyone can find it.

- **Reciprocity:** Reciprocity is not just about building those two-way links between your content and the content of others, though that's crucial if one is thinking about SEO benefits. Just as important is not being greedy. That means thinking in a joined-up way and acknowledging that what goes around comes around. Reciprocating encourages engagement – 'building strands of connection which can, over time, turn into powerful networks that can help you start, grow or develop your business or other endeavour' (Broomfield, 2013).

How should I engage?

Assuming you've joined your various forums, set up your Twitter account, created your LinkedIn page and joined some of the professional editorial groups, and got your Facebook profile up and running, it's time to think about what you can do.

Remember that the goals are to engage with your colleagues in a way that enhances your professional reputation, to create connections between online hubs that increase your visibility or findability (SEO), and to build awareness about your editorial service brand across the business community broadly.

If the traffic is all one way – that is, you only post content about you – it will backfire. Broomfield (2013) wisely suggests considering the 80/20 rule: '8 retweets or shares of other people's content via the social media sharing buttons on their blog posts to 2 promoting your own words or interests'. If you bear that rule in mind you'll be seen as a contributor instead of a free-rider.

For very detailed information about all the things you can do across a range of social media platforms (such as endorsements, sharing, liking, commenting, etc.) I'd recommend Liz Broomfield's (2013) blog post on 'Reciprocity and Social Media'. The following is a brief summary of how you can engage.

- Share your added value: tell people about posts on your blog, any new information added to your resource hub, or updates you've made to advice sheets, booklets, etc.

- Share others' added value: tell your network about good posts on their blogs, or updates they've made to their resource centres, advice booklets, etc.

- Comment on others' blogs, forum messages, tweets, Facebook posts and discussion board threads.

- Be helpful. If people ask for advice and you have something to offer based on experience, help them out. New entrants to the field often have a lot of questions about pricing, marketing and getting experience. Your responses will make them feel welcome, encourage a debate, and demonstrate to the professional community that you're 'driving' rather than 'parking'.

- When people take the time to respond to you, take the time to respond back so that they can see you've engaged with their contribution.

Questions to avoid when tapping your network

Effective networking tapping means asking the right questions. Too often, a new entrant to the field might ask a colleague something that's unanswerable. Examples include: How long will it take me to get my business up and running? How long before I start earning money? How long will it take for my marketing plan to work? Can you refer clients to me, or me to them? The first three are unknowns and the fourth is insulting unless the new starter and the established business owner have already built up a solid professional relationship.

Tapping one's network isn't about getting someone else to do all the hard work. Good marketing involves thinking about skills, background and experience. Our colleague networks are a wonderful way to learn about others' experiences, but ultimately each editorial business owner has to do their own planning and preparation to make themselves marketable because each of us is unique and has our own story to tell.

Instead, ask research-focused questions because these can be answered substantively. Bear in mind that it's essential that you come ready with information about your training, background knowledge (career and education) and intended service provision if you want an editorial pro to give you the most robust guidance. Examples of research-focused questions might include:

- What methods/channels have you found most effective in your marketing strategy to attract customer X?

- What particular USPs do you think customer X is interested in?

- How long did it take you to get a response rate from X marketing activity and would you recommend it?

- Given that I have the following educational and career background, what customer types do you think I'm most suited to targeting initially?

- Do you mind telling me how many hours a week you choose to work (approximately) and how long it took to get to the point where your work stream was solid enough to fill those hours?

How will I fit it in?

Set up a time limit and decide on various points in the day when you will check in with your social media platforms – use it as a way of enforcing a natural break from your work. Be disciplined about the amount of time you spend on it. It's not the be all and end all!

Using tools to schedule posts and manage multiple social channels at once can be useful for the busy editorial freelancer. Allan Beaton's article on how to manage your social media activity explains the benefits of using one such tool, Hootsuite:

> With up to 200 streams in your dashboard, you couldn't be any more organised! This means that you can organise your social media into tabs that are relative to each other, so that you can monitor everything more quickly and can recognise opportunities to engage for increased online profile. (Beaton 2013)

In 'The 1.5-Hour Daily Social Media Schedule' (O'Moore-Klopf 2013), editor Katharine O'Moore-Klopf offers the following guidelines:

> [T]here's no universally accepted schedule for engaging properly in social media [but] by following this schedule, I spend approximately 1.5 hours on any given weekday on marketing activities, excluding e-mail. That time is spread out in bits and pieces.

KEY POINTS

- Be gracious – watch your manners and be professional at all times.

- Be generous – social media engagement is a two-way street. If you help and share, others will do the same for you.

- Make use of the tools that each platform offers to reinforce your brand and maximize the impact of your profile.

- Be disciplined about the amount of time you spend on your social media platforms. Consider using tools like Hootsuite to manage your time more effectively.

- Be creative and research the opportunities available that you can use strategically to build awareness about your editorial business.

- It's fine to spend the most time on the platforms that you find work for you best. You don't have to do everything all of the time.

- When tapping your network, take care with the questions you ask. Framing them in a research-focused way is preferable.

TRY IT!

If you don't have a social media presence at all, start by building yourself a LinkedIn profile since this is increasingly being used by businesses, independent writers, students and publishers to locate professional editorial freelancers.

Visit your national/regional editorial society and see which social media platforms they're using. Consider joining the same platforms and connecting with them.

Find 30 colleagues with whom you can connect (via your professional editorial society perhaps, or by investigating some of the more active fellow freelancers on LinkedIn group discussion boards).

See if they've posted interesting content today, and share it on LinkedIn (or on any other social media platforms you have access to, e.g. a message board, discussion group, Facebook).

If you've already created some added value for your business in the form of a resource hub, a free advice booklet, a blog article, share it on your social media platforms.

16 BLOGGING FOR BUSINESS

What's in it for you?

- Massive SEO benefits
- Enables you to add value in a dynamic space that you completely control
- Connects you with your customers and colleagues

Why is blogging a stand-out activity?

I've dedicated a chapter to blogging for business because, caveats aside (and there are plenty of them), my own blog, The Proofreader's Parlour, is the single most important SEO tool in my marketing strategy. Not that this was the deciding factor when I began blogging, but I'll come onto that at the end of the chapter.

Successful SEO means you are findable. And the more findable you are, the more likely you are to have a choice of customers and projects from which you can choose. That choice might bring you more interesting projects or more financially lucrative projects, or both. To understand why blogging is so powerful, we need to put our joined-up-thinking hats on.

Thinking in a joined-up way

You'll recall how, in Chapter 3 on thinking in a joined-up way, we discussed how each activity we carry out (and the concepts we embrace) is linked to many of others. A directory listing that includes a link to a website means the two are connected. A guest article on a colleague's website that includes links to your own websites, and your various social media profiles, means all of them are connected. A comment on a LinkedIn group discussion thread that includes a link to a resource you've written about for an online magazine or newsletter means the two are connected.

A blog that's disconnected is just a blog – a log of musings that no one but you and a few friends will ever know about. Even if the content is fabulously interesting, if no one knows about it, no one will visit it. Successful blogging – and by that I mean successful from the point of view of marketing – therefore requires you to have the means to share that information, whether via social media, professional society membership networks, online discussion groups, professional print magazines, business cards, etc. Without a networking platform to bounce off, your blog could remain just an isolated entity rather than a dynamic part of your marketing strategy that engages you with your customers and colleagues.

Thinking about added value – where should you put your blog?

In Chapter 8, we discussed in detail the concept of adding value to your business website. Blogging is an excellent way of adding value because it provides you with a personal space in which you can offer advice and resources to customers or colleagues (or both), in a way that is designed by you. On your blog, you're not restricted – you control the message and the voice in which you communicate that message. And if your message is relevant to your business (and it should be, otherwise there's little point in doing it), it makes sense to embed that added value in a relevant space.

With this in mind, I'd advise attaching your business blog to your business website because it makes it easier for the blog visitor to bounce through to other relevant pages – those about your editorial services, the formats in which you work, your portfolio, your testimonials, and your business contact details. Of course, you can create links to all this information if it lies on a separate website. However, your business website will not benefit from the page-rank information that your blog does. Therefore, by placing the two within the same domain, the blog feeds the business SEO, and vice versa.

Given that the search engines are so fond of fresh, regularly updated content, your business website needs your blog more than your blog needs your website!

Business blogging and SEO

Once you start blogging, and have the means to share the valuable content on your blog, you begin the process of optimizing the chances of your website featuring higher up in your customers' and colleagues' searches for information on search engines like Google. The nearer you appear to page one, the more likely someone is to click through to your website.

Consider what a premium feature advertisement would cost you – guaranteeing a first-page listing on Google – and the benefits of regular and relevant blogging soon become apparent. Blogging costs nothing in terms of money, unless you add images from stock libraries.

If you do want to use images, Sophie Playle (personal correspondence) offers some useful advice:

> There are lots of websites that offer free stock images (usually requesting a simple attribution). For example: photopin.com, pixabay.com and freeimages.com. [Y]ou can even search Flickr for images with Creative Commons licensed content (using the Advanced search option).

Blogging does, however, cost time. If you're not enthused by the idea and don't want to put in the time to commit to it, think seriously about the degree to which you want to include it as a serious part of your marketing strategy.

Case study: business blogging

One of my colleagues, Mary McCauley, wrote a guest article for The Proofreader's Parlour in 2012 about how she used goal setting as part of the business-planning process during the start-up phase of her business. The article is excellent and a superb demonstration of a new entrant to the field strategizing in a professional and sensible way. Here's how she and I benefited mutually from that article:

- To start off with, it's high-quality content, so I knew that it was worth sharing. That's the bottom line when it comes to blogging.

- I used my social media networks to share that content: Twitter, LinkedIn, Google + and Facebook. Mary then used her own social media network to re-share that same content.

- That drove new visitors to my blog and they went on to share the article via their own social media networks, thereby expanding my readership base even further. With every extra share of Mary's article, the search engine bots that regularly scour the internet were getting the following information: this article is new, this article is interesting, and the website this article has been posted on therefore publishes fresh content that is of value to people.

- Mary's article also includes links to her own business website. People can click through to find out about her and the editorial services she provides. Her site and my site are therefore connected. Search engines like this kind of organic connection. Her website being linked to my website tells them she's interesting, too.

- Eighteen months on, and Mary's article is still a favourite for newbies searching on Google for information about starting out. Using keywords such as 'starting a proofreading business' brings up Mary's article as the second from top listing on page one of a Google search. It's consistently one of the most-viewed articles on my site. More engagement, more shares, more external inbound links, all of which help towards my rankings.

- The longer-term effect is that as long as my domain name is considered interesting to the search engines, the more likely I am to feature higher up in a more general keyword search, for example, 'proofreader fiction'. That keyword combination generates a Google listing of what it considers to be relevant links, and my website is the number-two listing on page one. So an independent writer will find my website quickly if he or she uses those keywords to search for someone to proofread their self-published novel. Actually, the link is to another article on my blog that I wrote six months before Mary wrote hers. It wasn't nearly as popular as Mary's but that doesn't matter. It's published on the same website.

While I'm grateful to the contribution Mary has made to my SEO, I'm not going to give her all the credit! It's absolutely not enough to host a blog that delivers high-quality content like this now and again. And it's not going to work if you repeat the same information. The content needs to be original and posted regularly. And it has to be something that people actually want to engage with – in other words, it has to be relevant.

Regular business blogging

Expert advice on how often you should blog varies; some say every day, some argue for twice a week. I don't have the time to blog every day – I'm too busy proofreading! Instead, I prefer to post a regular feature once a week (my Proofreader's Parlour Weekly Review) and other longer articles about the business of editorial freelancing once or twice a month. It really depends on what I have to say, and whether colleagues have original contributions they want to make. I don't obsess about the regularity of my business blogging – after all, it's just one of a number of marketing tools. And ultimately it's driven by the enjoyment of sharing information with the global network of editors, proofreaders, indexers and writers. If I don't feel I've got something useful to contribute to the Parlour in any given fortnight, so be it.

If you're serious about business-related blogging, here are a few ideas for how you might manage the regularity issue without sending your stress levels through the roof:

- Think about short but regular features that you can share with your readers. In addition to compiling a weekly review of newsworthy story links that are relevant to the editorial community, I sometimes publish a 'Link of the Week' on the Proofreader's Parlour. This might be a colleague's new editorial blog, a particularly interesting article on business marketing, the contact details for a professional society, a training course that's new to market, or a recently launched book or newsletter. The Publishing Training Centre publishes regular Grammar Bites posts that offer short, snappy explanations of various points of grammar in the English language. Liz Broomfield of Libro Editing includes a regular Small Business Chat feature. Nick Jones, owner of Find a Proofreader, hosts a regular Freelancer of the Month review on the directory's blog. And the Copyediting.com newsletter features a Questions for a Freelance Editor/Proofreader. All use a set-question format.

- Consider breaking down longer posts into several sections that you can post over the course of a few weeks. If you have a lot to say, you don't need to say it all at once. Serializing encourages visitors to return to your site while at the same time enabling you to provide fresh, regular content that the search engines value so much in terms of rankings.

- Invite colleagues or customers to contribute. There are SEO benefits to them, too, as the organic links from your site to theirs enhance their own findability.

- Return the favour, and blog for others. Those two-way links work for you, too. Even if you haven't posted on your own blog for a couple of weeks, writing valuable, high-quality content for someone else's business blog will have SEO benefits for you. If your guest article includes a link to your site, and if the blog you are posting on has a big following, you may attract new followers to yours.

Relevant business blogging

One of the easiest ways to work out how to be relevant on your business blog is to put yourself in your customer's shoes. You might like to go back and read Chapter 7, where we discussed this in more detail. Your customers and colleagues won't bother reading your business blog if it's not relevant to them, so imagine you are them and use this as a framework for your content.

- If you work with academic authors, are there particular questions that repeatedly come up and that you could address over a series of blogs?

- Do your independent fiction authors consistently struggle with particular element of English-language writing?

- Do your customers regularly misunderstand what you do?

- Are there lessons you've learned, which you wished you'd known when you started out, that newbie colleagues would be interested in?

- Do you have a specialist knowledge base (legal, medical, marketing, translation, technical, software) that you could use as the basis for your business blogging?

- If you're a grammarian or linguist, in addition to being an editorial freelancer, could these elements form the foundation of your business blog's focus?

Whatever niche you choose, make sure that it's not just interesting to your colleagues, but to you, too. You'll find it difficult to maintain the momentum of regular blogging if you are not excited by the opportunity of writing the content, never mind sharing it!

Things to include

As well as your interesting content, consider including some of the following, which will help your readers navigate your blog in a user-friendly way:

- Enable comments so that your readers can engage in a dialogue with you, critique your posts, and provide additional information. Always reply to them so that your audience knows you're engaged with their contribution. And get rid of the spam!

- Offer multiple subscriptions options such as email and RSS feeds.

- Invite guest articles so that visitors can read multiple viewpoints.

- Include sharing buttons so that people can distribute links about your content to their networks.

- Offer navigation buttons/links that help readers search for keywords, subject archives and related information.

- Take advantage of the opportunity to add Google Authorship to your blog. Says Joshua Duke (2013):

  Google Authorship is becoming more and more important. Properly setup blog posts will show up in Google results with the author's picture next to the meta description. While it doesn't seem like much, this picture tends to draw the attention of searchers, and some reports have even shown that the Google Authorship picture increases clicks by 150%.

  Google's developing AuthorRank algorithm benefits both the blog and the author, so it's a win–win solution.

Don't do it if you don't love it

This chapter has focused on how business blogging can be a stand-out marketing tool. There's a big caveat to this, though. To get the marketing benefits from business blogging takes a massive amount of commitment. I can't emphasize this enough. Therefore, I'd recommend business blogging only if you love doing it and derive genuine satisfaction from engaging with your customers and colleagues in this way.

Even if The Proofreader's Parlour hadn't had a huge impact on my SEO, and therefore my discoverability, I'd still keep posting, because it's something I love doing. It's one of many platforms on which I can connect with the people I work with and the people I work for. And, ultimately, that's what drives me.

None of us likes to spend even small amounts of time doing things we don't enjoy. The difference between business blogging and the other marketing activities discussed in this book is the amount of time it takes up. Let's imagine that the idea of creating your business cards bores you to tears. The fact is that you can spend a couple of hours sorting it out, and then it's done. With business blogging, the job's never done, so if you don't derive genuine pleasure from it, you'll find it almost impossible to keep up the momentum. If that's you, that's fine – focus your precious time on doing the activities that suit your work/life balance and that you are prepared to commit to. It's your business and you get to decide how to apportion your time to what you want to do.

KEY POINTS

- Business blogging has massive SEO benefits when it involves the posting of regular and relevant content. A joined-up approach is essential. You need to be able to share your content.

- Fresh, regular content tells search engines you are interesting. The more interesting you are, the higher you rank. The higher you rank, the more likely you are to be found by a customer via a search engine before that customer gets bored looking through a multitude of pages.

- Business blogging engages you with your professional community (and your customers). By adding this kind of dynamic value to your website, you can develop your business network and consolidate your brand.

- Put yourself in your customer's shoes to help you think about what to blog about and how you can add value for them.

- Share your own content, but share others', too. No one likes a greedy blogger. Blogging is about marketing but it's also about engagement with an international community. Poor reciprocation will reduce your colleagues' willingness to share your content.

- Reply to comments (except the spam ones, which you need to eradicate) to show your genuine desire to engage.

- It takes a huge investment in time, so only do it if you love it.

TRY IT!

If you fancy trying business blogging, why not first take a look at some examples in your sector. This will give you a feel for what your colleagues are doing. A selected list of editorial blogs is included in the Resources at the end of the book.

If you want to set up your own blog straight away, make a list of the things about editorial freelancing that you and your customers are most interested in and that you would most enjoy writing about – these might form the foundation of your business blog.

17 FACE-TO-FACE MARKETING: BUSINESS NETWORKING, EVENTS, WORKSHOPS AND MEET-AND-GREETS

What's in it for you?

- Enables you to engage with customers who may not be familiar with what you do
- Confidence – helps you to learn to articulate concisely
- Communication – encourages you to think about communicating with your customers' needs in mind

What are the opportunities?

Some face-to-face networking opportunities are more comfortable to contemplate than others. While the thought of turning up at a local or regional small-business networking event may induce anxiety, there are other less formal events that you may like to consider as a first step (for example, one of the local chapters run by your national editorial society).

Other face-to-face meet-ups could include professional conferences, training, seminars and workshops, writing groups, publishing events, discussions with university professors or supervisors, and appointments with publishers (either in-house or at a book fair).

Which types of meetings appeal to you will depend on who your core client groups are and what continued professional development courses you're considering.

Case study: colleague meet-ups

My local SfEP group (the Norfolk branch) meets once every two months. The structure of the sessions varies depending on what we want to achieve. Sometimes one or two people will lead a presentation on a particular aspect of editorial freelancing; other times the sessions will be social – people intermingling, catching up, saying hello to new faces, sharing advice and asking questions.

We keep the meetings informal and friendly. We share a meal together at the start of the session. But the real benefit comes from the diversity of the group. We vary in terms of age, gender, subject specialisms, and the time we've been running our editorial businesses. Together, we have a broad set of skills and lots of information to share, from fiction editors, social science project managers, manuscript critiquing specialists, legal editors, and finance specialists, to crime writers, bioscience researchers and adult fiction proofreaders.

We know each other, like each other, are interested in sharing knowledge about how each other works. But we also refer work to each other. I met my colleague Sophie Playle at one of our meetings and after having the opportunity to look at her work, I realized that she had a something I often needed – excellent copy-editing skills that many of my self-publishing novelists would really benefit from before working with me. She's now my go-to editor when I need to place this kind of work.

Our local-group meetings are therefore social and networking opportunities, but they're also a source of work on occasion. And newbies are always welcomed with open arms.

If you've not yet attended a meeting hosted by your national editorial society (or one of its local chapters), why not contact them to find out what opportunities are available. If there isn't a branch near you, you could set one up.

Getting personal

Face-to-face events and meetings can be excellent opportunities to meet other professionals both from within your field and from outside it. If it's your first time at an event, you may not know anyone. That means introducing yourself and being ready to explain what you do. And so we come to the verbal pitch.

The verbal pitch at a face-to-face meeting or event is possibly the thing that sends more people into a cold sweat than anything else. It's my least favourite activity, so I won't hold it against you if doesn't make your heart sing either. Even if you decide not to actively attend events or workshops, you may well accidentally find yourself in a situation where the chance to pitch your services face-to-face arises, so it makes sense to be prepared, just in case!

Don't forget that your colleagues are potential clients, too. If you perfect your verbal pitch, you'll be more confident about introducing yourself and explaining what you do if you meet fellow editorial freelancers on training courses or at conferences.

Tips for talking to others without fear

Back in 1996, I attended a course called 'Effective Presentations and Public Speaking'. Part of my in-house role with the publisher I then worked for required me, as part of a team, to present our marketing strategy to professional societies whose journals we were bidding for the rights to publish. My then director thought this course was an excellent training opportunity and something I could use throughout my career, wherever it led me. He wasn't wrong.

The best thing about that course was that it was run *for* people like us, *by* someone like us. The trainer wasn't a motivational speaker: there was no chest thumping, no group hugs, and no fire-walk at the end. Instead, she showed us how we might talk to others without fear. Here are the several lessons that most clearly stand out in my mind from that day. Perhaps they'll help reduce your fear, too:

- **You don't have to like it to do it:** You may never learn to love presenting or pitching, but you will become better at it with practice, especially if you bear in mind the points below. I still don't like presenting to people and I never will. Given the option of pitching to one stranger, or chatting to 10 friends, I'd choose the latter every time. I don't get a 'buzz' out of the challenge; I don't feel like it's an opportunity that I want to grab enthusiastically. In fact, face-to-face presentations make me feel sick with worry, but I've done a fair few of them and lived to tell the tale. Sometimes you just do what you have to do!

- **Your listeners don't want you to fail:** Most people to whom you present are on your side. Very few human beings enjoy seeing people squirm with discomfort. Look at your listeners' faces when you talk to them – not only is it polite to do this, but it also gives you the chance to see them smiling at you and encouraging you with their eyes. If your listeners look bored or aggressive, that's their failure not yours.

- **Be prepared:** Practise your pitch in your head so that you know it off by heart. That way you can look your listeners in the eyes, rather than at a piece of paper, while you talk. You might never learn to love face-to-face pitching but preparation is the single thing you have most control over. If there are key points you need to remember, have a cue card to hand.

- **Breathe:** Regular breathing is the most powerful tool your body has to offer in this situation. It keeps your heart rate steady, thereby physically calming you. But it also provides you with natural pauses in your speech that give you time to prepare the next few words coming out of your mouth, and that makes you feel more in control psychologically.

- **Speak more slowly than you normally would:** Most of us tend to speak faster when we're nervous, which means we're more likely to trip over our words or stammer. Use your breathing to force yourself to pause and slow down.

- **Smile:** When you smile you force your face to relax. You look more comfortable on the outside than you might feel on the inside, so it hides your nerves. Smiling makes you radiate warmth and engagement. Even if you do trip over your words while you're pitching, your listener probably won't notice, and almost certainly won't care, as long as you have a smile on your face.

- **Arms:** Hold your arms at the side of your body, hands relaxed, elbows just bent at waist-height (or thereabouts – whatever feels most comfortable and natural). Placing your arms behind your back can make you appear aggressive; folding them in front of your chest can make you appear defensive; and holding your hands together in front allows you to fidget if you are nervous. By placing your arms apart at your sides, you can gesticulate gently and comfortably.

- **You're good enough:** You don't have to be great at presenting – you simply have to be great at being you. Our tutor kept reminding us of this. Delivering a pitch isn't about being a fabulous orator; it's about being a normal human being with 20 seconds' worth of something interesting to say. You don't have to be Gandhi or Lincoln – you're good enough.

Our trainer videoed us presenting short pitches both before and after her tutelage. It gave us the opportunity to see how using the above tools improved our presentation skills. And it worked. I didn't return home eight hours later liking the idea any more than when I walked into the training room at 9 am, but I did feel more capable of carrying out the task.

You might also find the following useful:

- The BBC (n.d.) has a range of video clips on *The Speaker*

- Toastmasters International (n.d.), '10 Tips for Public Speaking'

Developing the verbal pitch

There's no definitive rule about how to tackle this, but one way of thinking about how to structure your pitch is to flip Daum's differentiation–solution–empathy framework on its head (see also Chapter 4).

- First, dive straight in with the empathy element.

- Then present your differentiation and solution in whichever order feels right to you.

Recall the example given in Chapter 4 for a verbal pitch to a business executive by Liz. The following is a real pitch that she created after we discussed this issue and how Daum's framework could be used to tackle it. Liz used the exercise to prepare for a local business networking meeting.

> Business exec.: Hi! I'm Mel. Nice to meet you. Who are you and what do you do?

> Liz: Hello! I'm Liz Jones. So, what do I do? Well, all businesses produce written documents: websites, brochures, reports, ads, flyers ... It's not easy to get the text right – but it matters. Well-written and presented text reflects well on your business, and makes you (and your products or services) more credible and trustworthy.

> I'm a professional editor. I take what is written and polish it so it's clearer and more accurate. I don't change what you want to say – I just help you express it in the best way possible.

- Everything up to and including '... more credible and trustworthy' is empathy.

- 'I'm a professional editor ...' is differentiation. It's the thing the customer can't necessarily do for themselves.

- 'I take what is written ... in the best way possible' is the solution.

And here's an alternative that could be used when talking to an independent author.

> Author: Hi! Good to meet you. Who are you and what do you do?

Krysia: Hello! I'm Krysia Cruz. What do I do? Well, all authors want their readers to get the maximum amount of enjoyment from their books. It's not always easy to get the punctuation, spelling and grammar right because the author's skill is in story building ... But it does matter because a lot of readers get irritated by little mistakes and find these distract them from the tale being told.

I'm a professional copy-editor and I stop that happening. I take what's written and polish it so that the text is clear and your readers are free to enjoy the world you've created. I don't change what you say – I just help you express it in the best way possible.

- Everything up to and including '... tale being told' is empathy.

- 'I'm a professional copy-editor' is differentiation. It's the thing the customer can't necessarily do for themselves.

- '... and I stop that happening ... in the best way possible' is the solution.

In Chapter 4, I gave the example of a short pitch that I could use as a basis for my written marketing materials. Here's a tweaked version I might use verbally to a publisher.

Publisher: Hi! Who are you and what do you do?

Louise: Hello. I'm Louise Harnby, and I'm a specialist social sciences and humanities proofreader with over 20 years of publishing experience. I worked in-house for Sage Publications for 15 years, and I know it's a really tough haul in the production department! That's why I always deliver on budget and brief, and I never, ever miss a deadline. I can work onscreen or on paper, and blind or against copy. I'm an Advanced Member of the SfEP and I trained with the PTC. So far, I've proofread 350 or so books for the likes of CUP, Edward Elgar, Sage, Yale, and Polity Press.

- Everything up to and including '... 20 years of publishing experience' is differentiation.

- 'I worked in-house for Sage Publications for 15 years, and I know it's a really tough haul ...' is empathy. It says, 'I've been there!'

- 'I can work onscreen ...' is the solution.

What else do you need?

Business cards are a must – they're a standard tool to close with at business meetings. If you don't yet have some, read Chapter 22 and then take the necessary action.

You might also take some CVs or brochures with you for anyone who wants more detailed information. Since they are more bulky, they are best used as a second option, particularly if you are at an event where there are lots of people sharing information.

As a final note, you may like to know that despite the idea of business networking being rather daunting, Liz found the actual experience really rewarding and plans to attend more events. For her, preparation was key because using Daum's framework helped her to avoid something we're all terrified we'll do – ramble – and think instead about her business in the context of her potential customers' perceptions. And she wasn't the only nervous person in the room – many of the other attendees were too, but that wasn't an obstacle to them communicating with each other.

KEY POINTS

- Put yourself in the customer's shoes so that you focus on the right USPs.

- Flip the differentiation–solution–empathy framework on its head – there's no set order; it's a guideline for how to think about what you're telling people about what you do.

- Be yourself – you're good enough!

- Be prepared – rehearse your pitch.

- Relax. If you can't relax, use your arms, mouth, eyes and lungs! They'll do a lot of the hard work for you.

187

- Remember – if you attend a local networking event, you're not the only person there who'll be nervous. Being nervous is normal.

- Don't attend a meeting without business cards.

TRY IT!

Prepare a couple of verbal pitches that you could use for different client types that you might come across.

Consider attending a local business-to-business networking meeting and try out one of your newly created pitches.

18 PROMOTING YOURSELF TO EXISTING CLIENTS

What's in it for you?

- Existing clients know you, and you know them
- They're low risk – you know what you're getting and you know they'll pay
- Little marketing labour required – you already have their contact details
- Having been chosen once, you're far more likely to be chosen again

You've already done the hard work

To some readers it will seem obvious to tap your existing clients for business, and yet it's something that less confident editorial freelancers either feel embarrassed about or forget to do.

Just to be clear, your existing client base is one of your most valuable resources. You've already worked for them and proved yourself to them. You're familiar with their way of doing things and you've already built up a professional relationship with them. You know the name of the person to contact so, unlike cold contact, there's no hard work to do in terms of ensuring your email or phone call gets to the right person.

Additionally, the client has proved themselves to you – you've been paid (ideally on time), so there's a risk-reduction factor to build in to the equation.

Shouldn't I wait for them to contact me?

Here are a few things to consider about your existing clients, particularly those like project managers and publishing houses or business clients who use editors and proofreaders regularly:

- They're busy.
- They can't read your mind.
- They don't know what your schedule looks like – they're too busy thinking about their own to-do list.
- If you're out of sight, you may be out of mind.
- The worst thing they can say is 'no'.
- The best thing they can say is 'yes'!

One of my existing publisher clients has seen a lot of staff changes recently – one project manager moved to another house, one didn't return from maternity leave, and another had just gone back on maternity leave. I hadn't heard from one of the remaining project managers for a couple of months and got in contact to say hello and ask about any new members of the team I might introduce myself to, given all the changes. He responded with a friendly update of the staffing situation (which was a nightmare for him – he and a temp were doing the jobs of four people) and an offer of not one proofreading project, but three. I liked the look of the jobs, so I agreed to take them. His response? 'That's great, Louise. Thanks for saying yes – I really appreciate it as I'm pretty busy trying to keep things moving!'

It wasn't that I hadn't heard from him because he didn't want to work with me. Rather, I hadn't heard from him because he was barely keeping his head above water. By contacting him I saved him the time of having to fire off an email asking about availability. And he ended up thanking *me*!

There may be lots of reasons why you haven't heard from an existing client for a while, but the likelihood of it being because you're not worth talking to is right at the bottom of the list. If you've been chosen once, you are far more likely to be chosen again, but your client may need a reminder, especially if they work with a lot of freelancers. So if you like working with someone, drop them a line to put yourself back on their radar. It's perfectly acceptable business practice and doesn't warrant any embarrassment on your part.

What should I say?

When it comes to existing clients, I think it's perfectly okay to get straight to the point. They're not your best friends but fellow business professionals, so while of course you'll want to be polite you don't want them to feel you're wasting their time. Here are some basic ways of tackling it, some of which are quite direct and some of which wrap the enquiry around a reason. I've included examples of both so that even those who are nervous about contacting existing clients have some ideas about how to frame the message in a way that seems to justify the contact:

- Post-holiday message: 'Hi James. Happy New Year to you. I hope you enjoyed the festive season. I'm just writing to ask if there's any proofreading I can help you with in the next few months. Drop me a line if I can be of assistance.'

- Unexpected opening: 'Morning, Astrid. I thought I'd drop you a quick line to see if you have any copy-editing projects that you need help with. The past few months have been pretty hectic, but today a regular client let me down unexpectedly and shifted a project forward for a month. Consequently I have a two-week gap in my schedule that I hadn't accounted for. If you have anything suitable, I'd be delighted to help out.'

- Straight to the point: 'Dear Jeanne, I haven't heard from you in a while and wondered if you had any upcoming projects that I can proofread or edit for you. I enjoyed working on the previous project together so if there's anything you'd like to place with me in the next month, I'd be happy to discuss.'

- Updated details: 'Hi John. I'm just emailing you to ensure you have my current contact details. I changed providers a few months ago and thought I'd just check that you have my up-to-date information on file. [Details provided]. And if there's any indexing work you'd like me to assist you with, please let me know. I still have a few slots in my schedule for June and would enjoy the opportunity to work with you again.'

- Follow-up to prior project: 'Dear Jane, I thought I'd drop you a line to see how things are going with the novel I proofread for you in January. I know you were a little nervous about the marketing side of self-publishing and I hope those links I gave you were helpful. There are a lot of really interesting things happening in the world of independent authorship at the moment, and I hope you've retained the enthusiasm that was so obvious in our correspondence earlier in the year! You mentioned that you were planning to work on a sequel. Do let me know if you need a proofreader. I'd love to have the opportunity to work with you again, and I'd be happy to quote for you at any time.'

And so on and so forth. You're only limited by your imagination. As long as you are friendly and polite, your client will not object to hearing from you. They may even be grateful for your contact.

KEY POINTS

- If you see a space in your schedule and want to get back on the radar of an existing client, get in contact. You'll save them the bother of having to do the chasing.

- Don't forget that you're not the centre of your client's world. So if they've not been in touch for a while it's unlikely to be about you – it's about them being focused on other things.

- If you've been chosen once, you're more likely to be chosen again.

- If you feel embarrassed about directly asking if there's any work going, frame your question around a reason: a holiday greeting, a change of contact details, a congratulatory message about the completion of their project, a thank-you for the opportunity to work with them, and so on.

TRY IT!

Is there someone you've worked for in the past who hasn't been in touch for a while? If you have space in your schedule and would like to work for them again, draft two emails asking for work, each taking a different approach – make the first one a direct enquiry that goes straight to the point; with the second, wrap your reason for contact around a supposed primary enquiry (change of contact details, holiday message, etc.). Does either of these emails make you feel uncomfortable? If one does, send the other and see what happens!

19 DIRECTORY ADVERTISING

What's in it for you?

- SEO benefits
- Makes you available to core customers and new customer groups
- Positions you alongside other professionals
- Increases the likelihood of customers finding you and therefore the choices you have over the work you do and how much you earn

You're halfway there

Directory advertising can be a powerful tool in any editorial freelancer's marketing strategy. What sets it apart from other media is the fact that if a potential client has decided to look in a directory then you can be almost sure that they are ready to buy one of the services listed.

> It is the place we often turn when we have already made a decision and we are ready to buy ... The person looking in the directory has identified a need and has picked up the directory with intent to spend money. ('Driving Results with Directory Advertising' n.d.)

From the client's point of view, then, a directory search is more proactive than an internet browse. If you're in the directory they are searching, half the job is done. This is something we need to take advantage of when we're considering how to promote our editorial businesses.

Sue Browning, an experienced editor and proofreader, argues that they can be particularly useful for new starters with few industry contacts:

> When I started out, I had no contacts in the publishing world so was building a client base from scratch, and such sites were a major source of work for the first few years ... They were also a source of a large variety of jobs, for people and organisations I wouldn't necessarily have thought of approaching, one or two of whom turned into long-term repeat customers. If you're in a similar situation they are certainly worth considering as one strand of your marketing strategy.

Choosing your directories

Put yourself in your customer's shoes. Different customer types will turn to different directory types, depending on their knowledge of our industry. Any old directory won't do – targeted advertising is what you're aiming for.

Editorial society directories

Publisher clients will no doubt be aware of the directories hosted by the Society for Editors and Proofreaders (SfEP) in the UK, the regional chapters of the Institute of Professional Editors (IPEd) in Australia, or the Editorial Freelancers Association (EFA) in the USA, to give just three examples (a full list of editorial society directories is provided in the Resources at the end of the book).

However, the first-time self-publishing author who needs their novel proofread or the dentist who needs their website edited may not be aware of our national editorial societies. Think about a time before you became an editorial freelancer. If you needed to find a plumber or a cattery, where did you look? Which general business directories did you use?

General business directories

In the UK, some of the most-visited online business directories include Yell, FreeIndex, Thompson Local, and Up My Street. In the US, Yelp, Local.com, WhitePages and YP are in the mix. Wherever you live in the world, most national business directories provide the option to place free ads, though what information you can include will be limited.

Don't forget social media when considering business directories. LinkedIn and, perhaps to a lesser extent at present, Google+ Local could be considered, too.

Specialist freelancing directories

There are a number of specialist freelancing directories that are worth considering. Find a Proofreader specializes in editorial service suppliers. Advertisers receive regular emails from the site from potential clients who use the Get A Quote function. The nice thing about this site is that you can customize your listing fairly freely, and there's plenty of space to include as much information as you want. I've found that my listing has generated mainly leads from potential business customers and students. There's also a review section that allows clients to post testimonials once you've completed work for them.

More general freelance directories include PeoplePerHour, Craigs List, Freelancers in the UK, GalleyCat, ODesk and Elance (the latter two are due to merge. See Empson 2013). I've not explored these sites so I'd advise you to talk to your colleagues to find out how effective they've found these tools for generating business leads. The responses will probably vary depending on the particular market being targeted so once you've done your research, make sure you put it in context – what works for one person might not be suitable for you.

Should I pay?

This is probably the wrong question. How much a directory entry costs is not the issue; the return on investment is what counts. If I spend a £100 a year on a listing but it generates £2,000 of work, in terms of ROI that's a cheap listing. If I spend £30 a year and I only break even, I might reconsider.

Use your network of editorial freelancers to see which directories (whether specialized or general) they rate in terms or ROI and test the water. If you set a time limit, then you can consider any financial outlay as a learning process. If it doesn't give you the return you hoped for, either rework the design of your advertisement and try again, or move on and try a different directory.

Things to be aware of

Some directory websites operate an open-bidding format whereby the jobs can tend to go to the person offering the lowest price. This can lead to a 'race to the bottom', and some freelancers (editorial and otherwise) feel that job-bidding sites undermine the profession by encouraging a supply of service at below-market rates. This doesn't mean you shouldn't advertise in them but it's a good idea to fix your parameters at the outset. Decide what price you're prepared to work for and stick with it. It's tempting for new starters to feel that they'll bid low enough to ensure they get the work, even if the price they end up securing the work for is below the national minimum wage. Of course, there's no law that says you can't do this and if you feel it will offer you some experience and a testimonial that will give you a ranking on the site which makes you more attractive to future customers, you might decide to use this as a start-out strategy.

Other directory sites are more traditional and encourage a closed, private system of negotiation between the client and the editorial freelancer. Although price will often be a factor, these types of requests for quotations will allow you to construct a pitch that focuses not only on price, but also skills. By highlighting your unique selling points in a way that is targeted to your customer's needs, you stand a better chance of securing the job based on a number of factors of which price is only one.

Case study: job-bidding directory

The following case study is taken from *Business Planning for Editorial Freelancing* (Harnby 2013a). My colleague Johanna

Robinson recalls how in her early days of developing her editorial business, she used PeoplePerHour to acquire her first piece of paid work. Johanna took a strategic approach, viewing the bidding process as part of a wider marketing strategy. As the study demonstrates, even with an open-bidding system, it doesn't have to be a race to the bottom if you are careful about the jobs on which you bid, the clients you are prepared to work for and the specific USPs you are 'selling' to the client via your profile.

I received my first job in August 2012 and, as it was a hard-copy proofread (on paper) using the BSI proofreading symbols, it was an excellent starting point. It was a book written by a solicitor on the legal issues surrounding branding, aimed at entrepreneurs. She had set up her own publishing company and is therefore essentially a self-publisher, although she did use a book consulting service. The job was posted on the UK freelance website PeoplePerHour and I got the job because, unlike most freelancers applying for it, I could use the necessary symbols (the document had been copy-edited and typeset) and because I had been a lawyer.

I am aware that such websites can be controversial for various reasons: the quality of the work; the quality of the freelancers; the fact that 'bidding' can drive down prices and hence earnings, not just for the individual but arguably across the board. While I am sure these arguments are often valid, my own experience does not actually bear them out. My first job paid in line with rates often paid by publishers. The client did not choose the lowest bidder, but the person they considered could do the job best. As it was then my only job, I could take the time to do the job well and do it accurately. The lack of feedback is often quoted as a downside to this job. However, I have received good-quality feedback via this medium.

I have since carried out another job for my first PeoplePerHour client and have had many interesting and decently paid jobs from the site. This is, however, due to various factors: I have a good, concise and well-written profile; I submit accurate and comprehensive bids; I have positive feedback for previous jobs; and I have a PDF CV that I attach to most of my bids. I also pay attention to the quality of the job. I am quite picky about what I bid for. I won't bid for badly paid jobs and I assess the quality of the language in the job posting itself. Now that I am an established freelancer on the site, I am being approached by clients rather than having to bid for work.

Constructing the listing

Selling anything, editorial skills or otherwise, in a limited space can be quite a challenge. Advertising in specialist directories is something most of us do in addition to having a website. Even if you struggle to promote yourself succinctly, you can use the limited space wisely by following three basic steps.

These steps can be applied to any promotional profile you're building but they're particularly appropriate when dealing with searchable databases. Whether you've paid for your listing or it's free, it makes sense to maximize your chances of being found and selected. Otherwise, what's the point in having it?

Back in my publishing days, our marketing director would always encourage us to approach our promotion plans with joined-up thinking: first comes the hook, then the pitch, and finally the call to action. We discussed these in the Part I of the book, but it's worth reviewing them in relation to directory advertising. Remember, all three are connected, and by thinking about them as joined, it becomes easier to see what needs to be included and why. In relation to how we manage our directory listings, the hook, pitch and call to action could work as follows:

Step 1. The hook

Unlike traditional print directories, the online equivalents have the added advantage of being searchable. This makes them more powerful because they're no longer mere category listings; they're powerful databases.

You may be one of hundreds, or even thousands, of colleagues who are listed in the directory. The types of clients you want to attract need to be able to find you. Using the most appropriate keywords is the first thing you need to crack. These are what clients will use to filter their searches.

Your keywords could refer to the service(s) you provide and the subject areas or genres you specialize in: 'proofreader', 'crime', 'erotica', 'sociology', 'law', 'politics', 'speculative fiction', 'race/ethnicity', 'theses' and 'science fiction' are some of mine. Yours will be specific to you.

Niche keywords can be effective because they can narrow down client searches; broad keywords are important because they make sure you're in the mix for the searcher who isn't too specific. I would advise a mixture of the two, as long as each keyword reflects your skill set.

Step 2. The pitch

If the hook leads the client to your listing, then the pitch keeps them on your page. Since you have limited space it's worth focusing on what your biggest selling points are. In addition to one or two sentences summarizing your business (e.g. 'I specialize in proofreading academic and professional books in the social sciences and humanities, as well as fiction and creative non-fiction'), you could add a short list outlining the things that you think will most impress the client:

• Any unique selling points that are relevant to your customer

• Truncated testimonials from several satisfied clients

• A list of clients for whom you've worked

• Highlights from your portfolio

• Number of jobs you've completed

• Length of service

Your list might look different. It doesn't matter. The point is to make sure that you highlight the things about yourself that will make you look interesting.

Again, Daum's differentiation–solution–empathy framework discussed first in Chapter 4 will come in useful when thinking how to present your pitch in a manner that speaks to your customer.

Step 3. The call to action

Having led the client to your page and impressed them with your pitch, you should now make it as easy as possible for them to take the next step. If you think your directory listing is so impressive that you can nail the job there and then, add in a call to action under your pitch inviting the client to contact you. If you want to drive them to your website because you think the information there will close the deal, add in a few words inviting them to do just that (e.g. 'Visit my website for more testimonials and a full portfolio of works').

Even if your website link and contact details are listed elsewhere on your page, writing a few words that encourages a particular step is still an example of best practice; it invites the client to engage with you. In the world of sales and marketing, this is nuts-and-bolts stuff, so why not apply it in the world of editorial freelancing, too?

Thinking about presentation

Order

Keep your pitch and call to action 'above the fold'. I realize that most web users are perfectly used to scrolling to find the information they want. However, clients looking for a service provider in a directory are often pushed for time and are looking at multiple entries. It makes sense to hit them with your pitch in a way that requires nothing from them – they land on your page and the information you want to sell is right in front of them.

Think also about the F-shaped reading pattern and the above-the-fold discussion from Chapter 14.

Highlighting

Directory listings are often restrictive in terms of design. You may have to follow a formula. If you can, use bold to highlight keywords or phrases, colour to set off headings, and bullet lists to express key selling points. Here's Gube (2011) again:

> According to an eye-tracking study by ClickTale, users fixate longer on bulleted lists and text formatting (such as bolding and italics).

Keep it short

This is one of the hardest nuts to crack, but all the online and print material I've ever read about advertising and direct marketing insists that you keep things short and snappy. Ensuring your personality is injected into the listing is a tough call when space is limited. This is why a call to action that moves a client to your website can be effective, because that's where you have the space to really shine.

Space it out

Again, the general advice from online and print marketing specialists is to not be afraid of white space. Text that is broken down into lists, or into short, line-spaced paragraphs, is easier on the eye. Margins count. Once more, Gube (2011) has some interesting stats to share:

> The spacing between characters, words, lines and paragraphs is important. How type is set [...] can drastically affect the legibility (and thus, reading speeds) of readers. In a study called "Reading Online Text: A Comparison of Four White Space Layouts," the researchers discovered that manipulating the [size] of margins of a passage affected reading comprehension and speed.

Giving space to white space works!

10 steps to getting it wrong – the 'Fromholzer fails'

Sometimes it can be as helpful to think about what not to do when tackling a particular marketing tool. Dennis Fromholzer of CRM Associates has identified 10 'fails' that impact negatively on a directory listing's ability to drive in customers ('Driving Results' n.d.). He identified these specifically in relation to Yellow Pages listings but they can be applied to any directory entry.

1. You've omitted where you're based and what your phone number is. Some customers want to work with someone local, and all customers want to at least know where you're based.

2. The headline doesn't stand out (colour, size or font). If a business name is used, it should reflect the service being offered, otherwise it's a waste of headline space.

3. Your pitch is too wordy and too cluttered. There's not enough white space.

4. Too much attention is given to the problem rather than the solution.

5. Failure to include a local number (with an identifiable STD code). Toll-free numbers can save the customer money but they are impersonal.

6. Graphics or pictures don't relate to the service being offered or the benefits it provides.

7. Your contact information is so small that it's either difficult to locate or uncomfortable to read.

8. Information included is too technical rather than using the language of the customer.

9. Your client testimonials are too long.

10. The business description is not clear or not credible.

Testing

Another good piece of advice that professional marketers like to reinforce is that of testing. You'll recall that this was one of the concepts we considered in Part I. If your directory entries aren't driving in the quantity or type of client you'd hoped for, try playing around with different hooks, pitches and calls to action. Different sets of keywords might be more effective; perhaps your call to action could be more prominent; or you could reconsider your pitch to make it more salesy, more academic, more publisher-focused, or more self-publisher-centric.

Case study

In June 2013 I received a phone call from a potential client looking for a proofreader to work on a number of screen plays, all dramas he was writing for television. I was full to capacity at the time, and had no experience of proofreading screen plays so I referred the caller to the Society for Editors and Proofreaders' Directory of Editorial Services.

The Directory has over 500 advertisers and my client was on a tight deadline. He clicked on the relevant page of the SfEP website while I was still on the phone with him. 'What shall I put in the search box?' he asked. 'Try screen play and drama,' I replied. Thinking that this was possibly a little too specific, I decided to suggest how he might broaden his search. Before I could get the words out of my mouth he said, 'Found someone. Ooh, found someone else!'

Using the right mix of keywords in searchable directories really does work, so spend some time thinking carefully about yours and ensuring that they match the terms used by the type of client you want to find you.

SEO benefits

Adding links to your website from your online directory listings enables you to boost your SEO. Search engines like to see websites that are linked organically from other sites. The degree to which others will link to you is not usually in your direct control. When it comes to directory advertising, you're invariably given the option, so use it. Furthermore, if the directory ranks highly in the search engines, you're enabling your business to jump on the back of this while you're still building your own ranking.

Other advertising opportunities

You might also choose to advertise in other magazines, professional trade bulletins, or newsletters, particularly if you can locate ones whose readership is one of your specialist markets (for example, legal or accountancy publications, or university student newsletters).

Again, consider the cost and the potential return on investment, and test the impact of any paid advertising you do over a limited time period.

KEY POINTS

- Use the joined-up framework of the hook, the pitch and the call to action to structure your advertisement.

- Test, test, and test again until you start to see the results you want.

- Keep things short and snappy, and don't be afraid of white space.

- Keep the most important information 'above the fold' by displaying information in an inverted-pyramid format.

- Put yourself in your customer's shoes and focus on using language and terminology that makes sense to the kind of customer you want to attract.

- Different types of customer use different types of directory. Bear in mind which client types you want to attract when you are choosing which directories to advertise in.

- Don't focus on the cost but rather on the return on investment. 'Free' isn't the be all and end all; it's value for money that counts.

- Take advantage of any opportunity the directory offers to add value to your profile: links to your website, CV attachments, opportunity for clients to add testimonials upon completion of work.

- Avoid the 10 'Fromholzer fails'!

TRY IT!

With your different customer groups in mind, make a list of the key directories you think are 'musts'. If you are not yet listed in all of these, make a note of anything you need to do in order to rectify this.

Note down two more advertising opportunities that are directly relevant to the market you want to access. You may decide not to exploit them but if you do want to test them over the next 12 months, you'll have the information available. They might be free or paid – consider the potential return on investment when making your decision.

20 GOING DIRECT

What's in it for you?

- Encourages you to be active and confident about the services you offer
- Allows you to be very targeted
- Forces you to put yourself in your customer's shoes

Active targeting

Whether you use a letter, the phone or email, when you make direct contact, you actively connect with an individual customer (rather than passively waiting for them to discover you). This is the most targeted you can be and it gives you the opportunity to tailor every single pitch to the individual.

The downside is that direct targeting is much more labour intensive. However, the corresponding upside is that the rewards can be much higher simply because you are able to put yourself in your customer's shoes, and their socks and shirts, too.

Of all the advice I've read about effective cold contact, Gill Wagner's article 'Cold-Letters' (n.d.) proved the easiest to digest. Plus, his way of thinking fits nicely into the core concepts that we looked at in Part I, including putting yourself in your customer's shoes and our two structural tools: 'hook, pitch, call to action' and differentiation–solution–empathy. Consequently, I quote him often throughout this chapter.

Hot and cold contact

There are two types of direct marketing to consider here: 'hot' and 'cold'. **Hot contact** is when you are responding directly to a request for information about your services. For example:

- A student emails you with a request for a proofreading quotation.

- A publisher, prepress agency or editing agency messages you on LinkedIn to ask if you'd like to do their editing test.

- A small business owner telephones you to ask about your website proofreading and content validation services.

Cold contact is when you make an unsolicited contact with a potential client. For example:

- You send a cover letter and CV to a publishing house whose list matches your USPs.

- You contact some of the senior lecturers at your local university with a view to offering your proofreading services to their postgraduate students.

- You ring the marketing director of a local business to ask them if they'd be interested in your website proofreading and content validation services.

- You email a direct mail marketing agency to ask for the opportunity to meet up and pitch your services.

In the case of hot contact, the most important thing is, of course, to supply the information requested. So if the potential client asks for a CV and a covering letter, do make sure you supply both. I think it's still a good idea to frame your response within a value-on framework, as discussed in Chapter 6 on pricing. Hot contact won't always be made with you alone, but with some of your colleagues, too, so if you want to make the best impression, give the potential client a reason to want to continue the conversation with you by highlighting your USPs and any useful information you can offer that shows off your added value.

In the case of cold contact, there is no one true way. One thing to consider about letters and emails is the opportunity they afford over the phone call, as this lovely quotation from Liz Carpenter reminds us:

> What a lot we lost when we stopped writing letters. You can't reread a phone call. (Quoted in Wagner n.d.)

The prospective client has something they can keep on file even if they don't have use for your services right now or they don't have the time to consider your offer. If the publishing desk editor or corporate marketing executive reviews the situation later, they have a reminder of who you are and what you do.

Ann Henderson (cited in Denicolo and Reeves 2014) reminds us that

> A covering letter is a connecting document ... [t]he covering letter is primarily about the [client] and the job you are applying for. Your CV is about you – the covering letter is about them.

Why go direct?

Some of your customers (such as commercial businesses) might not understand the relevance of your services to their work. By contacting them direct, you are in a position to explain what you do and why it's useful to them.

Other customers (like publishers) understand exactly what you offer but are so frequently contacted by trained editorial freelancers that they don't feel the need to trawl the internet to find them. Even if they do search online, they may use one particular national editing society's database. If you're not in that, you won't be found. If you can get in it, you therefore should. If you don't qualify, you can't compete. In that case, it's time to go direct.

In my experience, cold contact with publishers has proven a lot easier and has generated a much higher success rate than have my attempts with non-publisher clients, precisely because publishers understand what we do and expect to receive letters, emails and telephone calls from us.

Case study: the publishing industry

One of my preferred methods for accessing publishers and project management agencies is to send a cold letter and my hybrid CV/brochure, both of which are adapted specifically for the press I'm contacting. In-house production staff are some of the busiest and most pressurized people in the industry and don't often have time to search for editorial freelancers. If I sit around waiting for them to locate me, I might miss my chance – when they do find the time for a freelance recruitment drive, they'll be reading the cold letters sent by my colleagues.

What to include

Once again, you can use the 'hook, pitch, call to action' framework outlined in Chapter 4, and you can develop your pitch with the deeper differentiation–solution–empathy tool also discussed. Since you know exactly who the client is (either because they asked you to contact them, or because you chose them specifically), you can adapt your pitch to what you can find out about this prospect. Look at the client's website and use your network to find out if you have colleagues working for them. Then try to learn as much as possible about how their business matches your USPs and how you can provide solutions to the challenges they face.

Cold contact *is* different

Your hook and elevator pitch will be more critical than ever here. If someone searches for your services in a directory or online, they've already demonstrated intent to buy. This is absolutely *not* the case with the cold contact. Gill Wagner (n.d.) reckons that:

> [A]t most you have ... eight seconds before the decision-maker will make the first yes/no decision about whether to crumple and toss ... So, at most, you

have about 40 words with which to deliver your first compelling message.

Make sure you incorporate the elements of differentiation–solution–empathy into your elevator pitch (as outlined in Chapter 4). The cold client, more than any other, needs to know what's in it for them.

In the case of the snail mail option, you may even want to think about what happens before your recipient has even started to read your correspondence. The envelope may generate its own 'crumple and toss' response. Wagner therefore advises doing nothing that could make the recipient think that your letter is like hundreds of others she receives all the time – not allowing the client to make the decision too early. That means keeping it simple and unidentifiable – no logos, slogans or clever graphics; just a neat, clean, possibly hand-written address label.

> If you want the odds on your side, put nothing identifiable on the envelope itself – just a plain envelope with the prospect's name, title, company and mailing address, and a return address that contains your name, street, city, state and ZIP. (Wagner n.d.)

Using a named person

Do try to find out a named person to whom you can address the letter – not because it will impress the recipient (who probably won't even notice, such is the extent of the correspondence received with his or her name on it), but because it means it doesn't get shunted around from department to department and desk to desk. If you want to make a good impression on the person in charge of hiring the likes of you, you don't want your letter and CV to look like it was used to wrap someone's lunch by the time it ends up on their desk.

The same applies to email – if you don't target a named person, by the time your enquiry lands in the correct person's inbox, your beautifully targeted pitch and branded email signature will be consigned to the bottom of the message, a long scroll down, and surrounded by several layers of ugly forwarding chevrons. This is not the way you want to present yourself at first contact. In the worst case, your email will be deleted.

Look on the client's website first and see if you can work out who is the decision-maker for editorial freelancing services. If that's not obvious (either because the company chooses not to make that information public or because your service is considered a non-standard requirement), pick up the phone and ask.

In the case of publishers, you'll be asking for someone who most probably works in the journals or books production department. They may have various titles from production manager to editor, desk editor or project manager. In the case of commercial businesses, it's impossible to speculate, hence the importance of putting the effort into the research early on.

Wagner's top letter-writing tips – six 'P's to ponder

Wagner (n.d.) offers several tips to think about when you're writing a cold letter or email:

- **Personality and plain speaking:** Bring your personality into your words and write in a way that makes you sound like a polite neighbour rather than using salesy jargon and buzz words. It makes you sound more honest and engaged. Editorial freelancing is about relationships and trust. Clients will be letting you loose on their words – words that are valuable to them from an academic, artistic or business point of view – so they want to know they're dealing with someone who has a brain and a soul!

- **Perspective of the customer:** If you're still not convinced about using the differentiation–solution–empathy framework, then consider this. Wagner advises always assuming that the recipient doesn't 'give a hoot about you or your company, and offering to tell them about your company will almost always result in crumple and toss'. To clarify, he's not advising that you don't provide information about your business, but rather that those details need to be framed in a way that tells the recipient what's in it for them.

- **Promises:** Ensure your promises are ones you can keep.

- **Perfection:** It goes without saying that you should ensure the cold emails or letters you send are perfectly presented, with all grammar, punctuation and spelling errors eradicated. You need to be able to demonstrate that you can practise what you preach!

- **Position:** Don't ignore the standard layout conventions for letter-writing – the date, the recipient's address, salutation, message, close-off, your name, and a postscript. Include all these things in your letter.

- **Postscript:** Says Wagner, 'When reading business letters from people they don't know, 85 percent of readers will look first to see who sent the letter. And, in almost all of these cases, the very next thing they'll read is the postscript, if it exists' (Wagner n.d.). Not only that, it's the thing that's most likely to be read twice. With that in mind, it's worth ensuring that you use the postscript effectively, because it's potentially the most powerful line in your letter. It's therefore the ideal spot for an extra hook that makes the client **curious** and that forces them at least to think about whether they need to **take action**.

A word of caution on postscripts

Recall Wagner's advice about provoking curiosity and enabling a possible action. With this in mind, don't use the mistake-pointing strategy for your postscript if there's nothing the client can do to change it. An example would be that of contacting a publisher and telling them you found 30 errors in a book they published 18 months ago. It's too late for them to do anything about it, and you run the risk of provoking irritation rather than curiosity.

While I very much appreciate it when colleagues gently point out a typo in one of my blog posts, the reaction is quite different when supposed flaws are pointed out to me by people trying to secure business from me. I feel they're being smug and manipulative. And if I feel like that, perhaps a potential client will, too. No one likes to feel that someone is trying to bully them into submission by undermining their confidence. I certainly don't, and any attempt to do so will only send me running from the perpetrator as fast as possible. With this in mind, most marketers recommend a solution/skills-focused approach rather than the mistake-pointing method.

Examples of solution/skills-focused approach might include:

> P.S. I'd be happy to take a proofreading test for you in order to demonstrate my competence. I've passed the tests for Anyold Press, City University Press, and Academic Publisher with flying colours.

The idea here is that you make them think about taking action while at the same time piquing their curiosity regarding the competence you've demonstrated for similar publishing companies.

> P.S. I can supply you with excellent references from some of your colleagues in publishing houses with complementary lists. I work for Jane Doe at Anyold Press, John Smith at City University Press, and Charlie King at Academic Publisher on a regular basis.

Again, this is something they can action, but you're also piquing their interest; publishing is a small world and production staff often know each other – you might be mentioning names of people with whom your recipient is connected in some way.

Examples of a mistake-pointing approach could be:

> P.S. On page X of [title], I noticed a few spelling and grammar errors. There are only eight but I've enclosed them on a separate sheet so that you can amend them.

> P.S. On the nth page of your website, I noticed eight spelling and grammar errors. Call me if you'd like me to work with you to eliminate these.

Case study: cold letter to a business client

In the following, I've used the differentiation–solution–empathy tool to help me think about what I need to include, and I've used Wagner's six 'P's to help with tone and structure.

I've constructed a fictive example of how I could deal with a local government client. I've chosen the non-publisher sector because it's a far harder nut to crack. Client groups who are used to dealing with editorial freelancers and who understand the services we provide (e.g. publishers) will need far less convincing than will those for whom proofreading and editing services are perhaps a non-standard element of their business.

About the prospective client

I've looked at the website of my local county council. The fact that they have a website tells me that they are producing at least one form of written material, but I assume there must be others – reports, brochures, booklets, for example. I make some phone calls to find out whom I should approach. It takes some time because public organizations can be large and bureaucratic. Eventually I find out the name of the person in charge of production of web content. His name is Amir Sudath and his title is Manager, Marketing Services.

I've discovered that there are a lot of grammar, punctuation and spelling errors on the website, as well as at least one damaged link that forces the reader into a loop.

I use the differentiation–solution–empathy tool to think about the issues from Amir Sudath's point of view:

- Differentiation – unlike, say, a publisher, local government organizations don't automatically consider the benefits of hiring a professional proofreader. They might think it can be done in-house by people who have a 'good eye'.

- Offer solutions – local government differs from a commercial business in that it's publicly funded and is supplying a public service. Arguing that spelling and grammar errors/inconsistencies are going to cost them money is not going to work. What we do know is that local government is supposed to work for 'the people'. The relationship is one of trust. Written material needs to communicate that trust, and competence is a key element in the equation. Web content, designed to be of use to the tax-paying public, that is littered with spelling mistakes does not inspire confidence and trust. At best it makes the organization seem as if it doesn't care. At worst it seems that even if it does care, it doesn't have the competence to solve the problem.

- Provide empathy – local governments have to do a lot within a limited budget. During times of recession, budgets are likely to be shrinking, placing more pressure on already stretched human and financial resources. Amir will be ridiculously busy, possibly be managing a department with fewer people than three years ago, and servicing the marketing demands of multiple internal customers from different departments who all want him to produce results by yesterday!

What I can offer

Now I think about the relationship between my proofreading skills and Amir Sudath's business challenges.

- **Differentiation**: I have more than a 'good eye'. I'm a dedicated professional proofreader – it's what I do, and only what I do. I'm not distracted by the push and pull of interdepartmental politics and bureaucracy. I also used to work in marketing so I'm experienced in working with digital and print promotional material.

- **Solutions**: I can eradicate the errors in the text and highlight the link problems so that the words will communicate confidence and competence to the people whose tax pounds pay for the website and the services it describes.

- **Empathy**: I understand the pressures of fulfilling multiple tasks for multiple clients within a limited budget. I therefore offer an efficient, friendly and professional service that offers outstanding attention to detail at a cost-conscious price. And I can offer a fast turnaround.

Next I think about Wagner's six 'P's to ensure I've covered all the bases: Personality and plain speaking; Perspective of the customer; Promises; Perfection; Position; and Postscript. In the framework above, I've put myself in the customer's shoes and covered the promises about what I can deliver. Next, I remind myself to use plain language, as if I was Amir's polite neighbour. Then I think about how I position the information on the page, giving special attention to my postscript – something that will make Amir curious and want to take some kind of action.

Writing the cold letter

Using all the information I've compiled, I now write the cold letter, mindful that I've got eight seconds (or approximately 40 words) to prevent Amir's crumple and toss.

> Dear Mr Sudath,
>
> I'm writing to ask you if you would be interested in using my service to eradicate any errors in your website text (and any other marketing materials).
>
> I'm a professional proofreader, trained to ensure that your website's content communicates confidence and competence to its local community readers. I'm also a former marketing manager, so I'm familiar with promotional content (both digital and print). The enclosed CV includes further information about my training, experience and qualifications.
>
> I realize that the current recession means you're probably expected to do more, only with fewer staff and a reduced budget. It's with that in mind that I can promise you an efficient, friendly and professional proofreading service that will give you outstanding attention to detail at a cost-conscious price.
>
> I can also guarantee a fast turnaround for smaller projects if you need it. Any piece of text under 6,000 words can be delivered to you within 24 hours.

> If you think I can help, please call me on 01603 270073 or email me at louise@louiseharnbyproofreader.com and I'll answer any other questions you have.
>
> Yours sincerely,
>
> [signature]
>
> Louise Harnby
>
> P.S. I'd be delighted to offer you a gratis sample proofread of your home page at [URL] so that you can evaluate my services with a real example.

If Amir does what 85 per cent of readers do, and looks at the postscript before anything else, this is what he'll read in the first eight seconds:

> POSTSCRIPT: I'd be delighted to offer you a gratis sample proofread of your home page at [URL] so that you can evaluate my services with a real example ...
>
> THEN TO TOP OF LETTER: I'm writing to ask you if you would be interested in using ...

If he reads the words in the order they're presented, and he definitely will if it's an email, this is what he'll read.

> TOP OF LETTER: I'm writing to ask you if you would be interested in using my service to eradicate any errors in your website text (and any other marketing materials). I'm a professional proofreader, trained to ensure that your website's content communicates confidence ...

Tell the truth and be thorough

Probably the worst fail you can achieve when sending direct emails or letters is to write what amounts to a load of rubbish because you're either not being honest about what you can offer, you haven't researched the client thoroughly enough, or you've made assumptions about their needs that are based on flimsy evidence.

Examples of this appear in my inbox often. They're usually from SEO companies trying to sell their services. The solutions they offer are based on statements that are meant to make me feel so insecure that I'm impelled to take action and hire them to solve my problems. All of which would be fine if their statements rang true. Alas, 'your website doesn't show up in organic searches for keywords relevant to your business' isn't true. Nor is 'you're not generating any customers from your website'. This kind of poorly researched cold contact does nothing but aggravate the potential client and leads to a quick crumple and toss.

What about the indie author community?

I never contact independent authors with cold letters or emails. I recognize that some editorial freelancers might disagree with this decision but my view is that, more often than not, an *unsolicited* approach to an independent author gives the appearance of desperate spamming, not unlike that carried out by the SEO companies emails I mentioned above. Why?

Publishers expect to receive enquiries from editorial freelancers – we're a known and useful entity to them. Corporations are increasingly coming to understand our value. And, indeed, many self-publishing authors already commission our services. However, the relationship between a proofreader and a publisher is business-to-business. It's the same with the corporation. But the relationship with an indie author is very much person-to-person. Cold contact is far less likely to evoke a positive response. Indie author Ruth Ann Nordin (2012) concurs:

> Congratulations. You picked up a free ebook by an author and read it. You found something that didn't meet your expectations (whatever those expectations might be) and thought, "Oh goody! Now I can email this author who's never heard of me because I don't have any credentials to my name and offer my services." AKA I will go up to a stranger's door and pitch my product to make a sale.

Nordin argues that a better approach is one of participation, using writer forums to get to know writers, engage with their concerns and demonstrate your credentials over time.

KEY POINTS

- Going direct is the most targeted you can be in your marketing strategy.

- Direct contact can be hot or cold.

- When using the cold method, pay ultra-special attention to your hook and pitch, making sure you make your key points within the first eight seconds or 40 words.

- Put yourself in your customer's shoes. Research each client thoroughly to ensure you use those eight seconds effectively, ensuring the solutions you offer in your pitch are relevant to the client's business needs and challenges.

- Get a name so that you go straight to the correct person. Forwarded email messages and crumpled letters look awful and undermine your professionalism.

- Consider also Wagner's six 'P's to help you get the tone and structure of your pitch just right.

- Use the postscript to elicit curiosity and a need for action, but take great care with the mistake-pointing strategy, even if you do it in a way that enables the client to take immediate action. A softer alternative may be more effective.

- Tell the truth!

- Think carefully about which types of customer it's appropriate to make unsolicited contact with.

TRY IT!

Pick three businesses that you think might have use for a proofreader or editor. If you find them on the web, you know they're producing at least some form of written content. Consider focusing on those who are doing something that you are familiar with (e.g. if you used to be an estate agent, focus your research there; if you've worked for local authorities/state public bodies, then focus on this client type; if you have technical writing and editing skills, use these as your focus).

If you're more publisher-focused in your client base, do the same as above but concentrate on publishers that produce material in the subject areas in which you specialize.

An alternative might be the postgraduate department of your local university.

Read their websites thoroughly to ensure you understand what kind of written materials they produce. Find out the names of the people you need to contact. Create a cold cover letter or an email tailored specifically to each one and send it to them. The content should focus on solutions you provide rather than mistakes they're making.

21 BUILDING A CV/RÉSUMÉ

What's in it for you?

- Adds value to your website – lets customers download (and print) a summary that they can read at their own convenience

- Multi-purpose – can be printed and used as a brochure at face-to-face events if it's kept to one page

- Communication – helps you to think about how you communicate your USPs to your customer

- Content is usable on multiple platforms – you can use the pitch for other marketing activities

A backbone marketing tool

Having a CV (curriculum vitae) or résumé is a thoroughly useful addition to your marketing toolkit. It's something you can attach when you contact potential clients 'cold' or that you can upload to your website. It can look traditional or take the form of a less formal brochure/résumé hybrid. You can email it or print it out and snail mail it. CVs may have been around for a long time but they are still one of the main ways that business people communicate with potential employers.

Why do you need one?

Many of your potential clients won't have the time or inclination to crawl over every page of your website – they'll want a summary of who you are and what you do. If you don't provide the summary they're looking for, you could risk them losing interest. My CV is one of the most popular downloads on my website. CVs demonstrate professionalism and show clients that you can organize information and communicate succinctly.

Some clients will ask you to send one, so it makes sense to be prepared, particularly if you are under a deadline to get a quote in quickly.

They are no cost, high impact. Even in these days of extensive digital marketing communication, the CV (like the business card) is still an understood and valued form of communication.

Creating one-page summaries forces you to think about the information that is of critical interest to different client types. If you can't summarize it on a page for yourself, this is an indication that you haven't engaged deeply enough with the needs of your client base (you've not stood in your customer's shoes).

'I don't having anything to put in it ...'

'I wouldn't dream of creating a CV for my editorial business yet – I've nothing to put in it.' I've heard this statement from many newbies over the years; if it reflects your own feelings then I hope to persuade you otherwise by the end of this chapter.

Creating a CV can seem like a daunting prospect for the new editor or proofreader with little experience. It needn't be so. Even if you are a new entrant to the field of editorial freelancing, you can still build an effective one-page CV. Instead of thinking about what you don't have, think about what you do have. A few pointers to consider initially include:

- You can use the 'hook, pitch, call to action' framework for the structure (Chapter 4).

- You can use Daum's differentiation–solution–empathy framework specifically for the 'pitch' element.

- You don't need to be afraid of white space.

- It only needs to fill one page.

- Use positive statements that focus on what you have to offer – now (not what you don't, or what's in the pipeline).

223

- Put yourself in your customer's shoes and create multiple CVs for different client groups (with appropriate pitches that use the relevant language).

Putting yourself in your customer's shoes

Put yourself in the shoes of your customer – what do they want to know about you? Then consider how you can add value:

- Which services are you offering?

- What are your specialist subject areas?

- What training have you completed?

- What previous career experience do you have that is relevant to the services you are offering?

- Do you have relevant educational qualifications that would impress a customer?

- Do you have any other experience or skills that you could use as unique selling points (USPs) that make you stand out from the crowd?

- If you have managed to carry out a few pieces of work then summarize them.

- If you can get a testimonial from a client, do so.

If you've put yourself in your customer's shoes, and you want to target different customer types, it stands to reason you should have multiple CVs. I have separate ones for trade and academic publishers, but if I were to carry out a campaign that involved emailing or writing cold letters to businesses, I'd create a new one to tailor my hook, pitch and call to action to that client type.

In fact, you can go further than multiple client-type CVs. Every time you prepare to send a specific client a CV, put yourself in their shoes and ask yourself whether it needs tweaking, even if only slightly, to give you the best chance of making yourself look interesting.

Using the 'hook, pitch, call to action' framework for the overall structure

The **hook** might be an introductory headline, set out in bold or a different colour, which captures your business ethos. It might be a glowing testimonial. Or it could be a simple, clearly articulated statement in the first line of text that highlights your USPs. Whatever you choose, it should be something that grabs the customer's attention.

The **pitch** will include those key selling points that summarize what you do, e.g. your training, experience, relevant background, and subject specialisms.

The **call to action** is where you tell your customer what to do next: how to contact you to discuss a project. Here you can include your telephone number(s), email address, website and postal address.

Using Daum's differentiation–solution–empathy tool for the pitch

The 'pitch' element of your CV needs to incorporate the unique selling points (USPs) that will make you most interesting to your reader. They might include your training, previous educational or career experience that is relevant to the customer, and the subjects you specialize in (again, relevant to the customer). The differentiation–solution–empathy framework helps you to structure this content in a persuasive way. You can read more about this framework in Chapter 4, but to summarize:

- **'Differentiation'** is about the USPs that set you apart from the crowd or that enable you to do something that your client can't do themselves.

- **'Solution'** concerns identifying what the client needs and demonstrating how you can provide it.

- **'Empathy'** involves acknowledging the challenges a particular client faces and reflecting that you understand what these are, and that you can respond accordingly.

Case study 1: the brochure/résumé hybrid

I've created a one-page brochure/résumé hybrid. I include colour thumbnail images of jackets of some of the projects on which I've worked. I use a contrasting colour for the headings and for the testimonial at the top of the page. You can view my CV on the Qualifications tab at louiseharnbyproofreader.com.

- **Hook**: My primary client base is publishers, so my hook is a truncated testimonial from one of my regular publisher clients. It's in a larger font and in a contrasting colour to the main text on the page.

- **Pitch**: My bullet points focus on the USPs that will be attractive to publishers. I differentiate myself with my in-house experience, excellent testimonials from an existing extensive publisher client base, and an abridged portfolio of relevant projects. The solutions include my ability to proofread onscreen and on paper, and my ability to use industry-standard markup language. I demonstrate empathy by emphasizing that I always work to brief, to deadline and to budget.

- **Call to action**: At the bottom of the page I ask interested parties to contact me to discuss their requirements, and provide my contact details.

Case study 2: the traditional CV

My colleague Mike Faulkner has created a more traditional text-based CV that is equally attractive. He, too, uses a contrasting colour for his headings and has embraced the use of white space on the page to provide a comprehensive and attractive one-page summary of his services. You can view his CV at thebluecabin.com/proofreading.

- **Hook**: Mike's client base includes independent authors, publishers, students and academics. In addition to his editorial work, Mike is a writer and a lawyer, two USPs that he refers to in the first five words of his opening statement. He includes another hook at the bottom of his CV: several key testimonials from a range of clients.

- **Pitch**: He offers a range of editorial services from proofreading to light editing to text assessment. He differentiates himself with the same information he uses as his hook, by emphasizing his legal and writing background. He provides solutions by summarizing the value he brings to each service offered and the price he charges per 1,000 words. He also outlines his industry-recognized training and professional society membership. He demonstrates empathy by outlining his ability to work to brief and to deadline within the context of his experience as a writer and lawyer, and to provide a quick turnaround at a comfortable price.

- **Call to action:** Mike doesn't include a specific statement that calls his clients to action, though his contact details are prominently displayed at the top of the page. They are the second thing a client will read after his business title.

Case study 3: the new entrant to the field

This last case study is fictitious and demonstrates how even the recent entrant to the field who has very little experience can communicate a positive message. Let's call our newbie Margo Andersen.

Margo is British-born but her mother is from Denmark. She's bilingual, has a degree in English Literature, a Master's in Social Policy and Administration and is a qualified social worker with 10 years' professional experience of working in the Children and Family Services departments for two county councils.

The pressures of social work practice have affected her mental health and after some serious soul-searching she's decided to embark on a new career that she believes will be less stressful and enable her to have a healthier work/life balance.

In the past few months, she's taken an introductory proofreading training course with one of the UK's respected training institutions and has joined her national editorial society. She is in the middle of a mentoring programme that is giving her hands-on experience of live work under the guidance of an experienced colleague, has done some gratis proofreading for social work colleagues who needed a lengthy report checked for accuracy, consistency and readability, and has just completed her first piece of paid work for a Chinese Master's student.

However, with such little practical editorial experience how can she build a CV that sells her developing professional skills? She has few clients, no publishing experience and is still in the process of further training. What information might she include? Initially, Margo puts herself in her customer's shoes and decides to create a persuasive pitch for a CV aimed at students and social science academics for whom English is a second language. She starts with the **title**:

Margo Andersen | Proofreader

Next, she creates the following **hook**, which clearly states what her core USP is, and uses this as a headline at the top of her CV:

Bilingual proofreader specializing in clients for whom English is a second language

Now she focuses on the main content of the document, using the differentiation–solution–empathy framework to help her structure the information.

- **Differentiation:** She's bilingual and wants to present herself as a specialist ESL provider.

- **Solution:** She thinks that her client group will want someone who is familiar with the language of the social sciences and trained to professional standards.

- **Empathy:** As a previous Master's student herself, she understands the pressures of academic life and that flexibility, quick turnaround and approachability will be as important as her attention to detail.

Using this framework she writes the following **pitch** for her CV:

I am a bilingual proofreader specializing in working with students and independent academics, in UK universities, for whom English is a second language.

Training and membership
I am affiliated with the UK's top industry-recognized professional organizations – I trained as a proofreader with The Publishing Training Centre and I am an Associate of the Society for Editors and Proofreaders.

Subject specialisms
I have an MA in Social Policy and Administration, a Diploma in Social Work and a decade's worth of practice-based experience as a qualified social worker. I understand the language of the social sciences, particularly the sub-disciplines of:

child and youth studies • criminal justice • diversity • domestic disputes • evidence-based practice • interpersonal violence • family law • family studies • health research • learning disabilities • public and social administration • social policy • social work research and practice • women's studies • and youth community work.

Proofreading solutions
I provide a polished, professional finish to your manuscript, article, letter, personal statement, CV, website or report:

- addressing consistency with regards to layout and style
- attending to awkward non-standard phrasing
- eradicating grammar, punctuation and spelling errors

Your needs come first
I understand the demands of working in pressurized academic and professional environments and offer outstanding attention to detail, a friendly and approachable manner and, when you need it, a quick turnaround. I always deliver within budget, never miss a deadline, and pride myself on being able to follow a client's brief.

Margo adds a **call to action** at the bottom of the page, just above her contact information. As per the advice in Chapter 4, she uses an informative statement that tells her client exactly what to do and why they should do it.

> Contact me by telephone or email to discuss how I can help you with your project.

If she uses wide margins, effective line spacing, appropriate use of bullet points to make the information digestible, clear sub-headings that help the reader navigate the information, a readable font that is easy on the eye, and a simple colourway that matches her business brand, she will end up with a beautifully presented and professional CV.

Tweaking the pitch for other customer groups

If Margo puts herself in another customer's shoes, she might decide to create a second CV: one aimed at publisher clients.

In this case, she might adapt her pitch to focus on publisher-based solutions by including her ability to proofread onscreen, or to use the UK's industry-standard BSI markup language, while removing the information that explains what her service includes in terms of attending to grammar, spelling and punctuation errors (since a publisher will know exactly what to expect from a professional proofreader).

She could also amend her hook, either by asking her social work colleague to provide her with a testimonial or by developing an alternative statement of purpose on the lines of:

> PTC-trained proofreader with a practice-based social science background

Getting the design right

There are no rules as to whether you go for a more traditional text-based CV or more of a brochure style, nor the order in which you include the various elements of the information. What matters is that you communicate your message efficiently and that your design is pleasing to the eye.

Once you've put a large header with your business title on the page, added your hook, pitch and call to action, and embraced the concept of white space in your layout, you should find that you have a one-page summary of your small business that clearly articulates the services you offer and is attractive to the eye.

One page is absolutely fine. According to Paid to Learn (2012), 'Recruiters spend on average 20 seconds looking at each CV, so it's important to make sure yours is written as efficiently as possible.' If you only have one-third of a minute to grab a client's attention, you don't want to waste a second asking them to turn the page!

Fromholzer's checklist

It's worth reminding yourself of the advice from Dennis Fromholzer in Chapter 19 on directory advertising because much of the information applies to a CV, too.

- Include your address and local phone number.
- Make the headline stand out.
- Ensure there's enough white space and not too much clutter.
- Focus on the solution, in use the customer's language.
- Any images should be relevant.
- Contact information needs to be readable and easy to find.
- Keep testimonials succinct.
- Make the description of your services clear and credible.

KEY POINTS

- Use white space and headings to make it easy for the reader to find the relevant information.

- Focus on what you do have rather than on what you've yet to acquire.

- Use positive statements that focus on your USPs.

- One page is enough – it's quality not quantity that counts.

- Create multiple CVs for different client types.

- Use the 'hook, pitch, call to action' framework for the initial structure, and the differentiation–solution–empathy framework to get your pitch right.

- Experiment with different formats, depending on whether you want a traditional presentation or a brochure hybrid.

TRY IT!

If you don't yet have a CV, make a list of the client types you want to target and create a separate one-page version for each group.

If you do have a CV and you haven't reviewed it for some time, look at it now and check whether it embraces (1) the 'hook, pitch, call to action' framework and (2) the differentiation–solution–empathy framework.

When you are happy with your CVs, consider uploading them to your website so that they are accessible to your customers.

22 BUSINESS CARDS

What's in it for you?

* Low cost, potentially high impact
* Mobile marketing at any opportunity
* Professionalism and brand reinforcement

Don't underestimate them!

The business card is possibly one of the most underrated marketing tools, particularly in these days of online connectivity. If you've created your website, developed your social media profiles, created various directory advertisements, carried out your cold-calling campaign, and embarked on your networking activities, is there still a place for the humble business card? Absolutely! Here's a summary of why.

* **They are inexpensive:** You can buy a batch of 50 high-quality business cards for well under £20. This means that for the small business owner with a tight budget, they're a cost-effective way of carrying out highly personalized marketing.

* **They are quick to produce:** Many specialist business card printers (e.g. Moo) allow you to design your card online using templates, and take minutes to create and order.

* **They are small but beautiful:** They take up very little space but ensure you always have something to hand out, should the opportunity arise.

* **They facilitate marketing on the go:** You can take them anywhere, from the business meet-and-greet to the beach.

* **They are great for face-to-face marketing:** The digital world isn't all-encompassing. There are still times when only

face-to-face will do (e.g. networking meetings, training courses, interviews, etc.).

- **They enhance your professionalism:** First impressions count. John Williams, founder and president of LogoYes.com, argues that the business card '[is] often the first item prospects receive from you, so it's your first opportunity to make a strong, positive impression on them' (Williams n.d.).

- **They offer something for the client to keep:** Even if your potential customer doesn't use your services today, they have a reminder for tomorrow.

Business cards therefore give you a high benefit for a low cost. There are few professional marketing tools that you can create in less than half an hour, for the price of a couple of paperback books, and that will fit inside your wallet.

Acting like a professional business owner

Being an editorial freelancer means owning and running your own business, and that means presenting yourself in a professional manner, not an amateur one. Even if you're a new starter, you're still a professional new starter.

- **Put yourself in your customer's shoes:** A potential client asks for your details – what looks best? Scrabbling around for a pen and paper so you can write down your email address or handing them a ready-printed, high-quality business card? Your card needs to be eye-catching and attractive enough to give the reader a positive first impression and encourage them to want to know more. Every second you spend fumbling for that pen and piece of paper is a second for your client to think you are disorganized.

- **Think in a joined-up way:** Your business card is an extension of your other marketing activities. If your business card looks professional and attractive, a potential client is more likely to be interested enough to bother following the website URL you've provided on that card. And that means they're going to be confronted with a more detailed pitch about the services you offer.

• **Consolidate your brand:** Make sure you use the same logo, business name, slogan or photo on your card that you use elsewhere (online and in print). Chris Joseph (n.d.) of Demand Media argues that branding your business card appropriately makes your business more identifiable across the board. Remember that your colleagues are potential clients, too, so when you hand out your business card at a conference or training course, people are more likely to remember you and the services you provide if they can match the photo, business name or logo to what they're seeing or reading via other media (e.g. your blog, your Facebook, LinkedIn and Google+ profiles, or your website).

Design and content tips

John Williams (n.d.) lists five top tips for ensuring your business card conveys the right message and doesn't end up in the bin.

• **Quality:** Don't skimp on the quality of the paper for the sake of a few pounds. Cheap and flimsy paper is more likely to fall apart after it's been pulled in and out of someone's wallet a few times. A torn card is an unreadable card, and an unreadable card will end up in the trash can. More importantly, says Williams:

> When you choose to 'go cheap' on your business cards, what message does that send to those with whom you wish to do business? Are you really doing yourself any favors by missing out on the opportunity to start building a positive brand image right from the start? (Williams n.d.)

• **Keep it simple:** Don't be afraid of white space. The logo or business name needs to stand out, but not to the extent that any other key text is too small to read. Any call-to-action information (e.g. contact details) needs to be easy to identify and large enough to read without squinting.

- **Keep it standard:** Think carefully about using non-standard business card sizes or shapes. 'You must be willing to trade convenience for memorability if you choose an unconventional shape or size,' says Williams. If your card doesn't fit in an average business-card-holding device (e.g. a wallet/purse), it's more likely to get lost or discarded. To make your card stand out, focus on quality of design and simple differentiators (like colour or rounded corners). You might also want to consider the type of finish you use on a business card – a gloss finish may look attractive and render the card hard-wearing but it won't allow the receiver to write on it.

- **Consider the front:** The front should include all critical information – business name, branding (logo) and contact information. Make it as easy as possible for your customer to find the information you want to quickly convey.

- **Consider the back:** Keep the back blank or use it for non-critical information. Your customer is less likely to look at the back than the front. Consider also that any information you do place on the back will be competing for your reader's attention.

KEY POINTS

- Business cards are low cost and high impact.

- Take them everywhere with you – you never know when an opportunity might arise.

- Amateurish business cards are a false economy. Invest a few extra pounds and go for good-quality design and materials. Attractive and durable beats cheap and flimsy every time.

- Design the cards with the customer in mind – the critical information should easy to locate and comfortable to read.

- Reinforce your brand – match the design and colourway to your other business profiles.

TRY IT!

Ask colleagues to send you a business card. Review what you like and what you don't. Make a list of five providers and get quotations for 50 high-quality business cards. Jot down the critical information you want to include and how you will incorporate your brand (e.g. logo, colourway, slogan).

23 CREATING AN ONLINE PORTFOLIO

What's in it for you?

- It's an organized one-stop showcase of your experience
- Demonstrates that you've already done what you say you can do
- Provides you with a dedicated online confidence booster
- SEO potential

Leading by example

The online portfolio is the perfect way for the editorial freelancer who has notched up a creditable amount of work to show off their experience to potential customers.

When you give customers a portfolio to look at, you demonstrate by example that you have already done all that you claim you can do. Anyone can say they are a proofreader, editor, indexer, etc., but not everyone has a substantive portfolio to back up their claims. So as soon as you gain some experience that demonstrates your ability, start thinking about how you might construct a portfolio.

Put yourself in your customer's shoes

Imagine, for a minute, a young neuroscientist. Let's call her Dr Nell McManus. Nell has spent years training; now she's in practice. She's carried out a piece of exciting research and wants to publish. Nell decides to submit her findings to *Brain*, one of the premier journals in the field.

Her written language skills are good, but she knows that she's so close to the research, and has spent so much time writing it up, that it's hard to look at it objectively. She's almost positive that she's seeing what she wants to see on the page, rather than what's there in reality.

For the best possible chance of acceptance it's essential that her article is in tip-top condition and she decides to hire a professional copy-editor who has experience of working with article submissions to scientific journals and who is comfortable with the language of neuroscience. There are hundreds of copy-editors out there claiming to have the requisite skills. How is she going to choose, and how might you help her if you're one of her potential freelancers?

The online portfolio could be the clincher. If Nell looks at 10 directory entries, websites or online CVs from 10 different copy-editors, all with science PhDs, all with over five years' experience, and all accredited members of the same professional editorial organization, but only one of those freelancers has an online portfolio that lists related books and journals they've copy-edited, this is going to instil confidence and trust. If I were Nell, I know which freelancer I'd choose to call first.

When you put yourself in your customer's shoes it reminds you that however great you think you are, from the outside in you are just one among many. Your online portfolio makes you more interesting to the customer – it sets you apart from the crowd. Crowds mean competition and, as Janvey (2013) reminds us, 'In [a] competitive job market, every tool and potential advantage should be utilized.' That in itself should be the only reason you need to provide your potential customers with an online portfolio.

But do people *really* look at them?

Even if it makes sense to us that our fictitious Dr Nell McManus would be interested in looking at an online portfolio, is this reflected in reality? My own website analytics are enough to convince me that logic wins the day.

Looking at the pages on my site that are designed with the customer in mind (and excluding my blog), the top 10 in terms of page views were (during 12 months between March 2013 and March 2014) as follows:

- Home page: 26,354
- Portfolio: 16,918
- Qualifications: 8,681
- Subjects: 6,752
- FAQs: 5,863
- Contact: 4,952
- Formats: 4,664
- Rates: 4,492
- Testimonials: 3,907
- Guidelines for New Authors: 1,873

Note that the above numbers are page views, not unique visitors. There will be multiple hits to multiple pages from one visitor, and many of the visitors will be curious colleagues or accidental visitors. But some will be potential customers, too. So the numbers in themselves aren't what interest me – it's the proportions that tell a story. If you total up the hits for all 10 pages, my online portfolio represents the second biggest piece of the pie (20%).

If you weren't convinced by Janvey's argument that we should utilize every tool available to us due to the fact we're operating in a competitive market, then I hope the above data at least convince you that website visitors find this information interesting. And effective marketing is all about being interesting.

Designing an online portfolio

Your online portfolio could be a dedicated page on your website or a downloadable file such as a PDF. I opted for a text-based page on my website because:

- I wanted customers to be able to access the information with the minimum number of clicks.

- I wanted the SEO benefits of having the rich keyword information on my website.

- Updating is faster – it's two activities (amend site and publish) rather than four (amend document, save as a PDF, upload to site and publish).

You can test a variety of styles, depending on how creative you're feeling. It doesn't have to just be a list – you can add images, links, and even video if you think these will enhance the reader's appreciation of you. Here are three options to consider:

- You might opt for a **subject-based list of titles** if you work in a number of different genres or academic/professional fields. If you have a large portfolio this might be quite dense. Help your reader navigate the page by embedding jump-to instructions (e.g. Return to Top) so that they can move around the different sections of the text quickly and without having to scroll extensively.

- An interesting alternative is to use **the story-telling format** – here you describe the kinds of projects on which you've worked, telling your customer what the experience was like and why the projects you've listed excited you. You might add in images or graphics to enhance the reader's visual experience or video testimonials that link the client experience to the story you're telling.

- A third option could be the **resource-hub format**. If one of your target markets is scientific journal article authors, for example, you might list the journals you've copy-edited articles for, and add hyperlinks that open an external page to the journal's submission guidelines, thereby adding value for your customer.

Protecting yourself and respecting the client – ask first

Take care when uploading images to your online portfolio (or any other marketing materials). You do not own the copyright on book jackets or journal covers so it's essential to ask the publisher or owner of the image for permission to use these thumbnail images for promotional purposes. Most will be more than happy for you to do so, and will appreciate the free brand marketing.

The same caution applies to listings that name clients and publication titles. There are some well-known brands of business who forbid their freelancers to use their names or products for self-promotion purposes; a student may prefer you to wait until they've been awarded their Master's or doctorate before being listed; a journal article author may prefer their paper to have been accepted for publication first; and an independent author may not want you listing their book two months before they have a major blog tour arranged!

Always, always ask first, no matter how much you think a client will appreciate the exposure you're giving them – it's courteous and it protects you legally.

Thinking in a joined-up way

Since your online portfolio makes you interesting to potential customers, it makes sense to ensure it's not just hidden in the bowels of your website. Alexandra Janvey (2013) has some more sage advice:

> The purpose of creating the online portfolio [is] so others c[an] see it ... Make sure to include a link to your portfolio on résumés, cover letters, business cards, social media profiles, e-mail signature, article bios, and presentations. These are just a few ways to promote your portfolio and get it seen.

Make it easy for your website visitors to find your portfolio. Place links throughout your website where it's appropriate to do so – a call to action – and include a button in your main menu. And in addition to Janvey's suggestions above, consider linking to it in any directory listings.

An online portfolio is added value that demonstrates your experience and professionalism. It's high-quality, detailed, supplementary information that verifies the more condensed pitches that you'll be using in a lot of your marketing material.

Regular updating

Update your portfolio regularly so that your recent achievements are reflected. Remember – your portfolio is an online showcase of what you've achieved. It's accessible 24/7 by potential customers, so it needs to be checked regularly to ensure that it's doing the best job it can to tell your customer why you are an interesting prospect.

KEY POINTS

- As soon as you have a selection of works that demonstrate real experience, use them to showcase your business.

- Make sure your online portfolio is easy to locate – there's no point in having it if customers can't find it.

- Be creative or be traditional – there are no rules as to how you should structure your portfolio. All that matters is that the reader can navigate the information with ease.

- Keep it up to date so that it's a true reflection of the work you are doing.

- Link to your portfolio from other marketing materials and platforms (e.g. LinkedIn, Facebook, directory listings, CVs, quotation letters).

- Ask for permission if you are in any doubt as to whether a client would be happy for their name, their project, or an image they own to be included.

TRY IT!

If you don't have an online portfolio, create one on your website using either the story, subject listing or resource-hub formats as a

243

framework. If you're fairly new to the game and don't yet have a substantive amount of work to showcase, bulk out the page with a list of clients, some testimonials and perhaps some appropriate images. There's nothing wrong with white space!

Add links to it from any other marketing platforms that you can. LinkedIn is a good starting point, but look at your CV and any directory listings you have, too.

24 GATHERING TESTIMONIALS

What's in it for you?

- Gives both you (and your customer) confidence in your skills – social proof of your credibility

- Encourages you to seek something from others that you can sell on to future customers

- Encourages the customer to put *their* money where *your* mouth is

The power of the testimonial

If portfolios are the proof of what you've done, testimonials are the proof of whom you've done it for.

> A good testimonial tells potential clients as much about your ability to deliver as a training course and membership card. It demonstrates that you can do the job you were commissioned for, in both theory and practice. Testimonials are ultimately about building a sense of trust with the customer. (Harnby 2013a)

A testimonial is a statement from a person or an organization endorsing your ability to provide the service(s) you offer. Because they come from the mouths (or pens, or keyboards) of third parties, they provide what is sometimes called 'social proof'.

Social proof is based on two premises:

- Customers are nervous about committing to an unknown product or service provider.

- People are more likely to believe something that others believe (Neitlich 2004).

A positive testimonial from a prior customer is therefore more likely to persuade a prospecting customer that your editorial services are worth investigating. In other words, it can make the difference between that publisher, independent writer, business executive or student clicking on the contact form on your website, or moving on to someone else.

Ali Rittenhouse (n.d.), marketing specialist to online entrepreneurs, sums up social proof nicely: 'It's kinda like virtually wrapping your potential customer up in a soft, warm snuggie!'

Reassuring our customers by demonstrating that others have been pleased with our work is therefore a powerful tool that helps turn them away from cautious speculation and towards belief that hiring us is a safe decision and a wise investment.

Put yourself in your customer's shoes

All testimonials will not mean all things to all people. A testimonial from a PhD student will not hold much sway with a publisher, who will be more impressed with an endorsement from one of their colleagues from another press. That's because, for example, proofreading for a publisher may have different requirements to proofreading for a student (see Harnby 2014: 'Not all proofreading is the same: Part I – Working with page proofs' for an example of this).

High-quality and relevance is important. It's important to gather testimonials from clients that will make the best impression to the customer groups you want appear interesting to. If you want to demonstrate to independent authors that you can edit their novels with respect for their authorial voice, endorsements from self-publishers saying just that will have a powerful impact. If you want to prove to publishers that you can follow a complex in-house brief and meet strict deadlines, endorsements from production editors saying so will be invaluable. Likewise, if you want to show you can provide a thorough and fast turnaround for business clients, evidence from other corporate executives will provide the necessary reassurance. One well-written, relevant testimonial will say more than 10 that read as if you asked your teenage son or your favourite uncle to write a few sneaky words of praise.

While you might choose to list testimonials from a range of client groups on your website, you can be more targeted in your directory listings or CVs. I provide two CVs on my website: one that focuses on my academic work and one that's dedicated to my fiction proofreading. Each CV contains slightly different information – for example, the mini portfolio and testimonial are genre specific.

Making the best of testimonials

On which marketing materials should you include your testimonials? If you can fit in a testimonial, you should include it. Put them on your brochures, website, CVs, directory listings, print advertising, and social media profiles. You might also try putting one on the back of a business card.

To make the best of testimonials they need to be visible. That means placing them prominently. You might decide to put one or two at the top of your home page, or, like me, you might opt for a dedicated webpage that is signposted clearly in menu tab or sidebar button. They make great headlines on CVs and brochures, and if displayed in an attractive border, different font or alternative colour – anything to make them stand out – they draw in the reader's eye and work as a hook.

Don't forget the basics – include key information about the endorser (with their permission, of course), including their name, title, affiliation, and if possible a thumbnail photograph (Neitlich 2004). Why? Neitlich cites research by E.J. Newman et al. (2012) in the *Psychonomic Bulletin & Review*, in which the authors argue that photographs introduce a 'truth bias' whereby the image 'increased the likelihood that the subjects would judge the claim to be true'.

Be proactive

Don't be shy about asking satisfied clients whether they would consider putting their compliments in writing. It's perfectly okay to ask for endorsements – it's standard business practice. Encourage new independent clients to leave a testimonial for you by telling them how much it would mean to you if they could supply a few lines of praise. I've never had any other response to a testimonial request other than 'Of course – I'd be delighted to!' so even if you feel nervous about asking, take the plunge.

Using video (or audio)

According to Gregory Ciotti (2013), 'social proof works better with pictures'. If your endorser is prepared to offer you a thumbnail picture to include, great. But you could take it one stage further – video.

If simply adding a person's face to the written word embeds credibility in the testimonial, hearing them speak those words of endorsement moves things up another gear entirely. Even audio feeds are said to improve positive customer response rates by 'inflat[ing] truthiness' (Newman et al., cited in Neitlich 2004).

Nick Jones, owner of Full Media Ltd and Full Proof, is the king of the testimonial. The current strength of Nick's business was founded upon the positive written reviews provided by his customers from UK free-ads directory FreeIndex. Years later, his is still the top-ranked proofreading business on the site. However, you'll also find video endorsements on his professional websites.

Says Nick:

> Video testimonials make referrals and recommendations tangible yet transparent, giving them an honesty and attribution that can so often be lacking from the written word. The fact that your client has consented to be filmed in order to help you promote your business is a very public affirmation of faith in your goods and services. (Jones 2013a)

Videos don't need to be isolated on your website either. Consider uploading them to YouTube, and sharing the good news to your Twitter, Facebook and LinkedIn feeds. Indeed, 'posts that feature audio visual content are usually much more prominent in the home feeds of other users. Facebook's Edgerank algorithm is prejudiced in favour of such "native" content, as it believes it to be inherently more worthy than textual posts' (Jones 2013a).

Probably the biggest issue when considering video versus written testimonial is the ease of creation. If you're not a videographer (and don't fancy the cost of hiring one), producing a good-quality, professional video may be an obstacle, and that's before you've even begun the process of persuading a potentially shy customer to be filmed. Nevertheless, video isn't going away and for the more adventurous editorial freelancer it's absolutely worth investigating, especially given the ongoing 'truthiness' research.

KEY POINTS

- Testimonials increase credibility. Use them to socially proof your marketing materials.

- Gather testimonials that are relevant to the customer group you want to target.

- Don't be shy about asking – it's standard business practice. If your client is happy with the job you've done for them, chances are they'll be delighted to endorse you.

- Place your testimonials prominently so that they are easy for your customers to find.

- Experiment with images, and audio and video feeds. It's not just professional marketers arguing the benefits, but academics, too.

TRY IT!

With your different customer groups in mind, make a list of three people you can contact to ask for a testimonial within the next month. If you don't yet have any clients for whom you've completed work, extend the deadline until you're in a position to request them.

If you already have a solid bank of testimonials, consider enhancing your business's 'truthiness' by testing the use of images or even audio and video feeds. Keep a note of the date when you add these features, and monitor whether the test impacts on the number of requests to quote.

25 USING VIDEO AND AUDIO

What's in it for you?

- Offers your customer a more personal and visually interactive experience

- Shows clients that you are able to embrace current technology

- Expands accessibility and convenience for different customers with different preferences

- Consolidates the written message on your website

Complementing the written word

If you're quite technologically savvy, you might like to have a bit of fun by using video and audio as part of your marketing strategy. There are a variety of messages you could bring to life with video and audio: making your added value dynamic by creating tutorials or demonstrations; recording client testimonials; and explaining your service in a way that allows potential customers to hear your voice and see your face.

Audio and video files aren't intended to replace the valuable words you place on your website, social media profiles or advertising directories. They're there to enhance your words and provide dynamism to your message, while at the same time providing your customer with a more personal and, in the case of video, visually interactive experience.

Video-based testimonials

Using video as a delivery system for testimonials is something worth considering for the same reason as adding pictures of your referees and yourself on your website – as discussed in Chapter

14, pictures enhance trustworthiness. Recall the quotation from Jones (2013a) in the previous chapter:

> Video testimonials make referrals and recommendations tangible yet transparent, giving them an honesty and attribution that can so often be lacking from the written word. The fact that your client has consented to be filmed in order to help you promote your business is a very public affirmation of faith in your goods and services.

These won't work for every business. Not all your clients may want to feature on video. Even if they do, their delivery may not be strong enough to provide the positivity that you want your viewers to experience. Furthermore, high-quality videography is a skill in its own right, so unless you've a proven track record in this area, it's worth considering hiring a professional. If you're going to take a day away from paid work to do this, the end result needs to be top-notch without multiple reshoots. Do therefore think carefully about the cost implications when you're deciding if and how to generate your video testimonials.

Service-based video and audio feeds

Service-based video and audio feeds are another option to consider. These tell your viewers about your business and how the services you provide offer solutions to your clients. Like testimonials, both written and video-based, they enhance trust. Here's Nick Jones once again:

> 'People buy from people' is one of those annoying clichés you'll have heard a lot if, like me, you've ever worked in sales. But there is lot of truth in it ... a video is a very direct, effective way of getting your personality across and marketing your business at the same time. It's an opportunity for your potential clients to 'meet' you without *actually* meeting you. (Jones n.d.)

If you're nervous about appearing on camera, experiment with an audio description and series of images that show your brand-standard photo or logo followed by a series of images of projects you've worked on. Secure permission from your clients if you don't own the copyright on these images. These can be enhanced with a set of straplines that emphasize the keywords of an accompanying audio feed. Or you could have richer written descriptions moving across the screen that explain how you work, the various services you offer and how each of them is distinct. This could be accompanied by music. Remember, though, that if, out of shyness, you've sacrificed the use of your face, you might well benefit by compensating with the use of your voice.

Promoting your added value via video or audio

If you're already providing added value in written form on your website, ask yourself if there's an opportunity to present it in a different way. Video is a superb tool for presenting tutorials and demonstrations. Audio is equally good for podcasting the ideas you want to share. Examples might include:

- A video that shows your independent author client how you mark up using Track Changes in Word
- A video for your colleagues that demonstrates the use of a complex macro that you use to increase your productivity
- An audio feed for your colleagues in which you share your ideas about earning a fair fee for the job
- An audio feed for your customers in which you explain the different types of editorial intervention (substantive/developmental editing, copy-editing, proofreading, etc.)

In the two case studies that follow, I present real examples of how a video tutorial and a podcast provide alternative ways of presenting written information. Your skill set, specialist subject area(s), any ancillary services you offer as part of your service portfolio, and your target client groups will all factor into the decisions you make about what kind of content you could share and the multiple ways in which you can present it.

Case study: the video tutorial

Some of the most popular content on my website relates to the PDF proofreading stamps that I make available free of charge to fellow editorial freelancers. These stamps are a digital version of the British Standards Institution's proof-correction marks (BS 5261C: 2005 – Marks for copy preparation and proof correction). They're a useful complement to the built-in comment and markup tools provided by the likes of Adobe Acrobat and Tracker Software in their PDF editing/reading suites.

These stamps are part of the added value on my website. Not only are they my way of sharing a useful resource with colleagues from all over the world; they've also had a powerful effect on my search engine rankings – I'm number one on Google for this search term. Why? Because people have shared the stamps information widely via social media; as a consequence of this sharing, there are lots of external inbound links to my website, which the search engines use to determine how interesting my site is; the term 'proofreading stamps' is also a strong long-tail keyword (or keyword phrase) and features prominently on my website.

The written installation instructions don't provide too much trouble for most people, but I've still encountered colleagues who are a little technologically nervous and who've struggled to install the files without getting in a bit of a muddle. I realized that a solution might be a simple video tutorial that allowed viewers to watch me navigating the process on my own computer while listening to step-by-step guidance in which I explained what I was doing – a screencast with audio instruction.

Since the stamps are provided free of charge, I didn't want to spend a lot of money on expensive equipment. There are a number of free options available and some commercial options, too. I chose to download Microsoft's free Expression Encoder 4. The software proved quite easy to use and I was able to successfully make a trial video within half an hour of downloading the software.

I then found a super little online video that demonstrated how to make a video YouTube-ready, followed my fellow screencaster's instructions, and was able to upload my more polished version with no problems.

Case study: the podcast

I know several editorial business bloggers, but I know very few editorial business podcasters! In Chapter 5 on testing, I put forward an idea that I want to try out in the next 12 months – ParlourPods: audio feeds for my blog visitors who might prefer to listen rather than read some of the content I share.

One of my colleagues, Adrienne Montgomerie, is already leading the way, though. She uses the Dameditors website (which she hosts with her two editor colleagues, Helen Mason and Rita Vanden Heuvel) and the Right Angels and Polo Bears blog (Montgomerie 2013) to expand and retell, through audio, some of their most popular written articles. These podcasts are informative and easily accessible. I love the fact that I can sit back and relax my eyes for a few minutes while at the same time learning from a respected colleague.

But I love hearing Adrienne's voice, too. It makes the experience more real to me. In addition, I'm less likely to skim over important material just because it comes later in the piece. Instead, I focus on the whole experience. There's a meatiness to an audio feed that I feel a written blog post lacks.

What kit do you need?

What kit you use to make basic audio and video feeds for your website will all come down to what you want to spend, what you are trying to do and how technologically savvy you are. A poorly produced video testimonial might leave a negative impression on your viewer, whereas a podcast of a blog post to fellow editorial freelancers where a squeaky chair can be heard in the background will be easily forgiven.

As with all marketing activities, consider your audience when making your choice.

To make a video/audio (screencasting) feed for which the audience was my colleagues, I bought myself a Logitech headset with microphone and USB connector (£25 from my local supermarket) and downloaded Microsoft's free Expression Encoder 4. The software proved quite easy to use and I was able to successfully make a trial video within half an hour of downloading the software. Excellent advice for uploading Expression Encoder 4 videos was supplied by TheBenzVidz (2012).

If the point comes when I add video testimonials to my site, I'm going to hire a professional. That's because I feel this is beyond my skill set. It's not just the quality of the audio and video that needs to be spot on – it's the time out of the office to visit the client. If I'm going to take a day away from paid work to do this, I'd want to be absolutely sure that the end result was top-notch. Given that I won't have the ability to re-shoot again and again if I don't get it right first time, it makes more sense for me to leave it in the hands of someone who already knows what they're doing.

Can you include feeds on your website for free?

Some free website hosts ask you to upgrade to a pro version in order to embed videos in your site. Others allow a free YouTube upload. If you want to test audio and video feeds but you don't want to spend much money trialling the process, an alternative (less preferable, certainly, but a possibility nevertheless) is to create a YouTube account, upload your feed there and then add a standard link to your website.

If you are not using a free service (like Weebly) but are paying for your hosting, embedding YouTube videos is definitely the way to go as it uses YouTube's servers, which are very fast and are less likely to buffer. Furthermore, the videos won't use up any of the web space you're paying for. Some people might even use YouTube as their search engine so it could improve your discoverability.

Putting yourself in your customer's shoes

Ultimately, using audio and video to expand the delivery of your content is about putting yourself in your customer's shoes and thinking about how you can best supply what they want in a format that's convenient for them. The greater the convenience, the higher the take-up is likely to be from the broadest base.

Audio and video feeds enable your customer to hear your voice, see your face, or watch exactly what you're doing. They enable you to bring your personality to the fore. From a potential client's perspective, hearing or seeing you makes them trust that you are who you say you are. Given that some of our clients may not have used an editorial freelancer before, and are anxious to ensure they're dealing with a trustworthy individual, investing in the time and tools to reassure them makes sense from a business point of view. After all, if a customer has more trust in you, they're more likely to want to hire you.

KEY POINTS

- Audio and video feeds complement the words on your website and enhance trustworthiness.

- When thinking about which options to go for and how to create the feeds, consider the audience. Putting yourself in your customer's shoes will help you to determine whether you need to employ a professional or whether a DIY job will be effective.

- Use these tools to inform listeners and viewers about your services, your added value or your testimonials.

TRY IT!

Given that experimenting with audio and video might be a completely new experience for you, and therefore time-consuming, rather than jumping in to create your own feeds, consider first one of the following tasks:

Visit the Right Angels and Polo Bears blog and listen to one of Adrienne Montgomerie's podcasts on editorial freelancing. Make a note of how the experience differed to reading a written blog article.

If you have, or plan to create, your own added value (a blog or a client-focused resource, for example), can you foresee a situation where the customer's experience of this content would be enhanced by video or audio?

26 AND WHY NOT?

What's in it for you?

*   Encourages you to promote yourself creatively, regularly and across multiple marketing channels

*   Increases the likelihood of customers finding you and therefore the choices you have over the work you do and how much you earn

*   Helps you to embrace the concept of testing and ditch the idea of failure

Thinking outside the box

I've had an expensive marketing fantasy for years. It involves advertising on the London Underground. Visitors to the UK's capital will have noticed the array of linked advertisements that are placed on the walls by the escalators. And the trains themselves are full of ads, too. Oh, to have the budget to advertise in just one carriage! If you want clients, what better way of getting the attention of a ton of bored commuters rammed in a small carriage during rush hour! According to Transport Media, 'Transport for London (TFL) ensures all stations are kept in a bright and sparkling manner so you know your brand will be displayed in high-quality footfall locations.'

Hmmm, footfall or not, it's out of my league. The point is, though, that when it comes to marketing you are only limited by your imagination, your budget and your courage!

If your research (or a hunch) leads you to feel that one particular activity might work for you, and you are comfortable with the financial hit you'll have to take if your final return on investment isn't what you hoped for, give it a try.

Have you considered ...?

Here are some ideas to get you thinking. Some of them are quirky, some just common sense. Recall the message in Chapter 5 on testing: if you try something and it doesn't work, consider it a lesson learned; then tweak or shelve the idea and move on! There is no such thing as failure.

- Decals are relatively inexpensive and can be moved from one surface to another (or you can create your own digital image, print it and laminate it). Your new signage can then be placed in your vehicle or office window. Decals can be given to clients and friends, too!

- Postcard advertisements in local newsagents, community centres and supermarkets.

- Workwear, such as a branded t-shirt or a cap. My tree surgeon does this, and so does my electrician. Should I? Even if you feel it's not very 'this season', your partner might be prepared to wear it!

- Order a print-on-demand, branded bag with your colourway, logo and website address. Carry it around with you when you do your shopping.

- Run a competition whereby someone can win a free proofread (or other service).

- Make contact with your local university and invite some of the lecturers who teach Master's and PhD students to a meeting where you (and perhaps a few editorial colleagues) outline your proofreading services.

- Advertise in your local parish or village magazine.

- Get together with a group of local colleagues and take a stall at your village fete. They don't have to be fellow freelancers – they could be other small business owners.

- Place a sign outside your house or in your front garden. Builders do it – might you?

- If you live in, or near, a university town, do some research and find out where the students tend to rent property. Then do a leaflet-drop.

- Ask your local radio station if it would be interested in doing an interview with you about running a small business – you can plug your editorial services at the same time.

One of my colleagues asked me what I thought about one of the options above, as she was worried it 'might cheapen the profession'. My response was that when it comes to building your small business and sustaining your livelihood, there are only creative marketing solutions that enable you to find your customers and them to find you.

A sweet tale of inventive marketing

My colleague Rich Adin, curator of the American Editor blog, and creator the EditTools macro suite, gave me permission to share this story. I like it because it shows that you can have a lot of fun with marketing, and that even when things don't go quite as planned, there's often a silver lining (or a chocolate apple) to every cloud.

In the following anecdote, Rich is referring to the annual Communication Central conference, run in the US by Ruth Thaler-Carter, at which he was presenting some years ago:

> At the last conference I presented at for Ruth, I brought my usual, which was my business card wrapped in a custom-made business-card-size chocolate. The chocolate was a mold of my FES [Freelance Editorial Services – Rich's business] logo. Each chocolate cost me $2.25. (Years ago, when I was shipping hard-copy invoices, I started enclosing a couple of these chocolates with the invoice. Clients loved them and would even call me to ask me to send a few even if they didn't currently have work for me.) Anyway, I got to the conference and started to hand out the chocolate when I noticed that they forgot to include my business card. The chocolate itself was right, but the business card was missing. I called the person who

had made them for me and she offered to refund my money, but I told her I'd rather vent at her. After all, I was handing out the chocolate anyway so I'd pay for them. When I got home, she sent me a half-dozen chocolate apples as a consolation. She still makes my custom chocolates, including my 2-lb one that I send to clients at the holidays.

KEY POINTS

- Any marketing activity, however outside the box, is worth at least considering.
- You are only limited by your creativity.
- If it involves a cost, consider the potential return on investment carefully before you make a decision.
- If it involves a lot of your time, consider the potential return on time investment (see Gandia's advice in Chapter 11).
- Do what you feel comfortable with, not what others feel is the 'right' way.

TRY IT!

Every time you think of a new way to promote your business, make a note of it in your marketing plan. When you get a spare 10 minutes, go back to it and ask yourself whether it makes sense to test it, even if it seems a little outlandish. Even if you end up tweaking the original idea, or shelving it completely for another day, the thought process alone will be a productive enterprise.

27 CONCLUSION: BLOW YOUR TRUMPET!

The following is adapted from an article I wrote for the Full Media blog in November 2013. I've tweaked and republished it here because I think it sums up nicely how we as small business owners need to embrace marketing as an active and exciting process, and because it pulls together some of the main suggestions in this book.

Marketing is embarrassing!

One of the things I hear from quite a lot of new entrants to the field is how embarrassing they find the process of marketing. 'I feel like I'm blowing my own trumpet'; 'I hate showing off'; 'I don't want customers to think I'm arrogant'; 'I don't want people to see what I look like – all the photos of me are awful!' If that sounds like you, it's time to pick yourself up, dust off your insecurities and start promoting yourself with conviction.

A reminder about effective marketing

Effective marketing isn't about showing off – it's about communicating a positive message that tells your customer you know what you're doing.

Effective marketing isn't about being arrogant – it's about demonstrating that you are fit for purpose and can prove it.

Effective marketing isn't about curling up behind the sofa in the hope that a customer will somehow find your secret hiding place and feel imbued with confidence despite your red face – it's about instilling belief in them so that they hire you rather than someone else.

Ultimately, effective marketing is about being interesting, and if you don't tell your customers how interesting you are, they'll go elsewhere. You don't have to be a chest-thumping, fire-walking, motivational-speaking guru to be a good marketer. But you do need to be able to clearly articulate the solutions you offer to your potential client in a language they understand and on a range of platforms that enable them to find you in the first place. Even introverts can blow their own trumpets!

Be discoverable and verifiable

If your customer can't find you, how will they know you're even available to hire? Making yourself discoverable is key to an active marketing strategy. That means getting out there and engaging via the multiple channels that your customers use.

Making yourself discoverable is one factor. Another is verification. Customers might hear about you from their colleagues. That's fabulous, but wouldn't it be even better if they can easily verify who you are by finding information about your editorial business? Effective marketing helps you help your potential clients to do this.

Prove it

Once your customers can find you, it's not enough to tell them that you are focused on them and have a business solution for their business need. They need to believe it. Testimonials, photographs and portfolios all add up to what is sometimes called 'social proof'. You're in competition with hundreds, perhaps thousands, of other businesses offering similar services. The internet has expanded the number of customers who can find us, and increased the speed at which they do so, but it's also expanded access to all the providers who can service any given market. Presenting a strong, believable message has never been more important.

Imagine for a moment ...

Put yourself in a customer's shoes for a moment. A local author has decided to self-publish a guide for single parents managing the early-years rearing of twins. She needs a proofreader to knock the book into shape, so she searches an online directory for someone to help her. There she's confronted with two profiles – those of the embarrassed marketer and the trumpet blower.

The embarrassed marketer's listing tells the author about the proofreading service offered, the training they've completed, and that they are able to provide a professional service that is flexible and respectful of the customer's requirements. All the relevant contact information is given. All good stuff. It's all rendered cleanly and professionally ... but is it enough?

The trumpet blower's listing tells the author about the proofreading service offered, the training they've completed, and that they are able to provide a professional service that is flexible and respectful of the customer's requirements. All the relevant contact information is given.

AND they include a short list of clients for whom they've previously worked (a mini portfolio) and some high-quality testimonials written by previous clients who are prepared to put their name and business title against their words of praise. Furthermore, the trumpeter includes a mug shot so that the author can see their beaming face.

Think of it from the customer's point of view

The embarrassed marketer hasn't included the testimonials, portfolio or photography because, well, they're embarrassed. But here's the rub – the author doesn't know this. The author assumes the listing doesn't include testimonials or a portfolio because the advertiser doesn't have these things. And the author isn't sure why there's no photograph, but wonders if it's because the proofreader isn't an individual but rather an agency, or, even if they are an individual, they're not who they claim to be. The author wants to work with a real person, someone she can build a professional rapport with. And she wants someone whom she believes has done the job before, many times, and that the results were great.

Therein lies the problem with the embarrassed approach. The emotion behind the behaviour doesn't translate correctly in the customer's head. It's not perceived as humility, gentleness, or respect. Instead, there are just holes in understanding that the customer fills with their own questions and perceptions. The customer might fill those gaps correctly. But if they fill them in with negative perceptions, the embarrassed marketer can say goodbye to a potential lead.

Still don't fancy yourself as a trumpet blower?

If you're not convinced by putting yourself in your customer's shoes, put yourself back in your own and ask yourself whether you want to be without work. Something else I hear a lot in the self-employed world is that 'quiet patches are normal for freelancing'. I'm not convinced. I think that an effective marketing strategy can bring a small business owner to the point where they're in the position of turning down work rather than waiting for things to turn up.

I've not had a 'quiet' patch for years. The only time I don't have work is when I choose not to have work. But I'm a trumpet blower – I actively market my business on a regular basis, using a variety of marketing tools (digital and traditional). It didn't happen overnight, of course – it's taken a huge amount of work and a lot of commitment – but I've made my business discoverable, and, once a potential customer finds me, I've provided them with the proof to make me interesting enough to warrant first contact on many occasions. Don't get me wrong – this is not because I'm the only person who does what I do, or because there's no one out there who can do the job better. It's simply because I'm an active marketer.

Marketing with passion

Building a successful freelance business is hard, hard work. It requires regular investment in skills development, training, and the use of current technology. Sustaining that business is hard, too – many of us have experienced a situation where an established client tries to save a buck by cutting our rates, or by not increasing them in line with inflation so that we're worse off in real terms. Getting to a place where we're discoverable by clients who do respect our fee structures and the value we bring to the table is therefore more important than ever.

So blow your trumpet – sweetly, harmoniously, tunefully. Market your business with passion and conviction. If you want to feel embarrassed while you're doing it, go ahead. No one will know – they'll be too busy asking you to quote for them.

Be interesting, be discoverable and enjoy your own marketing adventure!

PART III:
SAMPLE OUTLINE OF A
MARKETING PLAN

28 THE FORMER SOLDIER'S MARKETING PLAN

The following outline is completely fictitious. Its aim is purely to show how someone with a particular background might go about structuring their marketing strategy. Depending on your own career and educational skills, the decisions might be very different.

Our new editorial freelancer's background

Jim Johanson has retired from the British Army after 15 years of service. He's served in Northern Ireland, the Balkans, Iraq and Afghanistan. During what was to be his final tour, an IED exploded nearby, killing several colleagues and leaving him severely injured and traumatized. He's made a strong physical and mental recovery but still has mobility issues with his lower limbs.

He has excellent written and verbal language skills, and proven team-leading abilities. By working primarily from home as a self-employed editorial freelancer he hopes to earn an income that will top up his redundancy package and his partner's earnings.

After putting together a business plan, he first focused on making himself fit for purpose by completing UK industry-recognized training. He completed the Publishing Training Centre's Basic Proofreading by Distance Learning course with distinction, followed by the Society for Editors and Proofreaders' Copy-editing 1 course. He'll continue to take improvement classes that consolidate his current skills and training, and that address any gaps in his knowledge base. He's also joined his national editorial society so that he can benefit from the networking, information-sharing and job opportunities.

Now he needs a marketing plan that addresses how he will promote his services and develop a steady work stream. He keeps in mind that ultimately he's trying to be interesting and discoverable – this will form the backbone of all of his marketing decisions.

Jim's market and services

Jim may diversify later but for now he's concentrating on the things he knows most about: military studies, strategic studies, defence, international relations, military intelligence, politics, peace research, peacekeeping, combat, weapons, the Middle East, war veterans, rehabilitation and PTSD.

Market

Jim has identified four groups that he believes will be most interested in his specialist practice-based knowledge and editorial training:

- Publishers with lists in military history, war studies, peace research, etc. Also academic journal authors writing in the same fields.

- Fellow military leavers and veterans, and the organizations that represent and support them. Jim has noticed that there are a lot of CV-writing services on the market that claim to be in a strong position to help former military personnel. He's also noticed that some of them have appalling typos on their websites and many are very impersonal.

- Military/defence businesses and government bodies.

- Self-publishers who are writing Andy McNab/Chris Ryan/Duncan Falconer-style novels, because he can use his military knowledge as a USP that would be relevant to the plot lines.

Services offered

- Publishers – proofreading

- Veterans/leavers – proofreading and assistance with written communication more broadly
- Military/defence organizations – proofreading and proof-editing
- Self-publishers – proofreading and proof-editing

Potential client materials

- Publishers and academics – books and journals
- Veterans/leavers – websites, CVs, personal statements, application forms and cover letters, verbal communication
- Military/defence organizations and NGOs – websites, reports, magazines, articles, books
- Self-publishers – books, websites, magazine articles and short stories

Jim's brand

Jim has chosen to call his business Frontline Proofreading & Communication Services. He wants his brand name to express clarity about what he does and differentiation from other providers. He chooses to include the phrase 'communications services' in his business brand because he feels this most effectively represents the kind of help he can offer to fellow veterans who need assistance broadly with their written material and verbal communication.

'Proofreading' is the element that tells publishers, independent authors and professional organizations what he does. He invests £50 in getting a logo professionally designed and asks a friend with a good-quality camera to take a head-and-shoulders picture of him that he can use as a thumbnail image on a number of marketing platforms. The 'Frontline' element is intended as a play on words that reflects (a) his prior career, (b) an element of written communication, and (c) a sense of commitment and immediacy regarding the job in hand.

As a nod to his prior career, the colourway he's chosen to brand his business with is grey-black, white and green.

Jim's domain name is www.frontlineproofreading.com. He elected to condense his full business name (Frontline Proofreading & Communication Services) because he wanted not only clarity and differentiation but also conciseness – something that was easy to remember and quick to type.

Jim's customers' shoes:

- Publishers – Jim's research has led him to understand that publishers want proofreaders who can work in a variety of formats, using industry-standard markup symbols, follow a brief, and meet strict deadlines. He's also completed an intensive distance-learning course provided by a training organization that is known and respected in the publishing world.

- Military leavers and veterans – as a veteran himself, Jim knows only too well how difficult it can be for ex-soldiers to make a new start in civilian life, where the language and culture are different. While Jim was recuperating, he learned of many colleagues who struggled to communicate the transferability of their skills. For some young leavers who had enlisted after struggling with academic school work, the standard of written English was such that their form-filling, CV creation and letter-writing abilities were preventing them from securing employment. For some, confidence was a serious problem.

- Military/defence organizations – Jim believes that this customer type will be looking for clarity, ability to mark up using lay annotation, and adherence to tight deadlines and strict confidentiality agreements.

- Self-publishers – Jim has thought about what the biggest issues for him would be if he were an independent writer, and thinks that self-publishers will be looking for someone who understands what they are writing about, is respectful of their authorial voice, makes them feel that they're in safe and nurturing hands, and won't rip them off.

Hooks, USPs and pitches

Initially Jim focuses on writing his hooks, elevator pitches and USPs. Then, when he starts to create his website, CVs, brochures, business cards, directory entries, social media profiles and advertisements, he will be able to use the information collated as a framework for each activity.

Hook

As part of his marketing plan, Jim has come up with several different hooks that he can use as slogans or straplines with different marketing activities, depending on which particular client group he wants to target.

- Publishers and academics – 'Professional proofreading to industry-required standards'

- Veterans/leavers – 'A fully customized writing, checking and communications service for those transitioning to civilian life'

- Military/defence organizations and NGOs – 'Clarity, consistency and confidentiality guaranteed'

- Self-publishers – 'Proofreading and copy-editing that respects your authorial voice'

List of USPs

Jim has identified a number of USPs that he could select from when creating long or short pitches for a range of marketing activities. Which ones he uses will depend on the space available and the client group he wishes to target.

- Basic Proofreading by Distance Learning (Publishing Training Centre), qualified with distinction

- Associateship of the Society for Editors and Proofreaders (abides by its Code of Conduct, thus providing a guarantee of editorial excellence)

- Fully conversant with BSI-5261 markup language

- Can work with PDF (using comment and markup tools or BSI symbols), Word (with Track Changes) and on paper (using BSI or lay annotation)

- Will proofread blind or against copy

- Ability to work to brief, to budget and to deadline

- Former sergeant in the British Army

- Specialist knowledge of military studies, strategic studies, defence, international relations, military intelligence, politics, peace research, peacekeeping, combat, weapons, the Middle East, war veterans, rehabilitation, field tactics, weaponry, defence strategy, warfare, combat tactics, military history, rehabilitation and PTSD

- Veteran who understands the practical and emotional challenges of moving to civilian life

- Knowledge of how to sell key transferable skills

- Excellent verbal and written English-language skills

- Range of fully customizable service packages available to suit client's requirements and budget

- Confidentiality strictly guaranteed

Short (elevator) pitch – written and verbal examples

As with the hook, Jim has come up with several different short (elevator) pitches that he can adapt for a variety of promotional settings, depending on which particular client group he wants to target. Each time he uses Daum's differentiation–solution– empathy framework to help him construct the text. See if you can spot the various elements in the following examples, and notice how I switched things round for the verbal example.

- Publishers and academics – 'Frontline Proofreading & Communications Services is run by Jim Johanson, a professional proofreader specializing in academic, professional and trade books in fields of military history, strategic studies, international relations, intelligence, politics and peace research. An associate of the Society for Editors and Proofreaders, Jim trained with the Publishing Training Centre, qualifying with distinction in 2013. Jim proofreads on paper or onscreen, on large projects or small, and blind or against copy. He offers a professional guarantee to work within brief, budget and deadline.

- Veterans/leavers – 'Frontline Proofreading & Communications Services is run by Jim Johanson, a former soldier, now proofreader and communications specialist, who offers a fully customized writing and checking service to those transitioning to civilian life. From application forms to CVs, cover letters, personal statements, papers and articles, Jim will ensure you've achieved consistency with regards to layout and style, iron out any awkward non-standard phrasing, and eradicate grammar, punctuation and spelling errors. Jim's understanding of the challenges involved in moving from military to civilian work life ensures you receive a friendly, flexible and confidential service that will bring clarity to your written materials, highlight your key transferable skills and provide you with the confidence to explore new opportunities.'

- Military/defence organizations and NGOs – 'Frontline Proofreading & Communications Services is run by Jim Johanson, a former serving officer in the British Army. He provides professional proofreading and copy-editing services for military/defence organizations and NGOs. Jim's specialist knowledge of military history, strategy, international relations, intelligence, politics and peace research ensures readability, clarity and consistency across all forms of written communication. Jim understands the sensitive nature of some of the documentation his clients generate and provides his clients with written guarantees of full confidentiality on every project.'

- Self-publishers – 'Frontline Proofreading & Communications Services is run by Jim Johanson, a former serving officer in the British Army. He provides specialist professional proofreading and copy-editing services for independent authors. Jim set up his independent editorial business in 2013 after completing his training with the industry-recognized Publishing Training Centre. His primary goal is to help writers achieve readability, clarity and consistency without interfering with their authorial voice.'

- Verbal pitch to the veterans/leavers – 'Hello, I'm Jim Johanson, and, like you, I'm a former soldier in the British Army. I've been where you've been so I understand the challenges of moving from military to civilian life and how filling out application forms and writing personal statements might seem daunting. That's where I come in. I'm now a professionally trained communications specialist and proofreader who can help you write and check your CVs, cover letters, personal statements and application forms to ensure they are error-free, highlight your key transferable skills, and give you the best chance of securing that first interview.'

Marketing activities

Jim now thinks about exactly which activities he will carry out in order to market his editorial business to various client groups. He is realistic about the time it will take for his marketing strategy to bear fruit and understands that he will not be able to do everything at once. He is also aware of the fact that some of his activities will be unsuccessful and that some of the clients he approaches directly will reject his offer of business services. He makes a promise to himself to remember that marketing is a process of exploration and that these negative outcomes are not failures, merely examples of lessons learned that he can add to his marketing knowledge base.

He'll be using multiple marketing channels because he wants to maximize the chances of a customer finding him by being present on the range of platforms that suit *their* particular preferences rather than his.

And by marketing regularly, and across multiple channels, he'll be able to spread the risk and grasp new opportunities as they unfold rather than putting all his eggs in only one or two baskets.

Prioritizing

Given that there's so much that Jim can potentially do from a marketing perspective, he decides to develop a time-management plan that utilizes the Client-focused Priority Framework (CPF) outlined in Chapter 11. He looks at his list of target client groups and orders them as follows:

- PRIORITY 1: Publishers and academics – he logs this group as his first priority because he believes that with his industry-recognized training and specialist background experience he will have a good chance of persuading them that he has a solid understanding of the subject matter. This client group is also used to working with editorial freelancers and will be able to provide regular work. Regarding publishers, the research to find out who to contact at which house will be initially time-consuming but straightforward.

- PRIORITY 2: Military/defence businesses and government bodies. While this group of clients might be less familiar with the idea of using a proofreader or editor, Jim's industry knowledge gives him an advantage, hence his decision to log it as the second priority. He knows who to contact and what language he'll need to focus on in his emails or letters in order to allay key concerns. He also believes this client group will be able to supply regular work.

- PRIORITY 3: Third on the list are self-publishers who are writing Andy McNab/Chris Ryan/Duncan Falconer-style novels, because he can use his military knowledge as a USP that would be relevant to the plot lines. However, he believes this client group will be difficult to find. It's more likely that these authors will find him and he wants a strong portfolio to be able to persuade them that he's a good fit. In the start-up phase, this will be a work in progress, and his website will not yet have the dynamism generated by an active SEO strategy at this point. Each individual client in this group will be less likely to supply regular work so the investment in marketing to them has to be balanced against the lack of repeat work.

- PRIORITY 4: Jim's last target group comprises fellow military leavers and veterans, and the organizations that represent and support them. While he has a good story to tell in terms of 'having been there', Jim believes that this group will require the most time to exploit and provide the least likelihood of repeat work.

Things to do in Phase 1

Using the CPF grid, he now fills in the marketing activities for his Priority 1 group.

SfEP Directory of Editorial Services

Jim wants to pay for an entry in the Society for Editors and Proofreaders' Directory of Editorial Services. However, to qualify he must upgrade from Associateship to Ordinary or Advanced membership. Since this directory is a popular resource for UK publishers (one of his target client groups), entry is a priority for him. While he's working on addressing this issue, he concentrates on directories that he does have access to.

Find a Proofreader

This is a vibrant specialist directory that attracts academic, business and student clients. A basic entry is good value for money and therefore a low-cost investment. It enables him to link through to his website, and provides plenty of space in which he can sell his skills. Jim also likes the fact that clients can leave reviews on his listing, thereby enabling him to build 'social proof' into his message. He can also add in searchable keywords that will enable customers to find him more easily. The site also accepts articles related to editorial freelancing, and he makes a note to himself to test this function later as a way of building his SEO.

CVs/résumé

Jim creates a template for a CV and brochure aimed at publishers and academics. He uses the appropriate pitch and USPs previously drafted as a point of reference. His CV will accompany the letter he uses for his direct contact with publishers.

Targeting publishers and going direct

Jim's keen to get on the freelance lists of various UK presses who publish in his fields of specialist knowledge. Securing work from this client base early on will be key to helping him upgrade his SfEP membership, and advertising in its directory. Furthermore, publishers are in a position to offer regular work to freelancers who can prove their worth so even though some of their fee structures may not be as lucrative as his non-publisher clients, the security and stability of the potential work stream is attractive.

Jim decides to target a few small, independent military history publishers who might allow him to do some gratis work in return for a testimonial/reference (see Chapter 6). He chooses Tattered Flag Press, Military Press, Hellgate Press, Woodfield Publishing, and Schiffer Publishing. This free work is not a case of doing something for nothing. Rather, it is designed to achieve two core objectives: provide references that will help him achieve the criteria necessary to qualify for an entry in the SfEP's Directory; and enable him to create a mini portfolio of work that he can sell on to mainstream publishers whose business model includes the hiring of professional editors and proofreaders.

He then starts to think about how he will structure his letter to potential paying publisher clients. He uses the differentiation–solution–empathy framework to think about the issues from the point of view of the publisher and adapts his covering letter and CV accordingly, using as reference the pitch and USPs that he's already drafted.

He can use the space in his postscript either to invite publishers to send him their proofreading test, or to show off the testimonials acquired via his gratis strategy.

He sends a covering letter and CV to the named in-house editor responsible for hiring freelancers at: Ashgate, Berg, Cambridge University Press, Chatham House, Edward Elgar, HM Stationery Office, IHS Jane's Group, Lawrence and Wishart, Oxford University Press, Palgrave Macmillan, Pearson Education, Plexus, Policy Press, Polity, Princeton University Press, Progressive Academic Publishing, Routledge, Sage Publications, Verso, Wiley-Blackwell and Yale University Press.

Jim wants to be active as well as passive in his approach to marketing. That means not sitting around waiting for people to contact him, particularly in the early stages of his business development when his company is unknown and his website has not yet become the dynamic, SEO-rich tool that it will be 18 months down the road. Actively contacting target client groups is therefore an important part of his strategy. He's hopeful that he will get some positive leads from these communications, but he's realistic enough to know that some of his letters will receive no response, and others will be outright rejections. He's therefore not expecting a 100% response rate and has made a note in his marketing plan not to be discouraged by negative or non-responses because these are to be expected, even by the most experienced marketer.

Building a website

Jim's ultimate aim is to have a dynamic website that has high search-engine rankings. This will bring clients directly to him and give him more opportunities to choose the work he takes. Building effective SEO takes time and he knows it will require a lot of work. However, building an online shopfront is something he can do now. It's his space where he can brand his services in a way of his choosing. He can begin the linking process by ensuring his domain name is included his CV, his letters, his directory listings, online networks, email signature and social media profiles.

He self-builds his website using WordPress – it's one of several recommended by colleagues and it's easy to use, customizable and stable.

Building a network

Networking is also a priority, both online and face-to-face. This could provide Jim with work opportunities from fellow freelancers who wish to refer work to colleagues with his skill set and subject specialisms. There are huge benefits, too, from being able to share experiences with fellow new starters and ask advice from more experienced editorial freelancers.

Jim's already an Associate of the SfEP so he sets up his access to the organization's online Forum (which includes a jobs board), and creates profiles for the primary social media sites – LinkedIn, Twitter, Google+ and Facebook. He begins the process of linking to fellow proofreaders and copy-editors using these platforms, engaging in group discussions, sharing any valuable content they post (or that he thinks they will be interested in), and taking the time to comment on articles that are useful to his business. He rightly believes that when he comes to later phases of his marketing strategy that involve creating his own added value and content, his online colleagues and friends will reciprocate. However, he's also building relationships, learning from others, and creating those valuable two-way links between his website and others'.

Keeping on top of priorities

To reiterate, there are lots of other things Jim could do or test, but right now he's concentrating on these objectives. Once he's achieved them, or done as much as he can to achieve them for the time being, he can move onto additional phases of his marketing strategy.

He pins his current to-do list of scheduled objectives on his desktop task bar. This ensures that it's easily accessible and encourages him to keep up the momentum – marketing his business on a regular basis. Not only can he monitor his progress, but it also embeds the process of marketing in his business mindset so that it becomes a routine part of his working day rather than a chore.

Activities in later phases

As Jim's business develops, he can move forward through his priority list of client groups and explore activities that are most likely to generate the relevant work leads. He can continue to use the CPF grid, adding in target groups and creating appropriate to-do lists.

All the time he should bear in mind that his aim is to be interesting and discoverable. The following are some of the things he could add to the next phases of his marketing strategy.

Creating an online portfolio

Jim decides to opt for a story-telling version of an online portfolio for his website. When his business has developed further, and he has a larger bank of projects to advertise, he may complement this with a more straightforward listing of projects, but in the early stages he focuses instead on the story he can tell about the jobs he's already completed and how his previous career background made him a good fit for the work.

Gathering testimonials

Jim will ask each client he completes a job for if they would be happy to supply a testimonial that he can post on his website, directory listings, CVs and his LinkedIn profile. He'll continue to update this as he moves through the phases of his marketing strategy.

Cold letters to military/defence organizations

Jim will make a list of military and defence organizations and NGOs that he'll contact with a CV and cover letter. He'll use the differentiation–solution–empathy framework, but this time focus on those key selling points that will be of most interest to this client group. These include:

- Associateship of the Society for Editors and Proofreaders
- Basic Proofreading by Distance Learning (Publishing Training Centre), qualified with distinction
- Can work PDF (using comment and markup tools or BSI symbols), Word (with Track Changes) and on paper (using BSI or lay annotation)
- Ability to work to brief, to budget and to deadline
- Former sergeant in the British Army
- Specialist knowledge of military studies, strategic studies, defence, international relations, military intelligence, politics, peace research, peacekeeping, combat, weapons, the Middle East, war veterans, rehabilitation, field tactics, weaponry, defence strategy, warfare, combat tactics, military history, rehabilitation and PTSD
- Excellent verbal and written English-language skills
- Confidentiality strictly guaranteed

Potential clients include the British American Security Information Council (BASIC), Esri UK, the International Institute for Strategic Studies (IISS), the Ministry of Defence Publications Department, Saferworld, Sarkar Defence Solutions Ltd, and SAAB Defence and Security – he'll call beforehand to find out the name of the person responsible for quality control over the website and any publications or internal communications. Unlike publishing clients, his role may be unfamiliar to these types of organization, so finding the right person to write to will a more labour-intensive process.

General directory listings

Yell, FreeIndex and Hotfrog are three UK business directories that offer free listings. Jim thinks that some of his clients (particularly self-publishers) might be more likely to use these more general directories, and, since the advertising is free, decides it would be a wasted opportunity not to experiment with them. With the limited space available, Jim will focus on Fromholzer's advice, making sure the information given is clear and easy to read. He'll use the relevant hook as a headline, the appropriate short pitch to construct the main text, a link to his website, a local phone number, his address, and a call to action.

Finally, Jim has his eye on the Career Transition Partnership's Preferred Suppliers List. The CTP is part run by the Ministry of Defence and specializes in resettlement guidance for military leavers. There is a rigorous application process to go through before a supplier can be accepted (though there is no cost to applying or being listed) so Jim decides to put this on hold until he has more experience. However, he makes a note of the contact details and the URL of the application form so that it's available in his marketing plan when he needs it.

Advertising to military leavers

Jim might test advertisements in *Quest Magazine*, *Civvy Street* and *Pathfinder*, three recognized resettlement publications for those transitioning from military to civilian life.

Another option is Remploy. He discovers this organization through his LinkedIn searches. Remploy runs regular events around the UK that help people who've left the military in the past two years to transition to civilian life. He will contact the company with a view to placing leaflets in conference packs, and also to find out if they hold a bank of specialist freelancers like himself to whom clients can be referred.

Social media and military leavers

LinkedIn's UK Army Veterans in Business is a perfect forum for Jim to build links with other independent business owners offering a diverse range of transition opportunities for military leavers and veterans, and the people they serve. Not only are the discussions about the issues vibrant and informative, but by integrating himself in this network, and joining in the debates, he can build at platform on which he can share his added value (blog, booklet) and drive people to his website.

Cold letters to agencies

Jim will search online for CV-writing agencies who specialize in working with ex-military personnel who need help selling their transferable skills. He'll stick to those whose websites impress him and who offer detailed information about the consultants who work for them. He'll make a list in his marketing plan and email them in the first instance to find out more information about their requirements.

Possible pricing structure

Jim's research has led him to believe that most publishers set their own editorial rates for freelancers. When it comes to quoting for non-publisher clients, Jim decides to base his pricing structure around the suggested minimum rates provided by the SfEP. He's nervous about this at first – after all, he's new to the field and doesn't have experience. However, he wants his quotations to be valued for what he does bring to the table (his USPs), not what he doesn't (an extensive editorial freelancing career), so he frames his quotations in terms of value rather than money, as per the advice in Chapter 6.

If he puts himself in his customers' shoes, he realizes that most of his clients are looking for the solutions he can offer to their problems, not a cheap deal. They want quality (otherwise they'd have done the job themselves). He doesn't want to undermine this by talking about how cheap he is – it's not the message he wants to communicate; nor does it reflect his professionalism, his investment in quality training, or the years of service to his country.

Adding value

Jim has also decided to create a blog called 'Frontline Talk' within his business website. It will feature articles, resources, links and news features that are relevant to veterans and leavers – the challenges they face, the organizations and networks that can offer support, and a special focus on employment advice, writing tips, self-proofreading/writing help, advice on basic grammar usage, and assistance with effective verbal and written communication more broadly.

He plans to encourage guest articles from fellow veterans, support organizations and currently enlisted soldiers who have stories to share and constructive advice to offer on moving forward.

He will use his social media platforms and other networks to promote the valuable content he posts, thus driving people to his site and increasing his discoverability.

He also plans to add further value by creating a free communication skills booklet that visitors can download from his website (or from Smashwords). The booklet will contain top tips for CV creation and letter-writing that focus on transferable skills for military leavers transitioning to civilian life.

Meetings

Jim spent his own recovery period at the UK's Headley Court, a rehabilitation centre that specializes in enabling military servicemen and women to return to operational duty as soon as possible. He plans to contact the centre to arrange for a meeting with a senior member of staff. In the meeting, he will outline the services he now offers and pitch to them the idea of running small-group onsite workshops for those who cannot return to active service and who need assistance with CV- and letter-writing, personal statement development, and application form-filling for their journey into civilian life. He's considering running a free trial workshop so that the unit staff and veterans can assess the usefulness of his services. The staff at the centre know Jim and acknowledge that his own experience of military life and post-trauma rehabilitation bring added value to the service he offers. Veterans may be inspired by him and feel comfortable working with a fellow serviceman.

When Jim completes the workshop, he will give each attendee a brochure about his company and a business card so that they can contact him for one-on-one help in the future if they wish.

Cold letters to veteran rehabilitation centres

If this workshop is successful, Jim will send cold letters to a further 12 regional defence medical rehabilitation centres across the UK. He'll get on the phone and establish the names of the individuals to whom he should send the letter. He'll send this in a plain envelope with a hand-written name and address.

He'll use the differentiation–solution–empathy tool to think about the issues from the point of view of the veterans and the support centres:

* Differentiation – Jim's been in the very situation some of the recovering veterans face. He's an ex-serviceman who has experienced post-trauma rehabilitation and recovery. That, combined with his editorial training and his natural verbal and written language skills, sets him apart from the crowd.

* Solution – defence rehabilitation centres focus on enabling servicemen and women get back to operational duty, and in many cases this is possible. For some, like Jim, it's not, and the so the journey into civilian life begins. This transition can be an additional trauma, particularly if they left school with poor grades and have little or no work experience outside of the military. Their application forms, personal statements and cover letters need to sell their transferable skills and this is where Jim can help. He's 'been there' and understands the challenges ahead, and he has the requisite skills to help the veterans communicate effectively, thus maximizing their chances of securing that crucial interview. In view of the mobility issues that some veterans will face, Jim will offer onsite assistance or remote working if they prefer.

* Empathy – rehabilitation centres will be dealing with people with a wide range of needs, both physical and psychological, and have stringent budgets to which they must stick. Jim can offer a 'been-there', dedicated service targeted at the niche of

vulnerable patients for whom military life has ended, and at a price that is sensitive to the broad range of facilities and services that the centres' budgets must work within.

Business cards

Business cards are quick to produce and have a high impact for a low cost. They'll be particularly useful if he pursues the workshop idea. He has a budget of £30 for his first batch of cards and opts for a simple design that features his business title, his name, website, telephone and email address. He uses his brand colourway and opts for a standard size card that will fit into the average wallet. The stock he selects is of high quality and has a matt finish for durability. The reverse features a QR code that enables users to access his website directly via their smart phones or tablets.

What else could Jim have done?

This sample marketing plan is just that – a sample. I'm not a former soldier so it was quite a challenge to put myself in Jim's shoes and create an outline marketing strategy for him!

You may have come up with other ideas while you were reading – better ideas even. You may have worded his pitches in a different way, or chosen different advertising platforms. You may have used a different focal point for his blog or come up with a more appealing business name. You may have prioritized differently.

And that's just it. All the advice in the world from someone else won't give you all the right answers. All it can hope to do is guide you to think creatively about what might work for you given your skill set, your background, your business objectives and your time limitations.

Jim's situation reminds us that the world of editorial freelancing is a diverse one, and the opportunities are therefore diverse, too. Ultimately, though, we all need to be interesting and discoverable to our potential clients, whoever we are, whatever we've done before and wherever we're going.

PART IV:
RESOURCES

Works cited

Adin, R. (2013). 'Implied Promises & the Professional Editor', An American Editor. Accessed October 2013 from http://americaneditor.wordpress.com/2013/08/21/implied-promises-and-the-professional-editor/

Adin, R. (2013a). 'Business of Editing: What to Charge' (Parts I–V), An American Editor. Accessed September 2013 from http://americaneditor.wordpress.com/2013/08/05/business-of-editing-what-to-charge-part-i/

Adin, R. (2013b). 'The Business of Editing: Thinking about Invoices', An American Editor. Accessed September 2013 from http://americaneditor.wordpress.com/?s=invoices

All About Cookies (n.d.). 'What is a cookie?', All About Cookies. Accessed January 2014 from http://www.allaboutcookies.org/cookies/

American Marketing Association (2007). 'Definition of Marketing', AMA. Accessed January 2013 from http://www.marketingpower.com/aboutama/pages/definitionofmarketing.aspx

BBC (n.d.). The Speaker. Accessed October 2013 from www.bbc.co.uk/speaker/improve/

Beaton, Alan B. (2013). 'Social Media Marketing for Business – Hootsuite is the Answer', Nick Lewis Communications. Accessed March 2014 from http://www.nicklewiscommunications.com/social-media-marketing-business-hootsuite-answer/

BizBest Media Corp. (2005). 'Satisfied Customers: What Do Customers Want?', Startup Nation. Accessed August 2013 from http://www.startupnation.com/business-articles/1103/1/AT_What-Customers-Want.asp

Brooks, R. (n.d.). '37 Calls to Action to Get People to Read, Click and Buy at Your Website', Flyte. Accessed June 2013 from http://www.flyte.biz/resources/newsletters/06/10-calls-to-action.php

Broomfield, L. (2013). 'Reciprocity and Social Media', Libro Editing. Accessed July 2013 from http://libroediting.com/2013/07/31/reciprocity-and-social-media/

Broomfield, L. (2013a). 'How to maintain a good online reputation', Libro Editing. Accessed October 2013 from http://libroediting.com/2013/09/02/online-reputation/

Broomfield, L. (2013b). 'Searching for jobs on Twitter', Libro Editing. Accessed January 2014 from http://libroediting.com/2013/12/23/searching-for-jobs-on-twitter/?utm_source=feedburner&utm_medium=email&utm_campaign =Feed%3A+Libroediting+%28LibroEditing+blog%29&utm_content= Yahoo%21+Mail

Cardell, C. (n.d.). 'Marketing = Testing', Chris Cardell's Official Website. Accessed May 2013 from http://www.cardellmedia.co.uk/marketing-testing.html

Chartered Institute of Marketing (n.d.). 'An Overview of Marketing', CIM. Accessed May 2013 from http://www.cim.co.uk/marketingplanningtool/intro.asp

Ciotti, G. (2013). '7 Things You MUST Understand When Leveraging Social Proof in Your Marketing Efforts', KISSmetrics. Accessed October 2013 from http://blog.kissmetrics.com/social-proof-factors-2/

Clay, R. (2007). *Learn How to Grow Your Business … in Just Two Hours*. Milton Keynes: Marketing Wizdom Ltd

Denicolo, P. and Reeves, J. (2014). *Developing Transferable Skills*. London: Sage Publications

Daum, K. (2013). 'Give the Perfect Elevator Pitch', Inc. Accessed June 2013 from http://www.inc.com/kevin-daum/give-the-perfect-elevator-pitch.html

'Driving Results with Directory Advertising' (n.d.), Sensis. Accessed July 2013 from http://about.sensis.com.au/IgnitionSuite/uploads/docs/Chapter14.pdf

Duke, D. (2014). 'How can transferable skills be marketed effectively to enhance employability?' in Denicolo, P. and Reeves, J. Developing Transferable Skills. London: Sage Publications

Duke, J. (2013). 'How to add Google authorship to your blog' in Standing Dog. Accessed December 2013 from http://www.standingdog.com/blog/how-to-add-google-authorship-to-your-blog/

Empson, R. (2013). 'Everything You Wanted To Know About The Giant Elance, oDesk Merger & Ensuing Backlash (But Were Afraid To Ask)' in Techcrunch. Accessed April 2013 from http://techcrunch.com/2013/12/22/everything-you-wanted-to-know-about-the-giant-elance-odesk-merger-ensuing-backlash-but-were-afraid-to-ask/

Fishkin, R. (2007). 'How to Choose the Right Domain Name' in The Moz Blog. Accessed August 2013 from http://moz.com/blog/how-to-choose-the-right-domain-name

Forster, M. (2000). *Get Everything Done and Still Have Time to Play*. London: Hodder & Stoughton

Frankel, L. (2010). *Nice Girls Don't Get the Corner Office: 101 Unconscious Mistakes Women Make That Sabotage Their Career*. New York: Business Plus

Gandia, E. (n.d.), 'The 3 Pillars for Landing Progressively Better Clients' in International Freelancers Academy. Accessed December 2013 from http://internationalfreelancersacademy.com/the-3-pillars-for-landing-progressively-better-clients/

Gube (2011). '7 Best Practices for Improving Your Website's Usability', Mashable. Accessed October 2013 from http://mashable.com/2011/09/12/website-usability-tips/

Harnby, L. (2012). 'Editorial Annual Accounts Template (Excel)', Proofreader's Parlour. Accessed January 2014 from http://www.louiseharnbyproofreader.com/4/post/2012/11/editorial-annual-accounts-template-excel.html

Harnby, L. (2012a). 'Website Tips for Editorial Pros: Get Yourself a Favicon', Proofreader's Parlour. Accessed January 2014 from http://www.louiseharnbyproofreader.com/4/post/2012/08/website-tips-for-editorial-pros-get-yourself-a-favicon.html

Harnby, L. (2013a). *Business Planning for Editorial Freelancers*. Norwich/London: Louise Harnby in Association with The Publishing Training Centre

Harnby, L. (2013b). 'Lessons Learned: Marketing for the Small Business Owner', Proofreader's Parlour. Accessed July 2013 from http://www.louiseharnbyproofreader.com/4/post/2013/03/lessons-learned-marketing-for-the-small-business-owner.html

Harnby, L. (2014). 'Not all proofreading is the same: Part I – Working with page proofs', Proofreader's Parlour. Accessed January 2104 from http://www.louiseharnbyproofreader.com/4/post/2014/01/not-all-proofreading-is-the-same-part-i-working-with-page-proofs.html

Harnby, L. (n.d.). 'Selling Yourself – Adding an Editorial Portfolio to Your Website', Find a Proofreader. Accessed November 2013 from http://findaproofreader.com/adding-a-portfolio-to-your-website/?utm_source=rss&utm_medium=rss&utm_campaign=adding-a-portfolio-to-your-website

Harris, H. (2013). 'Seven ways to make your LinkedIn profile more appealing to editorial project managers', in Editing Mechanics. Accessed May 2013 from http://www.wordstitch.co.uk/blog/seven-ways-to-make-your-linkedin-profile-more-appealing-to-editorial-project-managers/

Heuman, D. (n.d.). 'Building a website for your freelance business: five excuses that shouldn't hold you back' in Find a Proofreader. Accessed October 2013 from http://findaproofreader.com/articles/building-a-website-for-your-freelance-business/

International Freelancers Academy (n.d.). 'How to Create a Marketing Plan You'll Actually Enjoy Implementing', International Freelancers Academy. Accessed September 2013 from http://internationalfreelancersacademy.com/create-a-marketing-plan/#

Janvey, A. (2013). '4 Reasons You Should Have an Online Portfolio', Come Recommended. Accessed September 2013 from http://comerecommended.com/2013/06/4-reasons-you-should-have-an-online-portfolio/

Jones, N. (2014). '10 tips for perfecting your website in 2014 (Part 2)', Full Media. Accessed March 2014 from http://full-media.co.uk/10-tips-perfecting-your-website-2014-part-2/

Jones, N. (2013). 'Which social media channels are right for your business?', Full Media. Accessed October 2013 from http://full-media.co.uk/which-social-media-channels-are-right-for-your-business/

Jones, N. (2013a). 'Why you need a testimonial video for your business', Full Media. Accessed October 2013 from http://full-media.co.uk/why-you-need-a-testimonial-video-for-your-business/

Jones, N. (2013b). 'Why your business needs a responsive website', Full Media. Accessed November 2013 from http://full-media.co.uk/why-your-business-needs-a-responsive-website/

Jones, N. (2013c). 'How to monitor your online marketing performance', Full Media. Accessed December 2013 from http://full-media.co.uk/monitor-your-online-marketing-performance/

Jones, N. (2013d). 'The EU Cookie Law – An Overview', Nick Lewis Communications. Accessed January 2014 from http://www.nicklewiscommunications.com/the-eu-cookie-law-an-overview/

Jones, N. (n.d.). 'Web videos – inject personality into your online marketing', Full Media. Accessed January 2014 from http://full-media.co.uk/web-video-inject-personality-into-your-online-marketing/

Joseph, C. (n.d.). 'Importance of Business Cards', AZ Central. Accessed July 2013 from http://yourbusiness.azcentral.com/importance-business-cards-1527.html

Kania, W. (2012). 'The most lucrative ways to specialize', The Freelancery. Accessed October 2013 from http://thefreelancery.com/2013/09/the-most-lucrative-ways-to-specialize/

Kiisel, T. (2012). '4 Tips to Manage Your Online Reputation', Forbes. Accessed August 2013 from http://www.forbes.com/sites/tykiisel/2012/11/20/4-tips-to-manage-your-online-reputation/

McCauley, M. (2012). 'Spotlight: Building a Freelance Proofreading Business – The Usefulness of Objectives', The Proofreader's Parlour. Accessed August 2013 from http://www.louiseharnbyproofreader.com/4/post/2012/12/spotlight-building-a-freelance-proofreading-business-the-usefulness-of-objectives-bymary-mccauley.html

Montgomerie, A. (2013). 'Subscribe to the Podcast', Right Angels and Polo Bears. Accessed January 2014 from http://blog.catchthesun.net/2013/11/subscribe-podcast/

Montgomerie, A. (2014). 'Is this social media? No', Right Angels and Polo Bears. Accessed January 2014 from http://blog.catchthesun.net/2014/01/is-this-social-media-no/

Moran, G. (2008). 'Maximize Your SEO', Entrepreneur. Accessed 30 July 2013 from http://www.entrepreneur.com /article/198608

Neilsen, J. (2006). 'F-Shaped Pattern For Reading Web Content', Nn/g. Accessed September 2013 from http://www.nngroup.com/articles/f-shaped-pattern-reading-web-content/

Neitlich, A. (2004). 'The Importance of Testimonials', Marketing. Accessed November 2013 from http://www.sitepoint.com/the-importance-of-testimonials/

Newman E.J., Garry, M., Bernstein, D.M., Kantner, J., and Lindsay, D.S. (2012). 'Nonprobative photographs (or words) inflate truthiness', *Psychonomic Bulletin and Review*, 19(5): 969–74

Nordin, R.A. (2012). 'For Freelance Proofreaders/Editors: How to Not Get a Business Deal and How to Get One' in Self-published Authors Helping Other Authors. Accessed September 2013 from http://selfpubauthors.com/2012/07/28/for-freelance-proofreaderseditors-how-to-not-get-a-business-deal-and-how-to-get-one/

O'Moore-Klopf, K. (2013). 'The 1.5-Hour Daily Social Media Schedule', KOKEdit Blog. Accessed August 2013 from http://editor-mom.blogspot.co.uk/2011/05/the-15-hour-daily-social-media-schedule.html

OpenGlobal E-commerce (2012). 'How to comply with the new cookie laws (EU Privacy and Communications Directive)', OpenGlobal E-commerce. Accessed January 2014 from http://www.openglobal.co.uk/articles/192-how-to-comply-with-the-new-cookie-laws-eu-privacy-and-communications-directive.html)

Oxford Dictionaries Pro (n.d.). http://english.oxforddictionaries.com/

Paid to Learn (2012). 'Why Do I Need a CV?', Paid to Learn. Accessed June 2013 from http://www.paidtolearn.co.uk/video-hub/cv-stuff/why-do-i-need-a-cv/40010447

Playle, S (2013). 'Manuscript critiquing: The inside story', The Proofreader's Parlour. Accessed October 2013 from http://www.louiseharnbyproofreader.com/4/post/2013/09/manuscript-critiquing-the-inside-story-by-sophie-playle.html

Rittenhouse, A. (n.d.). 'Social Proof Your Business!'. Accessed November 2013 from http://alirittenhouse.com/social-proof-your-business/

Sharman, A. (2013). 'Working for Academic Editing Agencies', The Proofreader's Palour. Accessed November 2013 from http://www.louiseharnbyproofreader.com/4/post/2012/06/working-for-academic-editing-agencies-by-anna-sharman.html

Society for Editors and Proofreaders (n.d.). 'What is Copy-editing?', SfEP. Accessed February 2013 from http://www.sfep.org.uk/pub/faqs/fedit.asp#q1

Strauss, S. (2008). 'Ask an Expert: Should you have a website? You bet', USA Today. Accessed March 2013 from http://usatoday30.usatoday.com/money/smallbusiness/columnist/strauss/2008-02-11-getting-a-website_N.htm

TheBenzVidz (2012). 'How To Upload Microsoft Expression Encoder 4 Videos To Youtube', TheBenzVidz. Accessed January 2014 from http://www.youtube.com/watch?v=WdOL0y5oiOI

Thompson, M. (2013) *Pricing a Project: How to prepare a professional quotation*. London: SfEP

Toastmasters International (n.d.). '10 Tips for Public Speaking'. Accessed September 2013 from www.toastmasters.org/tips.asp

Twitter (n.d.). 'Using Twitter Lists'. Accessed September 2013 from https://support.twitter.com/articles/76460-using-twitter-lists

Wagner, G. (n.d.). 'Cold Letters', Honest Selling, Accessed 25 June 2013 from http://honestselling.com/books/your_name_here/chapter09.htm

Whelan, B. (2012). 'Have You Joined The Irish Twitter Party?' in Sage Ireland Blog. Accessed October 2013 from http://www.sage.ie/blog/index.php/twitter-irishbizparty/

Williams, J. (n.d.). 'The ABCs of Business Cards', Entrepreneur. Accessed May 2013 from http://www.entrepreneur.com/article/159468

Tools and other online resources

BookMachine: connecting publishing professionals including editorial freelancers: http://bookmachine.org

BrokenLinkCheck: online broken link checker: www.brokenlinkcheck.com

Boxshot: reasonably priced software for rendering images in 3D. http://boxshot.com/boxshot3d

Dropbox: file-transfer and backup tool: https://www.dropbox.com

Editorial job-tracking/accounts template: www.louiseharnbyproofreader.com/4/post/2012/11/editorial-annual-accounts-template-excel.html

Find a Proofreader: specialist editorial freelancing directory: http://findaproofreader.com

Google Analytics: provides website analytics: http://www.google.com/analytics

Microsoft Expression Encoder 4: easy-to-use free software for screencasting: http://www.microsoft.com/en-us/download/details.aspx?id=18974

MS Office Training Tutorials:
http://office.microsoft.com/en-us/training-FX101782702.aspx

Oxford Dictionaries Pro: including online access to OUP's dictionaries and thesauri, *New Hart's Rules* and *Pocket Fowler's Modern English Usage* (free to UK library members): http://english.oxforddictionaries.com

Parallels Desktop: allows users to run Windows and Mac applications side by side: http://www.parallels.com/products/desktop

PDF proofreading stamps: Louise Harnby's BS-5261 PDF proof-correction symbols: www.louiseharnbyproofreader.com/4/post/2012/08/roundup-pdf-proofreading-stamps-quick-access-links.html

PDF-XChange Viewer: PDF editing software from Tracker Software; alternative to Acrobat (free; pro version $37.50): www.tracker-software.com/product/pdf-xchange-viewer

PerfectIt: www.intelligentediting.com

ReferenceChecker www.goodcitations.com

StatCounter: website traffic analysis program: http://statcounter.com

VMware Fusion: conversion software for running Windows programs on a Mac: www.vmware.com

Weebly: web-hosting service with drag-and-drop interface and customizable templates (free and pro versions available): www.weebly.com

WeTransfer: large file-transfer tool with no sign-up necessary (2GB free): https://www.wetransfer.com

WordPress: blogging tool and web-hosting service with plug-in architecture and customizable templates: www.wordpress.com

Blogs and resource hubs

An American Editor: editing and business advice from Rich Adin: http://americaneditor.wordpress.com. See also Adin's (2013) book: *The Business of Editing: Effective and Efficient Ways to Think, Work and Prosper*. West Valley City: Waking Lion Press

Beyond Paper Editing: tips for writers and editors alike: http://beyondpaperediting.weebly.com

Copyediting.com: editing and language blog

Copyeditor's Knowledge Base: Katharine O'Moore-Klopf's international editorial resource hub: http://www.kokedit.com/ckb.php

Editing Mechanics: Hazel Harris's blog 'about how people work together to create great text': http://www.wordstitch.co.uk/blog/

Editorial Inspirations: editing and proofreading blog from April Michelle Davis: www.editorialinspirations.com

EditorMom: editing, medical editing and business aspects of freelancing: http://editor-mom.blogspot.com

Freelance Feast: Meg E. Cox shares ideas about working independently in healthy ways: www.freelancefeast.com

Freelance Folder: freelance tools, resources, tips and advice: http://freelancefolder.com

Full Media blog: insights and opinion of online media, with a strong marketing focus: http://full-media.co.uk/blog

Kateproof blog: covers all things proofreading and editing: www.kateproof.co.uk/blog

Katy McDevitt Editorial Services blog: for editors, publishers and authors: http://katymcdevitteditorial.com.au/editor-blog

Letters from an Irish Editor: Mary McCauley's blog for writers and editors: www.marymccauleyproofreading.com/blog

LibroEditing blog: editorial freelancing business and grammar tips from Liz Broomfield: http://libroediting.com/blog

Marketing Wizdom: general marketing ideas and tips: http://marketingwizdom.com

Nick Lewis Communications blog: marketing information for small businesses: http://www.nicklewiscommunications.com/blog

PenUltimate blog: editing and publishing blog from Arlene Prunkl:
http://penultimateword.com/blog

Proofreader's Parlour: Louise Harnby's blog for information, advice,
opinion, comment, resources, tips and knowledge-sharing:
http://www.louiseharnbyproofreader.com/blog.html

Publishing Training Centre blog: freelancing, publishing knowledge
base and grammar tips: www.train4publishing.co.uk/blogs

Right Angels and Polo Bears blog: lots of tips, tools and resources on
editing: http://blog.catchthesun.net/

Subversive Copy Editor: advice from Chicago:
www.subversivecopyeditor.com

The Editor's POV: forum for freelance editors of fiction:
http://theeditorspov.blogspot.com

Editorial societies

Most of the editorial societies listed have searchable membership
directories.

Australia: **Institute of Professional Editors (IPEd)**; regional chapter
links include searchable membership directories:
http://iped-editors.org

Canada: **Editors' Association of Canada (EAC)**: www.editors.ca

Germany: **Verband der Freien Lektorinnen und Lektoren (VFLL)**:
www.vfll.de

Ireland: **Association of Freelance Editors, Proofreaders and
Indexers (AFEPI)**: www.afepi.ie

Japan: **Society of Writers, Editors and Translators (SWET)**:
www.swet.jp

Netherlands: **Society of English Native-Speaking Editors (SENSE)**:
www.sense-online.nl

South Africa: **Professional Editors' Group**: www.editors.org.za

Spain: **Asociación Española de Redactores de Textos Médicos
(AERTeM)**: www.redactoresmedicos.com

Transnational: **BELS: Board of Editors in the Life Sciences**:
www.bels.org

Transnational: **Council of Science Editors (CSE)**: www.councilscienceeditors.org

Transnational: **Eastern Mediterranean Association of Medical Editors (EMAME)**: www.emro.who.int/entity/emame

Transnational: **European Association of Science Editors (EASE)**: www.ease.org.uk

Transnational: **Find a Proofreader** (specialist directory): http://findaproofreader.com

Transnational: **International Society of Managing and Technical Editors (ISMTE)**: www.ismte.org

Transnational: **Mediterranean Editors & Translators (MET)**: www.metmeetings.org

Transnational: **PeoplePerHour**: www.peopleperhour.com

Transnational: **Professional Copywriters Association (PCA)**: www.the-pca.org

UK: **Editors' and Proofreaders' Alliance of Northern Ireland (EPANI)**: http://www.epani.org.uk

UK: **Publishing Training Centre** (specialist training organization with freelance directory): www.train4publishing.co.uk

UK: **Society for Editors and Proofreaders (SfEP)**: www.sfep.org.uk

UK: **Society of Indexers**: www.indexers.org.uk

USA: **American Copy Editors Society (ACES)**: http://stl.copydesk.org

USA: **American Society for Indexing**: www.asindexing.org

USA: **Bay Area Editors' Forum (BAEF)**: www.editorsforum.org

USA: **Copyediting-L**: online discussion group and directory: www.copyediting-l.info

USA: **Editorial Freelancers Association (EFA)**: www.the-efa.org

USA: **Northwest Independent Editors Guild**: www.edsguild.org

USA: **San Diego Professional Editors Network (SD/PEN)**: www.sdpen.com

ABOUT THE AUTHOR

Louise Harnby owns an editorial business specializing in proofreading for academic and trade publishers. Over the past two years her client base has expanded to include independent authors and business practitioners. She has worked in the publishing industry for over 20 years, initially with Williams & Wilkins and then for Sage Publications. The birth of her child and the resulting desire for more flexible working arrangements led her to set up her own company in 2005.

Louise completed The Publishing Training Centre's Basic Proofreading by Distance Learning course with distinction in 2006 and is an Advanced Member of the Society for Editors and Proofreaders.

She is the owner and curator of the Proofreader's Parlour, a blog for editors and proofreaders, dedicated to providing information, advice, opinion, comment, resources, and knowledge-sharing related to the business of editorial freelancing.

Louise lives in the heart of the Norfolk Broads.

Visit her website, Louise Harnby | Proofreader, at louiseharnbyproofreader.com

ABOUT THE PUBLISHING TRAINING CENTRE

The Publishing Training Centre is an educational charity dedicated to the pursuit of excellence in publishing. It grew from a small department at the Publishers Association more than 30 years ago and remains at the heart of the industry.

The PTC's courses are focused on providing specific learning outcomes that are designed to thoroughly prepare freelancers for the work they will be asked to do. All the tutors are practitioners first and foremost, which means that they bring their real-world experience with them to the courses they teach, enriching the experience for students and making the training more practical.

In addition to its distance learning programmes, The Publishing Training Centre also offers a full range of classroom-based courses covering all aspects of publishing.

Visit its website at www.train4publishing.co.uk for full details.

Made in the USA
San Bernardino, CA
28 February 2018